WHAT'S IN A NAME?

The Sermons of Dr. T. V. "Corky" Farris

Volume 1

PENIEL UNLIMITED, LLC

Michael and Kelly Marcades, Publishers
326 Valley Star Drive
Canyon Lake, Texas 78133
Website: http://www.penielunlimited.com
Email: michaelmarcades@gmail.com

PENIEL UNLIMITED, LLC . . . the "author's choice."

The vision of PENIEL UNLIMITED, LLC, Dr. Michael Glenn Marcades founding President, is to provide superior publishing services regarding manuscripts worthy of public access. Since its inception, PENIEL UNLIMITED, LLC has taken a particular interest in manuscripts associated with, but not limited to, the assassination of President John F. Kennedy, choral music pedagogy, children's literature, faith-based books, and more.

Book Cover Design & Production by Daniel Whisnant
(www.suissemade.com)
10 9 8 7 6 5 4 3 2

WHAT'S IN A NAME?

The Sermons of Dr. T. V. "Corky" Farris

Volume 1

Edited by Mike Farris

Published 2024 PENIEL UNLIMITED, LLC

ENDORSEMENTS

"Corky Farris was a remarkable man, and some of that adjective has rubbed off on his sermons. Here are 16 sermons transcribed from old cassette tapes by his son, Mike, which are superb in so many ways. Illustrations and word pictures abound. Corky Farris knows how to turn the ear into an eye. His sermons are so visual you can reach out and touch the words. He is a master with humor. And of course, to top it off, he leaves you with an understanding of the biblical text and a desire to walk with God. Interspersed between sermons are delightful comments about Corky and the situational background of the next sermon or two by Mike. This context creates an atmosphere where the sermon comes alive to the reader. In a day when sermon books are on the wane, this volume will stir your heart and soul. Take up and read!"

—Dr. David L. Allen, Distinguished Professor of Practical Theology and Dean of the Adrian Rogers Center for Biblical Preaching at Mid-America Baptist Theological Seminary

"I did not have the privilege of knowing Corky Farris, but I feel like I have come to know him a little through the writing of his son, Mike. This collection of some of his messages has been a source of great blessing and encouragement for me. I recommend this work to anyone with a love for God's Word and a desire to live according to its truth. Pastors will be blessed by his exposition, students will benefit from his faithful commitment to the text, and believers will be encouraged by his warm approach and relevant application."

—*Dr. Deron J. Biles, pastor of Sunnyvale First Baptist Church*

"Dr. T. V. Farris was my mentor in Seminary. He was truly a scholar and a gentleman. I still use his brilliant approach to Hebrew verb analysis with my students. I met him when he was preaching on a Sunday morning at Bellevue Baptist church in Memphis. That Sunday, he witnessed to a young Japanese exchange student who was my guest. It was a divine appointment, as the young man trusted Christ and Dr. Farris invited me to one day attend his Hebrew class. He was truly blessed with keen intellect and a kind heart. I was blessed to have studied under his direction, and I whole-heartedly recommend this volume."

—*Dr. R. Kirk Kilpatrick, Professor Emeritus of Old Testament and Hebrew at Mid-America Baptist Theological Seminary*

"When I think of Corky Farris, I think of a faithful man. There are a lot of people who are not, but he was faithful. He was faithful to his call. God called him to preach. Anybody who ever heard him would never doubt that God called him to preach. And for all of those years after God called him, he worked at preaching. Marvelous, wonderful preacher. Studied the Word of God, prepared his messages, and all the times I heard Corky preach, I never heard him when he wasn't prepared, never heard him when he didn't have a real message from God, right out of the Word of God. Never heard him when there was any wavering at all. Because he was faithful to the call God had given him to preach the Word.

—Dr. B. Gray Allison, former president of Mid-America Baptist Theological Seminary, at Corky Farris' memorial service

"When I was a graduate student. I had really four mountaintop spiritual experiences or remembrances or impacts at seminary. . . One was the chapel service Corky Farris was in charge of. He talked about soul winning. I can remember it like it was yesterday. He was so good-looking, so facile with his speech, so deep in conviction, so winsome and so very sincere. I never thought I would have the privilege of being his pastor later on. It was a blessing to have him in the congregation, but always a little intimidating. I always cleared my throat a little bit before I said, "In the Hebrew . . . ." Many times, I would call Dr. Farris and say, "I want you to explain this to me," and ask him about some point of language or some point of theology. Ever gentle, never put me down. Always ready, always open to explain things to me."

—Dr. Adrian Rogers, former pastor of Bellevue Baptist Church in Memphis, Tennessee, at Corky Farris' memorial service

DEDICATION

In memory of Corky and Juanita Farris, my parents.

ABOUT THE EDITOR

MIKE FARRIS, the elder son of Dr. T.V. "Corky" Farris," is a retired attorney whose law practice in Dallas included commercial litigation and entertainment  law focusing on the movie and publishing industries. He is a 1983 cum laude graduate of Texas Tech University School of Law, where he was associate editor of the *Texas Tech Law Review* and was inducted into the honor society Order of the Coif. He has served as chair of the Dallas Bar Association's Entertainment Art and Sports Law Section and the State Bar of Texas Entertainment and Sports Law Section, where he also served as editor of the section's *Entertainment and Sports Law Journal.*

Mike is a multi-time published author of both fiction and nonfiction, including the Amazon best-selling Hawaiian true crime book, *A Death in the Islands: The*

Unwritten Law and the Last Trial of Clarence Darrow. His most recent non-fiction book, the Amazon bestselling *Blowhard: Windbaggery and the Wretched Ethics of Clarence Darrow*, is an analysis of, and commentary on, four seminal cases in the career of Clarence Darrow.

Mike is also an adjunct professor in the Political Science Department at the University of Texas at Arlington, where he teaches Constitutional Law, Entertainment Law, and a course of his design called *Lawyers in Popular Culture*. In addition to writing and teaching at UTA, he is a book reviewer for the *New York Journal of Books,* with more than 85 published reviews.

CONTENTS

CONTENTS continued . . .

ACKNOWLEDGMENTS

I cannot overstate my appreciation to Michael and Kelly Marcades for their belief in this volume and their faith in me. Without them, this would not have been possible. Thank you. Thank you also to Daniel Whisnant for his beautiful work on the cover art.

I also greatly appreciate those who willingly donated their time to read a draft and provide blurbs. They include Dr. Deron Biles and Dr. Frank Harber from my church, Sunnyvale (Texas) First Baptist Church; Tim Ahlen, senior pastor at Forest Meadow Baptist Church in Dallas; Dr. David Allen and Dr. Kirk Kilpatrick from Mid-America Baptist Theological Seminary; and Tom Bledsoe, who served as Minister of Music with my dad at both Gaston Avenue Baptist Church and Forest Meadow Baptist Church and remained a dear friend for the rest of Corky's life.

And last, but certainly not least, my wife Susan, who has dutifully read multiple versions of everything I have ever written . . . or at least most of everything I have ever written . . . or at least most of everything I have written since we were married in 1983.

FOREWORD

Michael Spradlin, Ph.D. – President
Mid-America Baptist Theological Seminary
Mid-America College – (Copyright 2024)

It is not every day that a pastor has himself arrested to illustrate a point in his sermon, and yet that story, told by T. V. Farris about himself, has never left my imagination. Long before I became a seminary president, I was a seminary student at Mid-America Baptist Theological Seminary (MABTS) and one of the best professors I ever met was T. V. "Corky" Farris. His specialty was Old Testament and the Hebrew language, but his gifting was to capture your heart and soul in the classroom, make the biblical stories as alive as today's news, and change your life spiritually without blinking an eye.

I was a Doctor of Philosophy Student in 1988-89 and studied, for two semesters, a subject called "Old Testament Soteriology." Little did I know that the notes of this class would later become an influential book by Dr. Farris on the subject of salvation in the Old Testament entitled *Mighty to Save*. As doctoral students, we sat in Dr. Farris's office, with his suit of armor watching over us, but in reality, we sat at the feet of a preeminent Bible scholar who, from the Hebrew Old Testament, shaped our view of Biblical Theology and Soteriology, the doctrine of salvation. Dr. Farris could lecture with the greatest minds of Christendom or tell a humorous anecdote about a recent preaching trip to some church in the delta of Mississippi. In fact, as I travel and preach even 30 years later, some church members will often talk with me after the service about the time Dr. Farris preached in their church long ago.

I had met author Mike Farris but reconnected with him when he came to our MABTS campus to lecture about a major event in the life of Dr. Farris, his near-fatal plane crash and miraculous recovery. What a delight to discover that Mike was an author and incredible storyteller in his own right with numerous books (and, apparently, some amazing legal briefs) to his credit.

Mike has done all of us a great service by publishing a sampling of sermons from a great preacher and professor and sharing the testimony of how our awesome Lord Jesus can bring a preacher back from death's door and use him again in ministry. As a new faculty member at MABTS in 1993 I was an honorary pallbearer at Dr. Farris's funeral. It may be one of the most powerful worship services I have ever attended. Adrian Rogers and Gray Allison both spoke. A third preacher shared how Dr. W. A. Criswell, pastor of First Baptist

Church of Dallas, Texas, lay on the hospital floor by the bedside of Dr. Farris's broken body and prayed for his healing.

And about that arrest during a sermon. Well, Dr. Farris was preaching in his church on the second coming of the Lord Jesus and how we should be ready for the end times at any moment. He had arranged for a police officer to come into the pulpit, stop the sermon, and arrest the preacher and say Christianity was now illegal. I'm sure it got the congregation's attention. The point was, are you ready to meet Jesus? I guess that question is as relevant today as it was then.

Corky and Mike at Mike's wedding in 1983.

INTRODUCTION

Mike Farris – Editor / Son of Dr. T. V. Farris

I suppose it's only natural for a son to have pride in his father, but I firmly believe that my dad, Dr. T.V. "Corky" Farris, was the best preacher I ever heard. Bias notwithstanding, I have heard many people say the same thing. After he passed away in Memphis, Tennessee, in December of 1993, one of the things I cherished the most was bringing home a collection of cassette tapes containing recordings of many of his sermons. He had preached them during pastorates at Gaston Avenue Baptist Church and Forest Meadow Baptist Church, both in Dallas, as well as at chapel services at Mid-America Baptist Theological Seminary, where he was Chairman of the Old Testament and Hebrew Department for the last seventeen years of his life, and at various other churches while he was on the faculty at Mid-America.

His sermons, although certainly scholarly, were accessible to any in the congregation. He didn't preach to or preach at or preach over the heads of people; he simply preached the gospel in plain understandable language. His sermons were marked with humor and, often, music. He had once contemplated entering the ministry in the field of

Christian music so, when he made the switch to preaching, he often used music as part of his sermons.

Dr. B. Gray Allison, president of Mid-America at the time, told a great anecdote at my dad's funeral that went something like this: Dr. Farris had been serving as interim pastor at a church in Mississippi, but had another engagement on a particular Sunday, so Dr. Allison filled the pulpit for him. Before the service, one of the deacons asked him, "What are you going to sing in your sermon today?"

Dr. Allison responded, "Man, I don't sing in my sermons."

"Dr. Farris does."

Taken aback, Dr. Allison said (tongue-in-cheek, of course), "Well, if I couldn't preach any better than that, I'd sing, too."

With the collection of cassette tapes, I have endeavored to transcribe some of my favorites, with the goal of producing this book. Here, I will present transcriptions of sixteen of Dr. Farris's sermons as well as a talk he delivered to students at Mid-America about the circumstances of his plane crash in 1965, in which the pilot was killed, and he broke his back. I listen to the tapes often, and even in editing the transcriptions, I could hear his voice echoing in my head.

Dr. Farris was still teaching at Mid-America when he passed away on December 14, 1993, at the age of sixty-six, shortly after publication of his book *Mighty to Save: A Study in Old Testament Soteriology*.[1] On his last visit to Texas, in July of 1993, he gave a copy of the book to my wife and me with the inscription: "To Mike and Susan, As a token of my love—and something to remember me by. As ever, Daddy (Pop) 7/1/93".

It was almost as if he knew his days were numbered. But oh, how much life he packed into his sixty-six years. When my mother, Juanita, died of breast cancer in September of 1978, it culminated a roughly 18-month span in which he lost not only his wife, but also his mother and his sole surviving brother, his other brother and his father having passed away years earlier. Still, he was able to write at the time: "It is at this point that the message of the Gospel and the hope of eternity take on a new and sweeter meaning. To be perfectly honest, I seem to have more investment in the other side than here. Won't it be a glorious day when we can be reunited with those we love?"

---

[1] "Soteriology" is defined as the doctrine of salvation.

Dr. T. V. "Corky" Farris

WHO WAS CORKY FARRIS?[2]

To get a full appreciation of the sermons, you first need to know a little about the man—who he was, what he believed, and how he became what he became. Dr. T.V. "Corky" Farris was born in Fort Worth, Texas, on July 4, 1927, with the given name Theron Vernelle Farris—a name he hated. That explains why he was typically more formally introduced, as an adult, as T.V. Farris, and why he long went by the preferred nickname "Corky" (which is how I'll address him in this narrative going forward).[3]

Of his parents, Corky wrote: "My father was an employee of the city, an electrical engineer for the water department, which position he held for about thirty years. My parents were fine country people who had moved to the city. They were regular and faithful in church attendance, my mother being a Sunday school teacher most of her adult life. Accordingly, my earliest memories are of our going to

---

[2] Much of this narrative is derived from autobiographies that he and my mother wrote in 1957 when they applied to the Foreign Mission Board of the Southern Baptist Convention for appointment as missionaries to Japan, as well as correspondence, other of his writings, and selected documents and materials I obtained from his personal files after his death.

[3] Although he had obtained a ThD from New Orleans Baptist Theological Seminary in the late 1950s, earning him the title "Dr.," I never heard him introduce himself as anything other than simply "Corky."

church, Sunday school and going with my parents as they participated in the various activities of the church."

I suppose it seems that, with this background, it was inevitable that Corky would become involved in church work and Christian ministry. But his path through his younger years was anything but direct. He started high school at Fort Worth Polytechnic High School ("Poly") when he was 13, having skipped a couple of grades during his elementary and junior high years. Though he liked football, he opted not to play his first year at Poly. He explained his decision this way: "During this year I began to be somewhat rebellious against parental discipline, and my church attendance became increasingly irregular and spasmodic. I did not go out for football my first year, feeling that my age, lack of size and ability would keep me from playing. I had something of an inferiority complex in general . . . ."

That rebellious streak intensified over the next few years. At age 14, "[I] found less and less time for Sunday school and church and almost quit going altogether. I found myself more and more interested in questionable amusements and non-Christian companions."

I'm not sure how "rebellious" he actually was, since he never provided any specifics that I am aware of, but at least part of it involved taking up pipe smoking, something he tried to hide from his mother. I know about this because I found a document in his personal files that he had kept for decades, which purported to be a letter his pipe supposedly wrote to him, but which his mother had actually written and tucked away in the drawer where he tried to hide the pipe. I don't know his age at the time.

The letter begins: "Dear Corky, I sure do hate it so bad that I smelled so bad that I was found by your mother. I could hear her sniff sniffing around & the next thing I knew she was going through the drawer cleaning everything. I dashed from one end of the drawer to the other trying my best to keep hid but she took every garment out and all I could do was to just hang my head in shame."

The letter closes: "I knew nice boys like you shouldn't own a nasty little old scamp like me. I am to be pitied, there really is no place for a thing like me so will you please bury me beneath the sod that I may rest throughout eternity in peace. Yours truly with regret, your little old Nasty Pipe"

When he was 15, a high school junior, Corky went out for football again but suffered some health setbacks that curtailed his playing time. He wrote: "I failed to letter and was extremely disappointed. World War II was in full swing by this time. I was strongly influenced by the restlessness that gripped the youth of our nation during those years. I became increasingly rebellious at home and quit going to church completely. I suppose I was no worse than the rest, but I became a thoroughly unmanageable young tough. In brief, I became the kind of boy my mother didn't want me to run around with."

At 16, as a senior in high school, he played first string in the Poly backfield, earning honorable mention All-District honors on "one of the best [teams] in the history of the school. I became quite cocky and vain and was impressed with my own ability on the gridiron and the impression I thought I was making on others." I'm sure that's hard to believe for those of you who knew him to be a man of humility, with a self-deprecating sense of humor.

He graduated from high school in 1944 at the age of 16, turning 17 the summer after graduation. He was offered a football scholarship to SMU, but what he really wanted was to join the Marines. Because he was a minor, he needed parental approval, but his parents refused to sign the necessary papers, so he enrolled at SMU in September to play football. Only two weeks into the school year, he chipped a bone in his ankle that knocked him out for the season, so he dropped out of school after the first quarter.

His mother only agreed to let him drop out in exchange for a promise to start going to church again, which he did at Polytechnic Baptist Church in Fort Worth.

At Poly Baptist, Corky first became acquainted with music director Dallas Alford, who got him involved singing in a quartet. It was there that he turned his life around, attributing some of that to Alford. He wrote: "I was trying so hard to have a good time in worldly pleasures, but for some strange reason he [Alford] was obviously getting much more out of life than was I." On New Year's Eve of 1944, he went with his mother to a "watch night" service at Poly Baptist, but then left "immediately after the service and went to town to meet some of my friends. I went to practically every nightclub in Fort Worth but failed to find them," so he returned to the church for a second service that was being conducted. He wrote that, as he listened to the preacher in that second service, "I suddenly became aware of my own personal shameful predicament. I was running with a crowd that was going straight to hell, and I was helping to get them there."

It was after that night that he made a change in his personal behavior and determined to go into full-time Christian ministry, though his initial direction was not the way he ultimately ended up going. "Of course, I was conscious of my limitations, but I could sing a little . . . . I suppose that at that time I had no personal sense of any divine call, but I did see a need and felt an irresistible compunction to try to meet that need . . . . At that time, however, I felt that the Lord could best use me in the field of Christian music, and I never dreamed that he would ever want me to preach."

SERMON: *For God So Loved the World*[4]

What is it? The most familiar Verse in all the Bible—John 3:16. Christians around the world have that Verse committed to memory in their own tongues and dialects. But regardless of the language, the meaning is the same. However, because of the very familiarity of the Verse, the deep significance and meaning of it may elude us. So, right now, let's think about that Verse and see if we can reconstruct the total story behind it.

To do so, let's call upon the powers of our imagination and see if, in our fancy, we can reconstruct that scene. In our minds, now, let's stand on top of Calvary, in the long ago, on that eventful day that changed the course of history.

As we stand here on top of the hill and shield our eyes against the slanting rays of the morning sun, we study the strange, walled city in the near distance: ancient Jerusalem. Then the gates nearest us open and slowly a great mass of humanity is disgorged. At first, just a conglomerate of human forms.

---

[4] This is one of my favorites. I first heard him preach this at Gaston Avenue Baptist Church in Dallas. He also preached it later at Forest Meadow Baptist Church. This, however, is from an undated and un-noted typed transcript, so I can't tell where or when this specific one was preached.

What's up? A demonstration? A protest march? It looks more like a disorganized parade, and . . . sure enough, it's coming this way. As it does so, we are gradually able to pick out the leader of the procession. He is a tall, deeply tanned, broad-shouldered young man. But instead of carrying a protest placard, he staggers and totters beneath the oppressive weight of a massive wooden cross.

The mob churns and swirls toward us. The crowd seems to be shouting. Are they speaking words of encouragement to him? No! That's not it; they are taunting and tormenting him. To be sure, one is trying to help him carry the weight of the cross, but most of them are laughing at him.

The procession continues to move in our direction, until it comes to the base of the hill upon which we stand. Then, slowly, torturously, painstakingly, the bearer of the cross tugs and drags his burden up the side of the hill until he finally reaches the brow.

A tense hush settles over the throng. He drops the cross and, for a moment, it creates a little stifling cloud of dust. From where we stand, we can see across his back the long, red, oozing stripes that give mute but eloquent testimony to the effectiveness of the talons of the Roman scourge that clawed his back last night.

Strange—despite the evidence of his torture and the shadow of execution, there is something about the set of his jaw. Maybe it's the quiet dignity of his fearlessness or, perhaps, the way those burning eyes seem to bore right through you, but you get the impression that the victim is actually the master of the situation.

We watch in horrified fascination as he stretches himself out on the cross and, unflinching, extends his hands in either direction. A burly Roman soldier walks over with a handful of spikes clutched in one fist, a big heavy mallet in the other. Selecting one of the spikes, he places the point of it in the palm of a hand.

We watch the muscles that ripple and bunch underneath his tawny skin as he raises the mallet. Will he do it?

He brings it ringing down (hands CLAP) and the point of the spike bites into flesh. A splotch of crimson in the palm.

A second blow (CLAP) and the nail sinks into the wood. Blood fills the palm and trickles onto the cross.

The sound of that mallet echoes into the distance (CLAP), reverberates down one of the valleys (CLAP), bounces off the side of a hill (CLAP), and wings out across the heavens (CLAP).

It ricochets off the North Star (CLAP), whistles through the celestial gates (CLAP), races along the streets of heaven (CLAP), and at last it comes clattering into the throne room of God, himself. Somewhere down there on that little insignificant speck of cosmic dirt called earth, his only Son is being nailed to a cross.

Do you hear it? Listen! Do you hear it? Ringing down through the corridors of time to say forever that the wages of sin is death. If the only sinless flesh could not—or would not—escape the consequences of sin, what hope have you and I? We are the guilty ones. We're the perpetrators of the crime. We are the ones who deserve to be nailed to that cross. It is for our rebellion that he suffers.

Finally, the hand is firmly secured to the cross. The same painful process is repeated with the other. Then the feet.

Oblivious to the agony their action causes, a detail of soldiers elevates the cross. They drop its base into the socket carved in the earth. The body swings. The ripping of flesh. And he hangs suspended by bones and tendons. His lacerated wounds gush crimson, and scarlet streams down his arms, across his chest, and runs down his legs to cascade in a little rivulet from his feet into the dust of the earth. An expanding pool of red forms at the base of the cross.

As we stand and watch the blood spill to the ground, somehow it seems in our imagination that we can hear the combined saints of all the ages . . . .

We want to turn our faces to heaven and say, "All right, God. There it is! Your Word says that without the shedding of blood, there is no forgiveness of sin. Well, the blood is spilled. You surely must be sensitive to the excruciating pain that racks his body. Is this not enough payment, sufficient ransom, for all our sins? Now take him down from the cross. Let's halt this brutal spectacle."

But it doesn't stop!

Now, at least the people will come to express their appreciation and gratitude, to offer praise and devotion for his sacrifice.

But, oh no! Here they come, prancing by the foot of the cross to laugh at him and to jeer at him. "Oh, yes, you're the son of God, are you? If indeed you be the Messiah, then come down from the cross and we'll believe you. You saved others; now save yourself and we'll know that you are the Christ . . . . You see—you can't do it. You're a fake, an imposter! Just as we thought."

So, they ridicule him and bathe his feet with their spittle.

Fools!

Fools!

Don't you see them? Look yonder beyond the gaunt outline of the cross, there to the ramparts of heaven. Don't you see them? Row upon row, phalanx upon phalanx, legion upon legion, the innumerable hosts of heaven. See them as they lean over the battlements of glory and they, too, call to the figure on the cross.

"Master, bid us come and we'll take You down from the cross. Master, at Your command, we'll rescue You from this monstrous shame. If necessary, we will annihilate the unbelieving rabble. Lord, at Your command, we will destroy all of the physical universe to demonstrate that Thou art indeed the Creator and King of Glory. Master, bid us come. Suffer no more. Master, bid us come and we'll take You down from the cross."

Now the mob falls silent, for the parched lips of the figure on the cross part. He tries to speak, and the angels listen. They strain from heaven to pick up the sound of His voice. What will He say? Will He ask them to come and help?

He speaks in a hoarse whisper.

"Father, forgive them, for they know not what they do."

That's right! All the nails of Rome could not have kept Jesus clamped to the tree for thirty seconds if he had not chosen to stay there for you. Indeed, all the combined destructive power of the modern nations of earth with their thermonuclear arsenals could not have kept Jesus impaled upon that cross for one split moment had He not chosen to stay there for you, to pay the full penalty for your sin.

Again, we want to turn our faces to heaven and say, "All right, Lord, surely this is enough. Not only the agony that tortures His body, but the shame, the perverse rebellion of the mob—surely this is enough. Let's bring down the curtain on this frightful scene. Let's end it all."

But the spectacle still doesn't stop. Overhead, the clouds begin to drift together, as if God is closing a curtain of gray to shut out the awful view from His gaze. As the clouds gather, they begin to glower and grow dark. They start to rumble and mutter with a muted fury. The wind picks up; it tugs at the tops of the trees, ripples the surface of the field, and starts to moan and whine around the gaunt outline of the cross.

And those who were so smug and arrogant only a moment ago suddenly feel the chill of fear probing at the heart. So, they scurry off into Jerusalem, to find holes in which to hide, like rats deserting a sinking ship.

And it grows dark, so dark that it is almost like midnight at noontime. Then suddenly, a piercing scream erupts from the cross.

"Eli, Eli, lama sabachthani!" My God, My God, why hast Thou forsaken me?

Why does He thus scream? I'll tell you why. Because in that awful moment, all of the sins of the world are emblazoned across His breast. Your sins and mine. And so putrefying, so loathsome is the stench and corruption thereof that God the Father cannot look on his beloved Son as He becomes sin for us. In that moment, He receives in His own body the death, the consequence—the very Hell of our rebellion.

Then the figure speaks again. "It is finished. Father, into Thy hands I commend my spirit."

With a gentle sigh, His head sags upon His breast and He breathes no more.

But, before you leave the scene, for just a moment more observe the still form of the Savior. Watch the wind as it takes a wisp of blood-matted hair and blows it across a gray, bloodless cheek. There, in broad scarlet strokes on the crimson canvas of Calvary is God's great masterpiece of redemptive love. It's for you, as if you were the only person upon the face of the earth.

John reduced it all, the cross, the burial, and the resurrection, to the simple formula: "For God so loved the world that he gave his only begotten son . . ."

But the verse continues. ". . . that whosoever believeth in him shall not perish but have everlasting life."

If I were to ask you the question, "Do you believe in Jesus?" most of you probably would say, "Yes, I believe." Perhaps you would say, "I believe that what you have rehearsed is essentially correct. I believe that Jesus, the Son of God, died for the sins of the world, and that He is able to save all who trust Him. Therefore, I am a Christian."

Not necessarily so. You know, the Bible says that even the demons believe—they believe and shudder. Why, Satan himself could agree to everything I have said to you. But that wouldn't really be an expression of faith because he knows it is so. And it certainly wouldn't make him a Christian.

Well, doesn't the Bible say men are saved by simple faith alone? That's right. But it's one thing to believe *about* Jesus, and something decidedly different to believe *in* Him. There is a significant difference between intellectual assent to Bible truth and a faith that saves. The faith that saves involves commitment and surrender of one's heart and life to Jesus. Let me illustrate what I am talking about.

When I was in the Army, back in the dark ages, in a moment of rashness, I volunteered for paratrooper training. Did they ever pull a dirty trick on me: They accepted me and shipped me off to jump school. That first morning at jump school, we marched to the training area where the instructor began our orientation by explaining the nomenclature and operation of the parachute.

He held up a chute and began by calling our attention to a little metal gizmo that he called a snap fastener. He said that when we got into the plane, there would be a steel cable, called an anchor line, running the full length of the interior of the plane.

"You take the snap fastener, hook it onto the anchor line, jump from the plane, fall approximately ninety feet, and the static line will pull the canopy from the pack. The blast of the engine will blow your chute open. You'll receive an opening shock, and you'll be let down safe and sound."

Well, that sounded reasonable enough. I had seen pictures of that happening, and I bought the whole bit. And so it was that, a few days later, I strapped one of those things called a parachute on my own body. Along with a bunch of other guys nearly scared stiff, I climbed into a C-46 and took a seat across from the big, yawning door. In a moment, the plane lurched into motion. The runway blurred and then dropped away. We were airborne!

We thundered along through the sky, each man isolated by his own fear. As we approached the drop zone, the DZ, I heard the ring of the buzzer and the voice of the jumpmaster as he gave the command to the first ten-man stick to stand up and hook up. I saw those young would-be paratroopers as they leaped to their feet, stomped their boots against the floor of the plane, and yelled like a pack of Indians. They had told us, "If you stomp your feet hard enough and yell loud enough, you won't be afraid."

Well, that was the theory, anyway.

Then again, the voice of the jumpmaster with the order to examine equipment. I watched those men—tense, nervous, excited—as they went over last-minute equipment checks. Then the command of the jumpmaster to close it up and stand in the door. They pressed into jump position, each man jammed against his buddy in front, as tight as the E string on a violin.

The buzzer sounded again, the jumpmaster slapped the first man on the leg and, to the sound of scraping boots and jangling harnesses, one after the other they shuffled out the door.

Now, you know I didn't know any of those men, but I suddenly developed a keen interest in them. So, as the plane banked, I began to count parachutes: one, two, three . . . eight, nine, ten. They had all opened, and I felt a moment of relief. But it was temporary.

We circled the DZ for a second time. Once more I heard the jumpmaster as he gave the command to stand up and hook up. Again, ten young would-be paratroopers jumped to their feet, yelling their fake bravery, checked equipment, and stood in the door. Then the buzzer rang, the jumpmaster slapping the first one on the leg. They, too, one after the other, shuffled out the door just as quickly as they could.

The plane banked for a second time, and for a second time I counted parachutes. Once more, all of them opened.

Then we started the third and final run over the DZ. I heard the voice of the jumpmaster again, but this time it seemed to come from some great distance, as if it were filtered by a waterfall. I jumped to my feet, hooked that snap fastener onto the anchor line, and yanked down. I stomped my boots on the floor—but suddenly my knees turned to rubber, and I sort of dangled on my static line like a marionette.

I tried to yell, but it came out "*aaarrggh.*" Boy, I really felt brave.

The command came to "examine equipment," and I checked everything from the top button of my fatigue jacket to the soles of my boots.

"Close it up and stand in the door!"

As I took hold of the cold metallic sides of the door and I looked out over the green countryside, I wondered what I was doing so far away from Texas.

The buzzer sounded, the jumpmaster slapped me on the leg, and I kicked out into a cold, rushing roar of wind. There was a flash of color, a sickening lurch, and deafening silence.

I looked up, and there it was: my very own parachute. Would you believe it? That was the prettiest piece of material I ever saw in my life—an old G.I., camouflage, nylon canopy. Moreover, I told it so all the way to the ground.

Now, then, would you be willing to concede that I believed in that parachute? When did I believe in it? When I received ground instruction about how it operated? Well, I suppose there was some confidence, or I would have checked out the first day.

When I clambered into the airplane? This, too, demonstrated that I was going to express some faith. When I watched the others as they went out the door and saw that it worked just as they told us it would? Well, up to a point I believed.

But I'll tell you when I really began to trust in it: When I walked up to the door, stepped out, and committed myself—lock, stock and barrel, do or die—to that thing strapped on my back. For the first time, I began to believe *in* it!

Yes, you may believe that Christ has the power to save, give mental approval to everything in the Bible, but you are not a Christian until you step out the door of commitment and surrender yourself totally to the saving and keeping power of Jesus Christ. That's when you believe *in* Him for the first time.

John 3:16 concludes by saying, ". . . that whosoever believeth in Him should not perish but have everlasting life."

A number of years ago, there was a little boy whose mother read the Bible to him regularly. As a result, he began to realize that when the Bible said, "all have sinned," it meant him. He came to sense that there were some things wrong in his own life. Oh, he hadn't done anything very bad. But on the other hand, he hadn't done anything very good. There had been times when his mother said, "Son, you stay out of the cookie jar." But when her back was turned, he had sneaked out a cookie or two. When confronted with his disobedience, he had found it convenient to take some liberties with the truth.

He was just a little fella, but he was already a little thief and little liar.

However, as his mother continued to read the Bible to him, he gradually came to understand that this was the reason Jesus died—in order to do something for him and in order to do something to him.

One day while she was reading the Bible to him, he became very disturbed. In his heart, he knew he was not a Christian. He was miserable as he thought about it. To escape this uncomfortable feeling, he dismissed himself from his mother's presence and started down the back alley towards a little friend's house to play and forget.

About halfway there, he stopped and leaned up against a big oil drum that a neighbor had for a garbage can. As he stood looking down into that thing, he got to thinking about what his mother had read to him out of the Bible. He knew deep inside what he needed to do, but he was scared. He thought about it and decided that he wouldn't do it today—some other time—and he started on down to his friend's house.

But he got only as far as the other side of the garbage barrel. He paused again to look inside the barrel; it was filthy. Then it occurred to him that must be the way the inside of his heart looked to God. And if ever he was to be made clean, he must surrender to Jesus, and if ever he was to trust Jesus, it must be right now.

"I'll do it," he said.

Turning, he ran back to his mother and asked, "Mother, how can I be saved?"

She quoted John 3:16 to him. Then they went into the bedroom, got down on their knees, and there that little boy prayed a little-boy prayer and asked Jesus to come into his heart and save him. And you know what happened? Jesus saved him, and he's been the possessor of a new life—eternal life—ever since.

How do I know so much about that little boy? I ought to. I was that little boy.

It does work, you know. That experience can be yours, too, if you will just give your heart to Him.

Transitional Narrative: *Why doesn't someone go tell them about Jesus?*

It was also at Poly Baptist that Corky first met my mother (Juanita Peacock; I will refer to her as Juanita) in 1945, though he knew of her through her brothers with whom he played football at Poly, and they began dating. He joined the Army in April of 1945, going through basic training at Fort Sam Houston then he was assigned to Camp Hood (later Fort Hood and now Fort Cavazos), and was later reassigned to Fort Oglethorpe, Georgia, to the Adjutant General's School where he spent six weeks in administrative training. From there, he was reassigned to Japan, at his request, as part of the U.S.'s military occupation of Japan following the end of World War II, but not before a two-week furlough to Fort Worth, during which he asked Juanita to marry him.

In August of 1945, he arrived in Yokohama, Japan, where he made application to the 11th Airborne Division Jump School. He was transferred to northern Japan for training and earned his paratrooper "jump pin." One of the more interesting documents I found in his office after his death is a paper he wrote for a college English class at Baylor titled "My First Parachute Jump," a first-hand, blow-by-blow account of that jump.

All the while he was in Japan, it's obvious that Corky pined for Juanita. In a letter to his mother (whom he lovingly called "Pudgy Wudgy"), he apologized for not writing sooner but said that "Every time I write, I always write to Peacock first, and by the time I get through writing to her, I don't have much time to write to anyone else." He closed the letter by noting, "Peacock really messed up my overseas trip. I really wanted to go [to Japan] before, but now I don't want to do anything but sit around and drool. No kidding, in case you didn't know, I really love that kid. Surprise!"

After earning his jump pin, Corky was assigned to the Adjutant General section at Airborne Division Headquarters in Sapporo on the island of Hokkaido. It was there that he "really came to know Japan." In December 1946, just a month before his enlistment was up, he and a group of men, along with the chaplain, attended a Christmas pageant in a small Japanese church two days before the holiday. "The pageant itself was presented by the children, and they were so cute and pathetic that I really loved them and wondered what life could possibly offer them in Japan."

He and the other men decided to buy toys and "play Santa Claus" for those kids on Christmas Day, but his participation was derailed when he was summoned home on emergency leave after his father suffered a serious heart attack the day before Christmas. A month later, he returned to California to be separated from the Army and then went back home to Fort Worth.

It was during his time in Japan that Corky first felt a calling to minister to the Japanese people, although it wasn't something that came easily to him. Writing about leaving Japan aboard a C-54 the day before Christmas in December of 1946, he said: "After spending several months as a paratrooper with the 11th Airborne Division in an occupied Japan, I had had enough of it. I was tired of the whole country; I was tired of the people, the poverty, the hunger, the destruction, the everlasting stench, the narrow streets, the unpainted houses, the indescribable filth, the hopelessness that hems in the lightest heart. I had seen enough of Japan. And, as the runway melted into a blur and dropped beneath us, I cheerfully peered out the window to bid my last farewell to Japan. I hated it. I never wanted to see those islands again. This was good-bye for keeps—or so I thought."

But as it turned out, "the memories of little runny-nosed, dirty-faced children clothed in rags haunted my every thought."

After he returned to Fort Worth, Corky enrolled at Texas Wesleyan College and began taking classes. It took a while, he said, to adjust to civilian life. "One of the things that bothered me during this period . . . was the growing feeling in my heart that I wanted to preach. At first, I was certain that it was simply a personal desire, so I ignored it. Besides, I had enrolled as a music major in school, and I . . . had made some very definite plans around . . . full time music work."

Corky and Juanita were to be married in June of 1947, but by then he no longer believed that his call to Christian service was in music but, rather, was to preach. "By the time summer came the issue was settled in my heart, which matter I shared with Juanita while we made plans for our June wedding. Much to my surprise she wasn't surprised at all but had known for some time that the Lord was dealing with me about it."

After their wedding, they honeymooned in New Mexico, then Corky returned to classes at Texas Wesleyan but also enrolled in a Homiletics class, which is defined as "the art of preaching," at Southwestern Baptist Theological Seminary in Fort Worth. They bought a car so he could drive between the two campuses, and he even found a job at a downtown parking lot to help out with expenses.

I'm still having a hard time imagining "my father the parking lot attendant."

While at Texas Wesleyan, "with very little experience and much enthusiasm," he accepted a job as youth director at North Fort Worth Baptist Church, which also included handling the church's music program since they were without a music director at the time. There, he led a citywide youth revival in Fort Worth and set up and conducted mission Bible schools around the city using all volunteer help.

"One such Bible school was located in one of the slum sections of Fort Worth, and we used a convenient bridge for the roof of an auditorium by meeting underneath it. In this section . . . children lived together in the same shacks and lean-tos. They came to Bible school together in dirty, ragged clothes, and they were a rowdy lot. But bless their hearts, they were so hungry for someone to love them that they just swarmed all over us every morning when we arrived because we had taken an interest in them."

It was those Bible schools, and spending time with those kids, that triggered a memory from Japan. "For just a fleeting moment caught in the flicker of my imagination, I was seated again on a train coach somewhere between Sendai and Sapporo in northern Japan looking through the window into the faces of other little children with ragged clothes . . . as they gazed at the strange American soldiers who were enjoying the warmth of the coach while they shivered in sub-freezing weather . . . . That vivid memory set me to thinking. What about those little children in Japan? . . . . Yes, for the first time I was really concerned about the needs of Japan, and over and over I asked myself, 'Why doesn't someone go tell them about Jesus?'"

That question continued to gnaw at him as he transferred from Texas Wesleyan to Baylor University in Waco, where Juanita also enrolled and took classes. While at Baylor, in addition to his classes and serving as pastor at the Ninth Street Mission, Corky made three summer mission trips to Japan before obtaining his B.A. in Greek in 1951. The first trip was in 1949 along with a nisei (American born to Japanese parents) friend from Baylor named Henry Ikemoto. Other students helped raise funds for the trip and, "before we realized it, Henry and I had enough money to go to Japan. We didn't have enough money to get back, but it seemed logical that if the Lord had enough money to get us there, He must have enough to get us back and He would supply it when it was needed."

By the time of his second mission trip, in 1950, the Korean War had started and, if he went, "we faced the very real prospect of finding ourselves cut off from home in a foreign land by a war." But he went anyway, this time with a larger group of seven students, from various colleges in Texas, again including Henry Ikemoto.

He returned for the last time as a student in 1951, and this time Juanita accompanied him. She wrote: "We went to the island of Hokkaido and there did most of our work. I immediately fell in love with the Japanese people. I began to see how Corky could love them so much and began to see the need for myself as we worked among them."

After Corky and Juanita returned from that trip, it was on to New Orleans Baptist Theological Seminary (NOBTS) for his B.D. (Bachelor of Divinity) in 1955, followed by his Th.D. (Doctor of Theology) in 1958. The title of his doctoral dissertation was *Degrees of Definiteness in the Aramaic Genitive Relationships in the Book of Daniel*, fitting, I suppose, for someone who would end up an Old Testament scholar and a Hebrew professor. Juanita once told me that, as of 1958, he had received the highest grade on a written dissertation in the history of NOBTS (which dated back to 1917) and that when he went before a panel of professors for the oral defense of his dissertation, they told him they had no questions.

While at NOBTS, Corky served as the founding pastor of Goodwood Baptist Church in Baton Rouge—during which tenure both my older sister, Darlyne, and I were born—and as pastor of Osyka Baptist Church in Osyka, Mississippi. After my birth on June 30, 1955, he wrote, "I spent much of that summer in the delightful companionship of my new son." Certainly, the first time, and quite possibly the last, that anyone has referred to my companionship as "delightful," although I'm sure other adjectives have been used.

In the fall of 1957, Corky and Juanita were appointed by the Foreign Mission Board as full-time foreign missionaries, and in the spring of 1958, our family traveled aboard the ship *President Wilson* to Japan. Darlyne was four and I was two; brother Steve would come along later, born in Kyoto, Japan, in August of 1960.

The Farris family spent two years in Tokyo, where Corky and Juanita both went to language school to learn Japanese. Juanita became conversational in the language, while Corky took additional study to become fluent, allowing him to preach in Japanese. From Tokyo it was on to Sapporo on the island of Hokkaido for three more years. Darlyne and I both attended our first years of elementary school in Japan; I got my start at Hokkaido International

School in Sapporo, where I attended first and second grades.

The next two sermons have a bit of the flavor of Japan from stories told in them.

SERMON: *Curse of Half-Heartedness*[5]

I do not know whether you are alert to the fact or not, but the first person to get the preacher's message is the preacher. And so, with that in mind, may I direct your attention then to Jeremiah 48, Verse 10. We'll just read the first half of the verse. And in the King James, it reads in this fashion, "Cursed be he that doeth the work of the Lord deceitfully."

I'm not sure what kind of impression or reaction that verse stimulates. I'm free to admit, however, that across the years I read this particular verse, and it said practically nothing to me. I just couldn't quite grasp what was being communicated. "Cursed be he that doeth the work of the Lord deceitfully."

And then I happened to stumble upon an edition of the Old Testament that had a note in the margin alerting me to the fact that the word "deceitfully," the adverb there, could be translated differently. And I suppose I would never have noticed the distinction had it not been for the note in my margin. And as I looked at it, then it began to talk to me because the verse can be read, very legitimately, "Cursed be he that doeth the work of the Lord"—and here's

---

[5] Preached on May 13, 1973, at Forest Meadow Baptist Church in Dallas.

the shift— "negligently."

We're living in a time in which our pseudo-sophisticated society is telling us that if you really want to be suave and with it, that you need to be a little bit bored with life. You know what I mean? Now, you find it expressed with some frequency on the television screen. I think it's rather classically condensed in a woman movie critic who sort of sniffs partly down her nose at everything. She's seen all the movies, and she's read all of the plays and she's been to all of the productions. And man, she just knows the whole thing until she's just talking down to everybody all the time.

And this sophisticated approach to life suggests that if you really want to be a part of the now generation and the jet set, you need to be a little bit jaded and you need to be just a little bit reserved and you don't want to get enthused or excited or all steamed up about anything. And surely the last thing in the world that ought to captivate your energies would be religion. Because if you get excited about your religion, then that would put you in the category of being a fanatic. And of course, the last thing in the world we'd ever want to be is a fanatic.

Now, you know what a fanatic is, don't you? Nine times out of ten, that's just somebody who's closer to Jesus than I am. And he looks like a radical to me.

But I'm appalled, frankly, at the way in which the professing Christian community seems to be entranced with this siren song of sophistication. It just doesn't seem plausible to me that we'd buy this particular bill of goods in light of two lessons that ought to just thunder for our attention.

One is that modern history, if it teaches us anything at all, it is this lesson: That at the human level, those who are influencing the ebb and flow of events in the 20th Century are not people who are emotionally detached from the conflicts of life. But, to the contrary, they are individuals and they are groups who are irrevocably and zealously committed to a proposition or to a call. It really doesn't make any difference at which end of the philosophical or idealistic spectrum. It may be from the jack-booted storm troopers of Adolf Hitler's Third Reich to the snake dancing Zengakuren sect in Japan, right on down to the left-wing militants who've stormed the great universities and who've eroded the streets of our city, to the Arab guerillas who have terrorized Europe and the Near East. It really doesn't make any difference.

We are living in an age in which men find themselves in fiery commitment to their causes and to their propositions, and they're making the rest of the world dance to their tune and sit up and take notice. Win, lose, or draw, they are hammering out the events of the 20th Century. And in light of that, I'm deeply convinced that if we believe, in this era, that run of the mill, ho-hum, lukewarm, take-it-or-leave it, business as usual commitment to the cause of Christ is going to startle and to jar the events of our day, then I think we're sadly, sadly, mistaken.

They'll never even know we've been on the scene. But they'll hear the zealots, and they'll listen to the radicals, and they'll respond to the fanatics. I'm not calling for blind, irrational fanaticism, but I am saying that just fair-to-middling Christianity is not going to cut it now—if it ever did.

The second thing, as I read God's word, I don't think he ever puts his stamp of approval upon that kind of devotion. To the contrary. I think he's attempting to challenge us away from it. I think he's constantly making an effort to tear the middle ground out from under us. That's the thing the Lord was trying to drive Israel to when he spoke through Elijah, his servant, as he called all of the people there. On the pulpit stand of Mount Carmel, he said, "All right, now make up your mind. How long are you going to stagger between two opinions? If Jehovah is God, then serve him. If Balaam is God, then serve him. But make up your mind and go one way or the other."

Our Lord himself presented that same kind of response option when he said, "No man can serve two masters. He cannot serve God and mammon. He'll either hold the one and he'll despise the other, or he'll cling to this, and he'll reject the other." You just can't go in two directions at the same time, and he was speaking to that.

Same thing when he addressed the church at Laodicea. As he said, "I know your works. You're neither hot nor cold. I wish you were hot or cold, but because you're neither hot nor cold, but simply lukewarm, therefore will I spew you out of my mouth."

And here it is classically formulated, "Cursed be he who performs the work of the Lord negligently."

As I look at this verse, I'm reminded of that friend about whom I spoke in the message this morning, O.K. Bozeman, Jr., and his college days as an outstanding athlete in football for Vanderbilt and North Carolina State. I will never forget when he shared on one occasion, with some of the men in the church, his introduction to the coaching philosophy of one of the two schools, whichever one it was that he went to second.

He said that in the orientation, as the head coach talked to the men, he made this statement. He said, "Now men, if in practice you get confused and you forget your assignment and, let's say you're a pulling guard, and you pull out and you're supposed to lead to the right, and instead of leading to the right, you lead to the left and you crash into the other guard coming in that direction, and you just make a terrible mess out of the play. That's all right. Don't you worry about it. Just forget it. Don't let that bother you.

"Now, for that matter, even on the floor of the stadium on Saturday afternoon, suppose you're playing on defense, and you cover the wrong man, and you forget what your assignment is, and that guy out there catches a pass, goes down there and makes a touchdown. That's all right. Don't worry about it. Don't let that bother you. You can make a mistake. Any mistake in the book that's a lapse of memory. It is forgivable . . . provided you make the mistake going full speed."

Now, do you understand what he was saying? He was saying a lapse of memory is forgivable, but a lack of effort is not permissible at all under any circumstance. I think that's what the Lord is saying here by pronouncing his curse upon half-heartedness.

Now that makes good sense. That makes real good sense if you stop and think about it. Because, you see, our half-heartedness is the bane of the work of the Lord. It is this one ingredient that does more, I am convinced, to impede and obstruct the growth and the march of the Kingdom than anything else.

Now, you know, we can talk a good fight, and we can boast about how wonderful we think the Lord is, and we can extol his virtue and his grace. But when we reflect upon his instructions, and when we react to his commandment to be his witness and to disciple the nations and to preach the gospel to every creature, we really begin to communicate some things by the way we go about it.

We may boast of him as being the desire of the nations and the fairest of ten thousand and the lily of the valley, the lion of the tribe of Judah and the king of our lives. And we may speak of his banner as being the most noble cause around which men have ever assembled, but we reflect what we really think about his cause and about his banner when we respond to his orders and when we execute his commands.

And it's not only just what we do, but how we do it, and the dispatch and the excitement and zeal and the enthusiasm with which we respond when he gives his orders. And that is what tells the world what we really believe about our Lord. Not what we mouth and not what we repeat and not what we sing and not what we chant and not what we say, but how we act. That tells them what we really believe about Jesus.

Now, this is one of the reasons that the younger generation has pretty well got us older folks figured out, and we wonder why they have their question marks and have their doubts. They've heard us and then they've watched us. We may speak of our commitment and of our desire to serve, and we may boast, and we may pray with our lips, but what we are and how we respond, and our zeal and enthusiasm tells people what we really think and how we're really committed to him.

But you know, the second reason I think this curse upon half-heartedness makes sense is the fact that, I suppose, it is this facet or this feature of our operation that above everything else imperils the unsaved. Now, God's grace is adequate to redeem and to restore, and to reconcile all the nations. All the blood that's necessary to be spilled for the remission of sins has already been poured out on the top of Calvary. The Holy Spirit is able to take that message and to convict and to convince and, ultimately, to convert men. And this really does not need to be defended before the unbelieving throngs of our day. All it needs is simply a zealous declaration.

But if God's done everything that's necessary to save to the uttermost, why aren't they saved? Well, you know, I can remember back at the close of World War II we were saying that one of these days, we're going to do something very dramatic and something very exciting in world evangelism and global missions. The little drum that we were beating on in those days as Southern Baptists was that, as soon as we get a strong home base, and as soon as we get our buildings built and our programs manned, then we'll go out and we'll evangelize the nations of Earth.

Well, here we are 25 years later. And we've built our buildings, and we've trained our leadership, and we've staffed and manned our programs, and we have more resources. We have more trained leadership, we have more personnel, we have more experience, we have more everything. And theoretically, we ought to be aggressively winning the world to saving faith in Christ.

But to the contrary, here we are for the most part as a professing Christian community, hiding behind our stained-glass windows and wringing our hands in increasing anguish and lamenting the fact that the world is passing us by and they don't care whether we're even in existence or not, and we can't understand why.

Now, what's the reason? It's not the lack of money. It's not the lack of buildings. It's not the lack of leadership. It's not the lack of training. It's not the lack of opportunity. And it's surely not the lack of lostness. Sooner or later, if we are honest, we'll have to paint ourselves into that final corner. The reason we are not turning our world upside down is because we have lost our passion.

That's one of the reasons, to be very honest with you, that I'm pleased that some of this group right here will be making that trip to Germany just next month. We really don't need to be going to Germany. You know that. I do, too. We're looking at some very critical factors in our development. We'll be talking about them at the close of the service tonight and, I suppose, strictly speaking, none of us ought to go to Germany. We've got a building to build, and we've got a ministry to perform right here.

But I've heard that song too many times. When we get our building built and our program is all completed and we've reached our community—if we wait until that day comes, the world will continue to accelerate its headlong plunge into Hell. It'll just do it. And that's the reason they are not saved: because of our lack of real commitment.

As I think of that, I remember the story that our

Lord told concerning the Good Samaritan. I don't mean to misapply the illustration or the parable, but I think I see something here. You remember that wayfaring pilgrim set upon on the highway. Beaten within an inch of his life and left there to gurgle, to gasp in his blood and in his pain. And here came the priest and here came the Levite. And here was a man who was in urgent need of rescue and remedy and first aid and deliverance, but they were on their way to the temple to worship. And if they were to soil their hands with that man's blood and that man's gore and misery, they would be ceremonially impure. And they would no longer have access to that holy place where they would worship the Lord. And so, they hurried on down the highway to worship the Lord.

My soul! My soul! How callous, how seared over, how indifferent, how dumb can spiritual vitality be as it's reflected in the priest and the Levite. But before we pass too severe judgment on them, how many of us pass by homes, acre after acre of homes and houses where there may be people just as brutally beaten and just as bashed and just as bloody and just as hopeless and just as miserable and just as unhappy and just as lost as the man in the story? And it's our lack of commitment and excitement about sharing the message of life that really keeps the door shut upon his healing graces. If we could just understand that men are not lost ultimately in some dim, distant, eschatological future, but men are lost now, and they're hurt and they're scarred and they're tortured and they're wounded.

Some years ago, I was in a revival meeting in one of the churches out in El Paso. It was an Encounter Crusade that all of the Baptist congregations were sharing and participating in, and in this context a noon service, a meal, was planned down at First Church. The pastor of the church where I was the evangelist took me down there a little bit late. I'm accustomed to traveling late, but we were running especially late that particular day.

In courtesy of my condition, he let me off at the door of the First Baptist Church, right there in the heart of the city. I got out while he went to park the automobile, and I went up the steps inside the building, then into the chapel, which is self-contained in one of the larger buildings there.

And as I walked in, I saw that I was late, just way late. The service was already over, the lights out, and my first thought was, "Oh boy, I hope they haven't already gotten through the chow line." It's all right to miss the preaching, you know, but I sure hate to miss lunch. And so I sort of began to shuffle as quickly as I could down that aisle in the gloom.

Out the corner of my eye, I caught the figure of an individual over there next to the wall, still seated. And I thought to myself, "Well, one of those preachers went to sleep. I guess it wasn't such a fiery message after all. He went to sleep, and they went off and left, and they'll go ahead and eat, and he'll just have to do without lunch."

But as I moved on down to the front and toward the door, I got a second thought about that figure. There was something mutely pathetic about that shadow over there in the darkness. It was almost as if he were calling after me.

And as I left the chapel building, on an impulse, I just circled the chapel and went back and entered the rear of the room again. As I walked in, I came to the row where that figure was seated, and I went in there and sat down next to him. It was only as I took a seat beside him that I saw it was not a preacher, but he was a young man.

I introduced myself and I said, "Are you having some problems, son?"

And he said, "Yes, sir, I really am." He said, "I've got problems the likes of which I've never had before." He said, "I'm a student over here at the college. I'm a stranger in the city. I've had problems before, but never anything like this." And he said, "I've just been out there walking the streets. I didn't know which way to turn. I saw this church building, and it occurred to me that maybe God could help. And I walked in here and just sat down." He said, "Yes, sir. I do have troubles. I've got big problems."

Well, you know, I don't think he ever told me what the problem was, but that was secondary. Anyway, I began to talk to him about the one person I found who can unravel all of the snarled threads of my life and who can solve any and every problem if I commit to him. As I told him about Jesus and asked him if he'd like to have the Lord come into his life, he said, "Yes, sir, I believe I would."

As we prayed, there was a glory of heaven in that old, darkened chapel as he gave his heart to Jesus. At the last word I heard from him, he'd come and made a profession of faith and been baptized at First Baptist Church of El Paso.

But you know, as I left that dark room, it suddenly hit me. There was an ol' boy hurt! He was like a wounded rabbit, struggling beside some forest trail and he was hurt. He really couldn't even tell, I expect, exactly where it hurt the most. But he needed the healing graces of the Lord. And I came so close to letting old half-heartedness keep me from saying anything about Jesus to him.

Our half-heartedness not only deprives people like

that of his healing graces right now, but if we persist in our lukewarmness, and if we hang on in our half-heartedness, it can slam the door of heaven in the faces of some people.

Well, I've got a jim dandy of an illustration here that I wish I could forget. I wish I could blot it out. I wish I could erase it. I wish I could undo it, but there's just no way.

Soon after we settled into our missionary home in Sapporo, Japan, we employed a young Japanese lady to work in our home to help with the chores of the household and to take care of Stevie, who was just about five or six months old then, so that Juanita could share in missionary responsibilities. She was a very charming young lady and from a very fine home, and I shall never forget how favorably impressed I was with her parents when I first met them.

Her dad had worked in one of the banking enterprises there in Sapporo. He was not a wealthy man, but he was retired, and he was comfortably fixed. And I shall never forget my response to him. He was such a distinguished, aristocratic-looking Japanese gentleman. He appeared to be no taller than I, with silver, gray hair. He was just almost the personification of the Japanese spirit, the Samurai warrior, and he was Japanese aristocracy at its best.

His wife was just a little elf of a Japanese mother. I think, if I remember correctly, she could just about walk under my arm stretched out like that. She was so tiny, and she was almost the personification of one of these little Japanese dolls that some of you may have seen on the store shelves. But there was one gross contradiction in her appearance. Her eyes just snapped and sparkled with mischief. They looked like the eyes of a 16-year-old high school girl. I believe she was the most charming little Japanese lady I ever met in my life.

As I met them, immediately my heart went out to them, and I just responded so favorably and I loved them. And I yearned for them in the Lord. But I remember saying to myself, "Now, Corky, you don't want to be too aggressive, but you cultivate the friendship of this charming couple. And after you get to know them adequately and well enough, then you'll have the opportunity to talk to them about the Lord."

God being my witness, that's what I intended to do.

The first Christmas we were there, they came over on Christmas morning. I can still see it. The lights on the tree sparkled and winked, and here they came bearing a red sled for Stevie. Bright red sled. Very appropriate in the chilly snow country of Hokkaido. As we stood in the living room that morning, I thought to myself how sweet and gracious to bring a present for my son on the day that marks the birth of my Lord. And I coveted them for the Lord.

But you don't want to be too gung-ho. We had been told that if you were too aggressive, it would be offensive to the Japanese mentality. And so, I thought I would appropriately bide my time.

The telephone rang one day, however, and it was our housekeeper, flustered and excited, calling to say that her mother was stricken ill and had been taken to the hospital. She asked permission to go to her mother's side and, of course, permission was granted. We waited a day or so and then we journeyed across the city to the appointed hospital. And I remember that, too, just as clearly as if it had happened yesterday. We walked down that hospital corridor and I was thinking to myself that now was the time to talk to her. You don't know how ill she is. You don't know how serious the problem is. You need to talk to her about the Lord right now. And when we walked into that room, that's exactly what I went in there to do.

But when we got inside, she was so alert and so vivacious. Her countenance just sparkled. And it was obvious that she was recovering nicely, and it wouldn't be long until she'd be back in her own home. And I got to thinking, "You know what? That's kind of an underhanded thing to do to come into a hospital room and ask somebody if they're prepared to die, or something like that. You know, that's just kind of creepy. You don't want to do that sort of thing." And I thought to myself, "Well, that's hardly the proper way to do evangelism in the Orient." And so, I didn't say anything.

We went back to our own residence, and we waited for her to get out of the hospital and come home so we could go talk to her about Jesus. But she never did come home, and I never did talk to her. And she died, friends. She died without Jesus.

"Cursed be he who does the work of the Lord negligently."

When I realized what had taken place, I was absolutely devastated in my spirit. I said to myself, "Oh, what have you done? What have you done? Man, you've made a fatal blunder, and somebody else is going to have to pay the price." And then I thought about that husband, and I thought, "Well boy, it's gonna be a whole lot harder to witness to him now, but I'll not make the same mistake twice. I'll go to him, and I'll talk to him about my risen

Lord who has the power over death and the grave. I'll just wait a few days for him to indulge his grief and after his mourning period has been adequate, then I'll go and talk to him."

So, I waited what I thought was an appropriate period of time and, would you believe it? While I was waiting, that man that, so far as I knew, was in the peak of health for a gentleman his age, dropped dead of a heart attack. And I never did get talk to him either.

"Cursed be he who does the work of the Lord negligently." Because when we piecemeal it along and postpone it, procrastinate, and use all sorts of little devious dodges and excuses not to be a witness in his name, do we understand we are slamming the gate shut in their faces?

Now, this final observation. I think another reason the Lord places the curse on half-heartedness is what it does to us. It robs us of the most exciting part of being a member of the army of Jesus Christ; it robs us of our witness. When there is half-hearted commitment to the assignment to be a witness in his name, we somehow never do get around to it. And then we miss out on all of the real thrill and all of the real excitement of being in the game.

I remember when I first got to New Orleans Seminary, they were all in the middle of a year. I came in at midterm and down there, there's a field mission program where everybody has to go out and witness. Now, you don't really have to witness, but you do have to go out on an assignment two times a week, and whether you are pleased with it or whether you're Billy Graham or whatever, first year students have to go out for two witnessing assignments. Well, the first assignment that I drew was an assignment to go to a street service in the French Quarter.

Now friend, if you think that's not belling the cat, think again, because I want you to know, that's going right up to the jaws of it to give your witness. I've tried to give witness from the Orient to the Occident, but I don't think I've found any place that's any more hostile to the Gospel than the French Quarter in New Orleans.

We got down there, and we had gone down on the seminary bus, and these old hands who knew what was going on, they got the sound equipment out and they got the portable organ out and they distributed some song books. We were in one of those great big vegetable sheds and I was—I'll just be real frank about it—I was embarrassed to tears. Suppose some of my friends from Texas come down there and see me off down there in the French Quarter. Boy, wouldn't that be terrible!

And so, I stood over at the back of a little group and we sang a few songs, and it didn't look like anybody down there knew what was going on anyway. And I thought well, maybe we'll get by with this and if I stay on the back row, I could pull it off pretty well. And I was thinking, "I sure will be glad when we get through with this so I can get on that bus and go back out there to the seminary and study evangelism." You know, I was going to go back out there and study about it instead of doing it. And so, there was a song or two and a testimony or two and a fella kind of tried to preach.

And then in a minute, they finally got everything through, and they folded up that portable organ. I thought, man, I thought it was never going to end. And then all of a sudden somebody shoved a fist-full of tracts in my hand, and I looked in his face, boy, stunned.

And suddenly I saw the men and, as they scattered, they didn't go two at a time, they went individually. They just scattered out through that market. All across the streets, up and down. All the men went.

Everybody . . . except me and the lady folks.

And there I stood with a handful of tracts and those ladies standing right there beside that bus looking at me. Man, I want you to know I was scared to death to head off down there through that French Quarter by myself. But I'll have to admit, I was more embarrassed to stay there with the lady folks, 'cause it made those other fellas look more spiritual than I did.

And so, I took that handful of tracts, and I started off down that vegetable shed in the French Quarter. Friends, I want you to know that was when I began to find out what it's all about. Anything that won't communicate the Gospel in the French Quarter in New Orleans, I'm not real sure we need it in this church or anybody else's, because that's what it's all about. It's not to sing songs, it's not to pat each other on the back. It's not to bask in our fellowship. That's all good, but that's what Heaven is all about. We're here to work together, to train, to go out into the French Quarters of life and to tell people about Jesus. And cursed be he who performs that assignment negligently.

There was a preacher and a deacon walking down a road one afternoon, and they were in something of a dilemma. They needed a lift into town. They came up to a home in the rural section of the country there, knocked on the door, and the gentleman of the house came. They explained their problem that they needed to use the telephone and call the nearby Baptist church where transcription was available.

The gentleman very graciously invited them inside and they went in, and the preacher got the number of the Baptist church and dialed it. While he was waiting for someone to answer the receiver at the other end, he heard that deacon friend of his as he began to talk to the little old gentleman and his wife there in the den in the home. And he began the conversation by saying, "Where do you folks belong to church?"

And the man responded, as the dial tone began to ring at the other end, "Well, we belong to the Assembly of God."

And just about the time that the receiver was lifted at the Baptist church, out of the other ear, the preacher heard the man say, "Well, to tell you the truth, that's where my wife belongs, but I don't belong anywhere."

By the time the preacher got off the telephone and the ride was on its way, that deacon was talking to that man very earnestly about his need of the Lord. And it turned out that he really did desperately need him because, by his own admission, he was in his mid-sixties and an alcoholic. He said, "To tell you the truth, today's my day off, and I started to go into town several times. But I knew if I did, I'd get drunk and so I didn't go. I've just been hanging around the house here all day as if I were waiting for somebody to come."

When those two men heard that, then they really begin to press the claims of Christ. And before they left the house, that gentleman, 65 years of age, opened his heart to Jesus and the Lord came into his life.

Later that evening, after their business was over, the deacon and the preacher came back down that highway, back to the little landing strip at the airport, and got in their Mooney aircraft and started back toward Dallas. And of course, you know, they didn't make it.

I was the preacher. And the deacon, with his body broken down in the Big Thicket, breathed his last breath and stepped from that wreckage into the presence of the King of Kings and the Lord of Lords. And when Len Rogers stood before our Lord, he stood there to say, "Master, the last opportunity I had to be a witness in your name, I took it."

I took it! What a way to go.

"Cursed be he who doeth the work of the Lord negligently."

SERMON: *Settling for Second Best*[6]

Tonight, I want to read two verses that are very familiar, from the 12th Chapter of Romans, Verses one and two. "I beseech you therefore brethren, by the mercies of God, that ye present your bodies a living sacrifice, holy, acceptable unto God, which is your reasonable service. And be not conformed to this world but be ye transformed by the renewing of your mind, that he may prove what is that good and acceptable and perfect will of God."

When we arrived in Japan to serve as missionaries, we were assigned to a residence in the compound area of the language school housing that was provided for new arrivals. There were some advantages in this kind of a concept because it meant that we were placed in a living area with missionaries who'd been there a little longer than we, and who had studied the language and who knew more about it. So, this provided one of the positive benefits. It meant that we could have a carpool, and we could go together to the language school. We could even have the opportunity of studying together and getting to know each other until we knew each other so well that we could just, you know, just almost hate each other thoroughly.

But seriously, it was clear it had its benefits. But it

---

[6] Preached at Forest Meadow Baptist Church on July 22, 1973.

also had its negative side. And a part of it was the outgrowth of the missionary version of keeping up with the Joneses. Living in a foreign land with your children, there is for missionary parents a sense of the fact that here are youngsters away from other members of the family, away from grandmother, grandfather, and the desire to provide every benefit and every substitute that's available in light of those omissions in their experience. This expressed itself in some very tangible ways. For example, there were several youngsters living out there in the compound together, and some parent brought in some kind of a plaything for one of their children. Well, two or three days later, all the other children of the same age would have the same toy. Sometimes it would even be a little bit nicer than the original version. And you can see how this thing would build up.

After a while, though, this began to get a little bit out of proportion, with every parent trying to prove that they loved their child just as much as the other missionary families. It wasn't long until some pretty ambitious presents were being bought. It really reached its climax when one day we came in from language school and—there were four or five little boys about the same age as my number one son, who was the only son in the family at that particular time. Little old knot-head renegades out there running around, digging holes in the ground, tearing up shrubbery, and that sort of thing. Hammering down walls.

We came in from language school one day and there was a bright, glistening, shiny new bicycle, with training wheels on the back and all that.

Well, I said to myself, "This has gone far enough now. We can't afford a bicycle. I don't know how in the world that other guy could afford it. I don't know what he did. He had to write a prayer letter and pour out his heart or something to the folks back home. I don't know how in the world he got that kind of money. He sure didn't get it out of his missionary salary, but it's gone far enough and we're just not gonna do that. We're not gonna try to keep up with that."

I was pretty firm in my resolve. But, oh, I guess maybe three or four weeks later I came home and there was another bright, shiny new bicycle out there. Hmmm. Bunch of smart alecks. I'm just not gonna give in to that. And I just kind of muttered and grumbled around the house there for two or three days. I'm just not going to yield to that kind of pressure. And I did pretty good for a while.

But there were four of these boys. You know, this dirty quartet out there. You couldn't tell whether they were

Japanese or American when they came in, they were so dirty. Anyway, I came in about a month later and there was another bright, shiny new bicycle. Every kid had a bicycle except my boy. Well, that was just too much. And I got to thinking about that. I loved my kid as much as anybody else in that compound. So, we began to work around and figure around. Mike was gonna have a birthday before long, and we did a little reviewing of our budget and figured that if we went without food for three or four weeks, we could squeeze it out.

I wanted to get all the benefit and all the goody out of that opportunity, you know? And so, on the eve of his birthday, I called him into the house, and I said, "Now son, your birthday's coming up."

He said, "Yes, Daddy, I know."

And I said, "Now, if you could have anything you wanted, what would you like for your Daddy to give you for your birthday?"

I knew what he was gonna say. He wanted one of those bicycles. And he said, "Well, Daddy, I'd like to have a chicken feather."

"Uh, how's that?"

He said, "Well, we've been playing cowboys and Indians, and I'm supposed to be an Indian and I need a chicken feather. You know, get it tied around my head like that."

I said, "Now son, Daddy's not kidding. I'm serious about this. I mean, really, if you could have anything you wanted, I mean, just anything you wanted, boy, just anything, you know, don't worry about it. What would you like to have for your birthday?"

"Well," he said, "I'm serious. I really would like to have a chicken feather."

"Now son, your Daddy's real serious. Your birthday's coming up and we've been kind of counting our yen here, and we're prepared to get you something real nice. If you could have anything you wanted for your birthday, I mean even a bicycle, what would you like to have most?"

"I'd rather have a chicken feather."

I said, "Well, you smart aleck kid, you're gonna get a bicycle anyway." And that's exactly what he got. I made him take it.

You know, isn't it amazing? Here's something much more fantastic available, and yet a child in a childish way can settle for something that is so unimportant and so inexpensive and so meaningless and temporary. And you know, sometimes we parents will force the good present, the more appropriate gift.

But the greatest gift of all, after salvation, doesn't come like that. It's God's will. God has a present beyond compare. He has a marvelous design. He has an impeccable blueprint. He has an utterly magnificent design, and he wants to work out the wonder and the excitement and the mystery and the fulfillment of his will in the life of every one of his children. Too many times we settle for a chicken feather. But God does not insist that we take the best gift.

As I'm looking at this and as I have wrestled with a quest for God's will in my own life, it's not a very simple thing, really. You can say put God's will first, seek God's will above every other desire, but that really doesn't solve all of it. Because you see, we are capable of some motivations that I think will frustrate even the remotest possibility of our finding God's will. For example, I continue to be intrigued, and somewhat perplexed, and altogether amazed by the experience of Jacob in the Old Testament. I shared this in another context before, but I see it in an entirely different light for this particular moment.

It's essentially the same principle in that strange vision at Bethel when Jacob saw the ladder with the angels ascending and descending from heaven. Following that remarkable disclosure, the scripture says, "Jacob vowed a vow, saying, 'If God will be with me, and will keep me in this way that I go, and will give me bread to eat and raiment to put on, so that I come again to my father's house in peace, then shall the Lord be my God. And this stone, which I have set for a pillar, shall be God's house, and of all that thou shalt give me, I will surely give the tenth unto thee.'"

I see this as a selection of God's will when it is essentially a selfish stratagem. Stratagem, according to the dictionary, is a trick or a maneuver in war for deceiving the enemy. That's what I see in Jacob. On the surface, it may appear that Jacob is coming to a real commitment, but I don't think so. I think Jacob, who was the arch-shyster of the Bible, who was the master manipulator of men, is attempting to try to play, as it were, a little cosmic game of chess with God. He's saying, "I'll let you do your will in my life, provided you will promise all of these benefits and you will vouchsafe all of these little goodies."

But when we look upon God's will as a means for securing the things we want from the Lord, I think we have shut the door solid and tight on the possibility of our experiencing His will. When we look upon God's will like that, His will is little more than a magic charm or a rabbit's foot or a horseshoe or a four-leaf clover or a little statue that we fix on our dashboard to keep us from running into somebody.

God's will just doesn't function like that, and we don't seek God's will in order to get things from him. Notice that Jacob said, "If you'll do this, I'll give the tenth unto thee." As I think about this, I'm reminded of some tithing testimonies I've heard. Now I don't mean to be critical, and I do not mean to pass judgment on intent or purpose, but I've heard some testimonies that seem to say to me, if you were to condense it into one formula, if you want to get rich quick, you go to tithing. You know what I'm talking about? I was down on my luck, and I began to tithe and man, money just poured in on top of me.

I'm still waiting for somebody to share a tithing testimony that'll run like this. Someone who'll say, "I hadn't been a Christian but about six months and, after I gave my heart to the Lord and I began to realize all that I owed to him, and that I could never begin to repay my debt of love, I decided that, as I understood that this was the minimum of God's pattern or standard of giving, that I ought to be giving a tithe. So, I began to tithe. And I've been tithing for the last four months, and I went bankrupt last week. I lost everything I owned. But the next dollar I earn, God's going to get the first fruits of it, and he's going to get the initial increase because it's his and because that's the very minimum that I can give to him."

If all we're interested in is to find God's will in order for him to rain and shower blessings upon us—I'll be honest with you, as I read God's word, I think you might just as well forget it because it doesn't work like that.

Well, there's another way in which we can seek God's will. I find this in the experience of Brother Jonah. I have a lot in common with Jonah. Most of us do. We've all been in rebellion, and we've all departed from God's pattern. You remember when the ancient prophet found himself cast overboard and he was swallowed up in the stomach of the fish. These words reflect, I think, the deep repentance and remorse of spirit and heart, where he said, "When my soul fainted within me I remembered the Lord; and my prayer came in unto thee, into thine holy temple. . . . But I will sacrifice unto thee with the voice of Thanksgiving; I will pay that that I have vowed. Salvation is of the Lord."

Now, do you understand the thrust of what he's saying? He said, "Man, I made a commitment down in there. Lord, I'll do your will. You just get me out of this awful spot here and I'll put your design first and I will be obedient to your directive, and I will comply with your instructions. I'll perform the vow that I've committed today if you just spare my life."

And so, did he opt for God's will? Well, not really. He *submitted* to it, but I suggest that what Jonah did was nothing more nor less than a very sullen submission. Because when he went to the appointed city of Ninevah and he preached the message of impending doom, just as God instructed him, and the people of the city repented in sackcloth and ashes, and God stayed his hand of devastation, then what happened?

The scripture says, "It displeased Jonah exceedingly, and he was very angry."

Now, he was willing to take God's will because he really didn't have any other option in the belly of the fish. And there are too many of us that pray "Lord, Thy will be done" as an addendum to our desires and our earnest requests and our ambitions and our goals. If I can't have what I want, and if I cannot realize what I choose, *then* I'll let you have your way.

Do you ever pray like that? Well, many of us have. It sounds pious on the surface, but the truth of it is that kind of surrender is more Buddhist in philosophy than it is Christian. It is simply a capitulation to the unavoidable and the inevitable and not really seeking God's will. But I observe that when this is the way we come to God's will, just as in the case of Jonah, just as soon as the stress comes and the pressure is brought to bear, we're going to cut out just like that.

I suppose we're all the product or the victim of our circumstances and our experiences, but you know, it's only at this point that we say, "Lord help me." I don't mean to be a cynic or a critic, but I talk to people who have all sorts of noble ambitions and high resolve. You know what I mean? I've stood at the front of too many aisles and too many decision services and I've heard too many people say, "I'm going to give my whole life to Jesus." Then I've turned around and it looked to me like their whole life apparently didn't last more than about two or three days. That distresses me and that upsets me. I'll tell you what, I think commitment to, and I think a real searching for God's will ought to reflect itself in sustained and persevering faithfulness and obedience.

Now, one of the reasons that I have this particular hangup is because of an event that took place with me when I was in the service a number of years ago. I have alluded to this before, but some of you have not heard this particular experience and maybe it'll tell you a little bit about me. And if you think sometimes I'm a little bit stubborn and bullheaded, then maybe you'll be a little bit more charitable with me in light of what I'm about to share.

I volunteered to go to the Airborne and, when I got up there, to jump school. It seemed like such a great idea before I got there. There was something that was so adventuresome and so romantic to me about those guys who could wear those little jump wings on their chest. I thought, man, that would really be great. When we got there that first morning and . . . I'll never forget. I should have known that it was gonna be a tough day. As the instructor came along, he came up to one fella and he said, "Soldier, raise your right foot." He raised his right foot.

He said, "Put it back down." He put it back down. He said, "All right, raise your left foot." He raised his left foot. He said, "Put it back down." He put it back down. He said, "All right, now raise both feet." And the fella jumped up and came back down. The instructor said, "Now wait just a minute. Who told you to put 'em back down? Get down and give me twenty-five pushups."

How can you beat a game like that? Well, I soon found out that when they stopped in front of you, it didn't make a difference what the questions were. The answer was, "Get down and give me twenty-five." After a while I had the feeling when they came in and said something to me, I just may as well get down and give them the pushups. You know, they were coming no matter what. There was no way out.

But that first morning, man, I'll tell you the truth, I've never done anything like that in my life. They just nearly killed me. I had been working in an office for about a year. The heaviest exercise I'd had had been pushing a pencil and man, they just ran us for five miles, and they did all sorts of terrible, strenuous things.

And then they got to the calisthenics period. And I thought, my soul! Calisthenics period! I'd already done more exercise than I had done in a year-and-a-half. And I'll never forget as we began the exercise period, we were doing what they call the side-straddle-hop. Now, I don't know what you call it these days, but it's that kind of a butterfly deal, you know? In the first 20 minutes, by count, not by approximation, but by count, we did eleven hundred side-straddle-hops. When I got through with the eleven hundredth one, I couldn't even see the guy in front of me. I could hear the voice of the jumpmaster out there, but I couldn't see a thing. And when we came in for the noon meal, my arms ached until I thought, man, they'll fall off. I'll never forget what a tremendous effort it was to have to pick up food on the fork. I'm telling you the truth, this is absolutely the way it was.

And boy, during that break at noontime, I just sat there and just let my arms sag, just limp. I didn't want to do a thing. And I thought, man, what in the world have I gotten myself into? It wasn't nearly as exciting, and it wasn't nearly as romantic as it was before I got there. I thought, well, this is an all-volunteer outfit, and I really don't have to do this. And it occurred to me that the best thing for me to do was to go on down there and find that sergeant and tell him that I was sick, or I'd changed my mind, or my mother had been run over by a truck. Or something. I just had to think of something to get out of that.

And then I got to thinking, well, I've only been here half a day. I ought to at least go back and see what's going to happen in the afternoon. So, we fell out in formation and we were marched out to the training area, and boy, that's when it happened. We stood there and here was this officer. There were about 500 men in that squadron. And he walked back and forth in silence for a moment, then he said, "All right, all you men who want to quit, fall out and fall in over here."

I want you to know that the formation broke. It looked to me like everybody was going and they just began to stream out of my platoon. And I found myself leaning way over like that, you know? And I thought, boy, that's exactly what I want to do. And then I got to thinking about it. Now, one of these days, I'll get married and settle down and I'll have children, and they'll say, "Daddy, what did you do in the Great War?" And I'll say, "Well, you know, I was fighting flies off the chow down there in Camp Hood during the war."

"Well, so you didn't do anything very exciting when you were in the service?"

"Well, I went to jump school. I went to the Airborne, you know, to be a paratrooper."

"Oh, what was it like?"

"Well, I only stayed a half a day."

I thought that's a terrible thing to have to tell a kid. I thought, well, I'll at least hang the day through and see how it goes.

But those men assembled—over half of our group, 250 or better, at least half of the number fell out. And then that officer walked back and forth between those two groups in what has to be the most obscene silence I had ever heard in my life. It just dripped with profanity and venom without a word being spoken. In a minute, he said to us, "All right, look at them. You see them? They're quitters, no guts. There's not a man among them." And then he said, "And there's some of you that haven't got any more guts than they've got. We're going to weed you out and you're going to quit, too, because you're not man enough to stick with it."

I want you to know that when he said that in my direction, I felt the starch in my fatigue jacket begin to stiffen. And I thought to myself, "Old buddy, I don't know what in the world you've got left coming, but if you have to crate me up and send me out of here in a box, God being my helper, you'll never say that about me."

I'm telling you the truth. And that hasn't always been good. I've been in some situations where it would have been the better part of valor to back off and quit and start all over again, you know, from another angle. And if you think I'm bullheaded . . . every once in a while, I'll have to admit I am, because I sure do hate to start something and then quit. And until this good day, that word "quit" has a negative tone. I just kind of want to wash my mouth out with soap when I say it.

And I tell you what, when we commit our way to the will of God just in order to get our own little purposes or simply because there's not any other option, the first thing you know, when the crossfire gets heavy and the going gets tough, we'll quit and sit down and let somebody else fight the battle.

You know, I think there's another reflection of how God's will is to be sought. It's in Paul's attitude. Luke reports, in the 21st Chapter of the Book of Acts, this interesting little interlude. He said, "And as we tarried there many days, there came down from Judaea a certain prophet named Agabus. And when he was come unto us, he took Paul's girdle, and bound his own hands and feet and said, 'Thus saith the Holy Ghost, so shall the Jews at Jerusalem bind the man that owneth this girdle and shall deliver him into the hands of the Gentiles.' And when we heard these things, both we and they of that place, besought not to go up to Jerusalem. Then Paul answered, 'What mean ye to weep and to break mine heart? For I am ready not to be bound only, but also to die at Jerusalem for the name of the Lord Jesus.' And when he would not be persuaded, we ceased, saying the will of the Lord be done."

I think Luke and his companions were sort of like Jonah. Okay, if this is all it could be, then your will be done. But what I think I see in Paul's heart is an entirely different level because he said earlier, "Behold, I go bound in the spirit unto Jerusalem, not knowing the things that shall befall me there, save that the Holy Ghost witnesseth in every city, saying that bonds and afflictions abide me."

Don't you see that it is not an option that he can turn away from, but it was Paul's first choice and, oh my, the magnitude of his desire to find God's will. I'm not sure that anyone short of a preacher can understand that, because here is a man in whom God has placed the call of the evangelist. He's called him to proclaim the Gospel to the nations, the great preacher to the Gentiles, and everywhere he goes, his voice is clear as he presses the claims of Christ. And for him, preaching is not just an avocation, it is not just a preoccupation. It is his whole life. He understands the spirit of Jeremiah when he said, "I came to the place that I was determined I would not speak anymore in his name, but his word became like a fire in my bones that I could not contain."

Paul said, "Woe is unto me if I preach not the Gospel." Paul didn't have long to live, but as long as he breathed, he had to preach. And now God was taking him to a place, back in a little cubicle, where he couldn't preach. I can't think of anything any more demanding of a preacher than that. And yet he said, "Man, I'm going to pursue God's will because that's my first choice. That's my destiny. I'm committed to him and to his design and his blueprint for my life."

And I think as he moved towards Jerusalem, he had in his own spirit the same attitude that we found in old Job, when he said, "Though he slay me, yet will I trust him."

When Stevie was born to us, we soon moved up to the island of Hokkaido, where we were to take our normal routine of service there in Sapporo. We hadn't been there very long, though, until we began to observe that there was something wrong. He had a little difficulty keeping his food down. Now, he was not our first child; he was our third. So, we were accustomed to the little decorations that you receive but this was ridiculous.

After a while, it got to be more than ridiculous. It got to be alarming, and I can remember—in fact, I cannot forget, the dread and the anxiety walking up and down the hall of that missionary house in the chill of the midnight hours. We would have given him a bottle, and I would begin to pace up and down that corridor, waiting, hoping, praying. I'd walk for a little while and think, boy, I believe he's gonna keep it down. And then here it came. And instead of growing and putting on weight, he began to grow thin and emaciated. Finally, we had to take him to a doctor there in Sapporo, and he examined him and gave him some medication, but he did not improve.

Finally, we found it necessary to fly him all the way

down to the hospital in Kyoto where he was born. After the doctors had run extensive tests there, they said, "We believe you ought to put him on a plane and take him back to the States. Wherever you'd like to go, we'll make contact with local medical authorities. We're not sure of the nature of his problem, but it's very critical, it's very urgent. And you need to take him back home."

So, with growing distress, we bundled him up and we made the long flight back here to Dallas and finally placed him in the hands of a medical team at Baylor University Medical Center. They began to explore and to run other tests, and finally they came up with what they'd been looking for. By this time, I was something of a specialist on the condition of pyloric stenosis. I'd seen enough textbooks, and I'd talked to enough doctors about what they thought was the problem, but they couldn't find isolated in an x-ray evidence that was sufficient proof of the condition to justify surgery. But when they took the x-rays here, the doctor called me into the viewing room and I looked and there it was, just classic in its form. It looked like something I had seen in some of those medical textbooks.

I knew what that meant. That meant surgery. So, we went across the street to the little motel where we had rented a room. Surgery was just minutes away. I got down on my knees and I began to pray, and I prayed the kind of prayer that you would expect a father to pray at a moment like that. I said, "Lord, he's very precious to us. We love him and we want you to spare him, if you will." I prayed at length, and then I got down to the end of that prayer and I prayed this little postscript: "But Lord, if it can't be that way, then your will be done."

Suddenly, the awful contradiction of it hit me, and I said, "Lord, I don't know whether you can erase a prayer or not, but if you can, I want you to erase that one. Let's start all over again, Lord. First, we want your will to be done. We want your will in our lives. We want your will in the lives of our children, and it's not an alternative to our desire. That's the number one desire of our hearts. We want your will to be done, because surely there are things that are more tragic than an infant dying on an operating table. Now, Lord, if in the circle of that desire for your will to be done in our lives, if you can spare him to us, we'll be so grateful. But Lord, that doesn't change it. Your will is our first choice. And we want that, whatever it means."

I believe that's the only way we find it. It's not a trade out. It's not a cop out. We find God's will only when it becomes more precious to us than our own personal desires, and when it expresses the supreme desire of our heart.

Thy kingdom come; thy will be done . . . in me as it is in heaven.

Transitional Narrative: *Intolerable Objections*

In 1963, our family (with the foreign-born addition of Steve, bringing our number to five) returned home from Japan on furlough, where Corky took post-graduate language courses at Oriental Seminary at Johns Hopkins University in Baltimore. Along with his classes, he pastored a Baptist church in Wrightstown, New Jersey, near McGuire Air Force Base. In September 1964, Corky and Juanita resigned their appointments as missionaries so that Corky could take a position as an associate evangelist with the Baptist General Convention of Texas, in Dallas, which brought him and my mother home to their native Texas. That fateful move led to one of the most significant events in our family's life.

In January of 1965, at the age of 37, Corky was injured in a private plane crash in the Big Thicket region of southeast Texas while on the way back from an evangelistic meeting. The pilot was killed, and Corky broke his back, paralyzing him from the waist down while he spent 40 hours on the floor of the Big Thicket awaiting an uncertain rescue. After months of hospitalization and physical rehab, Corky defied his doctors' consensus that he would never walk again, although he was forced to rely on a cane for the rest of his life.

That cane was both good and bad. Good, because he was able to walk. Bad, because it gave him something to wave in the air at school performances and football games to embarrass his kids in front of their friends. At an 8th grade choir performance while I was in junior high in the Dallas suburb of Duncanville, I was one of four boys designated by the director to perform a pitiful soft-shoe while the choir sang "East Side, West Side." Actually, she didn't assign us to perform a pitiful soft-shoe, just a soft-shoe; we improvised the pitiful part on our own. Even with the lights in my eyes on stage, I could see that cane swirling in the air at the back of the school auditorium.

In March of 1970, Corky accepted the pastorate of Gaston Avenue Baptist Church (GABC) in Dallas, which necessitated our move from Duncanville to the Lakewood area of east Dallas and brought me to Woodrow Wilson High School for the start of my sophomore year. While Corky was at GABC, and I was at Woodrow, the incident of the "Lake Lavon Four" occurred.[7] At the time I was involved in that incident, Corky was having some problems with a few of the church leaders (who, I might add, had already run off his predecessor), although I was unaware of

---

[7] I will address this "incident" in some detail, later.

the full extent of it at the time, and which culminated in his resignation in the spring of 1972.

Award-winning religion reporter Helen Parmley reported in *The Dallas Morning News*:

> The pastor and director of music at the Gaston Avenue Baptist Church unexpectedly submitted their resignations to a stunned group of worshipers attending the services at the church Sunday night. Dr. Theorn [sic] V. Farris, in an emotion-packed statement, *The Dallas News* learned, said he found objections to his ministry 'intolerable' and was therefore submitting his resignation, effective April 2. Dr. and Mrs. Farris then left the meeting followed by Tom Bledsoe, minister of music, who said his resignation was effective immediately.

Ms. Parmley wrote, "If the resignations stand, the 4,500-member church's staff will consist of one part-time minister of youth, since the minister of education resigned two months ago." She used the word "if" because the church membership voted to reject the resignation.

Among the "objections" that Corky found intolerable were criticisms that "encouraged him to minimize his evangelistic preaching" and that "questioned the emotional aspects of his preaching," as well as objecting to Juanita working (at the Baptist Building in

Dallas, where she was a secretary in the Evangelism Division) and questioning whether he could "effectively carry out his ministry with his 'handicap'"—a reference to that walking-with-a-cane business I mentioned above; you know, from the plane crash he was in while leading an evangelistic meeting in east Texas.

Sticking with his resignation despite the congregation's vote to reject it, Corky took a position as professor of Hebrew and Old Testament at Mid-America Baptist Theological Seminary, which had just opened in Little Rock, Arkansas. The founder of the seminary, Dr. B. Gray Allison, had been one of his professors at NOBTS and was even on the thesis committee that awarded him his doctorate. (By the way, Dr. Allison confirmed Juanita's story to me about that committee having no questions for Corky during his oral defense of his dissertation. As Dr. Allison put it to me, "None of us on the committee knew enough about the subject to know what to ask.")

Darlyne had already graduated from high school, but the plan was that our family would remain in Dallas, so that Steve and I wouldn't have to change schools, while Corky commuted to Little Rock during the weeks and home on weekends. But then the unexpected happened. A group of members from GABC split off and formed a new church, then called Corky to be their first pastor. He agreed, though only on a part-time basis since he had already committed to the new seminary in Little Rock. Over the course of the next semester, he commuted between jobs, living in Little Rock during the week and returning to Dallas on the weekends to serve as the first pastor of the newly formed Forest Meadow Baptist Church (FMBC). At the end of the school year, he resigned from the seminary to remain in Dallas as full-time pastor at FMBC.

SERMON: *Heart Failure*[8]

I invite you to turn please to the 32nd Chapter of the Book of Genesis. I would like to read, beginning at Verse six, the account of a very interesting event in the life of Jacob, one of the great founding fathers of the Hebrew kingdom.

"And the messengers returned to Jacob saying, 'We came to thy brother Esau, and also he cometh to meet thee, and four hundred men within him.' Then Jacob was greatly afraid and distressed; and he divided the people that was with him, and the flocks and herds and the camels into two bands; and said, 'If Esau come to the one company and smite it, then the other company which is left shall escape.'

"And Jacob said, 'Oh God, of my father Abraham, and God of my father Isaac, the Lord, which saidst unto me, "Return unto thy country, and to thy kindred, and I will deal well with thee." I am not worthy of the least of all the mercies, and of all the truth, which thou has shewed unto

---

[8] He preached this on several occasions, including at GABC in Dallas, but the cassette tape is from February 13, 1977, at Bellevue Baptist Church in Memphis, Tennessee. When he preached it at GABC, one of the church leaders who had lodged the "intolerable objections" demanded to know whether Corky had aimed the sermon at him; was he the Jacob in the sermon? I now know who the man was and I now know his part in the whole affair, and I can't understand how he could have made any correlation between his own conduct and that of Jacob. However, I suppose guilty consciences often have the ability to think outside the box.

thy servant, for with my staff, I passed over this Jordan, and now I am become two bands.

"'Deliver me, I pray thee, from the hand of my brother, from the hand of Esau, for I fear him, lest he will come and smite me and the mother with the children.'"

I'm skipping down now to Verse 22, and we continue in the reading. "And he rose up that night and took his two wives, and his two women servants, and his eleven sons, and passed over the ford Jabbok. And he took them and sent them over the brook and sent over what he had. And Jacob was left alone; and there wrestled a man with him until the breaking of the day. And when he saw that he prevailed not against him, he touched the hollow of his thigh, and the hollow of Jacob's thigh was out of joint, as he wrestled with him.

"And he said, 'Let me go for the day breaketh.' And he"—that is Jacob— "said, 'I will not let thee go except thou bless me.' And he said unto him, 'What is thy name?' And he said, 'Jacob.' And he said, 'Thy name shall be called no more Jacob, but Israel; for as a prince hast thou power with God and with men and has prevailed.'"

"And Jacob asked him and said, 'Tell me, I pray thee, thy name.' And he said, 'Wherefore is it that thou dost ask after my name?' And he blessed him there."

"And Jacob called the name of the place, Peniel, for I have seen God face to face and my life is preserved. And as he passed over Penuel, the sun rose upon him, and he halted upon his thigh."

Incredible as it may seem, there are still those among us who confidently insist that ancestry and environment alone will guarantee a right relationship with God. In other words, if one is born of the correct parents, has the right stock, and is reared in the right positive home environment, this will assure in and of itself an acceptable relationship to God. To be certain, this influence is positive. However, there are jarring exceptions. Consider, if you please, Jacob, who forevermore destroys the myth and the illusion.

Jacob, who was the child of Isaac, who in turn was the son of Abraham, the grandfather of Jacob. Abraham, the great father of the faithful. If ever there was a man who had the right ancestry to guarantee an acceptable relationship to God, it must have been Jacob. Moreover, Jacob was a part of the line of Messianic promise and fulfillment, ultimately, to find its expression in the birth of Second David: Jesus of Nazareth.

The positive influences, we can only imagine. But as we study the record of the earlier years of Jacob, obviously he was just a natural man, like all the rest of us. The ancient Hebrews frequently attached a great deal of significance to the giving of a name at birth. That principle is rather classically illustrated in the birth of Esau and Jacob.

The report of that event is described in the 25th Chapter of Genesis, where the writer said, concerning Esau, that he "first came out red all over like an hairy garment, and they called his name Esau."

Some scholars believe that the name Esau is the word "hairy"—not H-a-r-r-y, but h-a-i-r-y. So, they called this little infant, who had an inordinate amount of body hair, Hairy: H-a-i-r-y.

But the point of importance to us is the birth of his brother, who came soon thereafter. His brother, as he came out, "took hold on Esau's heel. And his name was called Jacob."

In translation, that seems to make little or no sense. May I alert you, however, to the fact that the name Jacob is built upon the Hebrew word for "heel"—the back part of the foot. And so, the name Jacob has some connotation of the word "heel." Consequently, some have insisted that the name means "the heel catcher."

I personally am convinced that there is more

significance to it than that. I cannot guarantee that this is the origin of the use of the term in our own language, but what a happy coincidence. We speak of people who are somewhat unsavory and undesirable in personality as being what? A "first class heel." And Jacob, from the beginning, was a "heel" by our standards of evaluation.

To understand the full import of what we say, look at the use of the name Jacob, and the verb that is built upon that same word by his brother Esau, after the second deceit or treachery on the part of Jacob. This time in Genesis 27, Verse 36, having been beaten out of his birthright and now having been robbed of the parental blessing that was legitimately his, Esau, in a towering rage of indignation, literally explodes in fury. He says, "Is not he rightly named Jacob? For he has supplanted me these two times. He took away my birthright and behold, now he has taken away my blessing."

There's a very significant play on terms in the original text here because the verb that is translated "supplant" is the root upon which the name Jacob is built, the root that means heel. In order to preserve that affinity, then, we could translate it something like this: "Is he not rightly named the supplanter? Because he has supplanted me these two times." Or perhaps even more incisively, the following. Consider: "Is he not rightly named the trickster? Because he has tricked me these two times." Or: "Is he not rightly called the deceiver? For he has deceived me these two times." Or: "Is he not correctly called the betrayer? For he betrayed me these two times."

Yes, that's Jacob. In concert with a conniving mother, he schemed to rob Esau of the blessing that was his. In fact, he so engendered the ire and the fury of his stronger brother that he had to catch a Greyhound bus and leave town in the middle of the night. Or at least do the Old Testament equivalent of the same.

As you read the record, up in Padanaram, where Jacob went to escape Esau, he continues to scheme, to manipulate, to negotiate. To be sure, he finds in some situations more than his match in Laban, his father-in-law. But here is Jacob: the manipulator, the user of people, the schemer, the negotiator. If you please, he is the prototype of the wheeler-dealer. He is the first of the big-time operators. That's Jacob.

Until the event at the ford Jabbok, where something takes place. I find in this particular account more than just an intriguing story of one of the Jewish patriarchs. I find here, uniquely isolated in the experience of Jacob, the essential ingredients of a new birth experience. I'm not suggesting that this was a new birth experience in and of itself, per se. I simply say that the ingredients of a new birth experience are uniquely isolated in the experience of Jacob.

Now, let's notice, Jacob has finally amassed a comfortable fortune, and he begins to reflect upon the days of his youth. The scenes from the early years come crowding in upon his reverie as he ponders and prays. It occurs to him that it would be appropriate to liquidate all of his assets, his holdings, and return to the scenes of his youth. He proceeds to do so, but as he journeys back to Canaan, drawing ever closer to the place of his birth, he remembers with growing concern and consternation the events that led to his sudden and hasty departure.

The question haunted and nagged at his consideration: Would Esau forgive? Would Esau forget? Would he find him positive and responsive now as the elder brother, or would he continue to harbor resentment? Never one to leave circumstance to blind fortune, Jacob appoints the equivalent of a reconnaissance patrol. They range far out in advance of the main body of his family and troops, and they return with the account that Esau is coming to greet Jacob with a band of 400 armed men.

That night, I think I see Jacob as he paces back and forth in his Bedouin tent, ringing his hands in anguish to lament again and again. "I knew he couldn't forget. I knew he wouldn't forgive. He was always one to nurse a grudge. What shall I do?"

And Jacob, the master manipulator, the consummate negotiator, for the first time in all of his experience, has exhausted his bag of tricks. He's down to the end of the string for the first time. At last, God has Jacob in checkmate. Well, it took him a long time to get him there, didn't it? But at long last, the self-made man, for the first time, finds himself in desperate, dire extremity.

Beloved, that's the first step to any kind of saving relationship with God. Did you know that? No man becomes a saint until first he recognizes that he's a sinner. No one ever turns to God for deliverance until he is first made aware of the fact that he has an urgent need.

The fact is, that's the most difficult part of it, particularly here in affluent mid-20th Century America. It is extremely difficult for us to recognize that we have need of anything, unless the thermometer plunges below freezing. But even then, somehow, we are assured that we shall be able to deal with our emergency on the basis of our own resources. That's the most difficult part, to recognize our need.

Several years ago, I received the name of a man

who was not a professing Christian. The circumstance was the pastorate where I served in Baton Rouge. With that bit of information, I had an address in one of the more affluent sections of the city. With some sense of hesitation, I drove out to the appointed address, parked my automobile in front of the most impressive, palatial mansion I think I had ever seen as a seminary-student pastor. I was totally intimidated by the magnitude of it.

I rang the doorbell, and, in a moment, a lady came in response. I identified myself as pastor of the nearby Baptist church and requested permission to talk to her husband. She very graciously invited me inside. As I stepped in, I was amazed at the small size of the living room for such an impressive house on the outside. It was not until we turned the first corner, though, that I realized that this was the foyer. And here was a football field of a living room. I had the distinct impression as I stepped out in it and sank down in the thick nap of the carpet that the tops of my shoes just disappeared in all of that luxury. And we started walking out across that football field of a living room.

And we walked and we walked and we walked and we walked. Until we got to about the 35-yard line. She motioned me to a chair, and I took a seat. She went across the field into the back of the house. Somewhere back there, apparently, they had a basketball court, a bowling alley, swimming pool. I don't know.

After a bit, the gentleman came in and he sat close enough to me for us to be able to converse if I kept my voice up. I began to talk to him about the Lord Jesus. I reached into my pocket and pulled my New Testament out as I warmed to the assignment and as I read from God's word and began to press the claims of Jesus in his heart.

Finally, he cut me off by saying, "Preacher, do you see this house?"

Yeah. As a matter of fact, I had noticed it was there.

He said, "Preacher, I was reared in deepest poverty. I never dreamed any man could live like this. You may be right. Conceivably, I am lost and under condemnation. Moreover, I may be on my way to hell, but if I were to repent of my sin, receive Jesus Christ as my Lord, I would have to change some of my business practices. I would have to forfeit some of my income, and I am not about to do that, even if it means I do go to hell."

I said, "Thank you, sir." I closed my New Testament. Put it back in my pocket. Walked out through the end zone and left. He had made his cold, calculated choice.

Ah, but the tragedy was that man, apparently with all of his business perception, could not understand that everything dear and precious to him could evaporate in one smoke-puff of reversal. He apparently could not grasp the fact that, in the presence of God, he was a pauper, helpless and alone. How difficult it is for us to realize that we need anything outside of ourselves, even God.

But the fact is, not only are we disillusioned by our wealth, sometimes we cannot perceive our need of God even when our health is in jeopardy. We were conducting a series of evangelistic meetings in the First Baptist Church of Wrightstown, New Jersey. I was, at that point in time, serving as pastor of this particular congregation while doing some study down in Baltimore. Dr. Gray Allison, the president of Mid-America Baptist Theological Seminary, who at that time was a full-time evangelist, was our visiting preacher.

Once more, I received the name of an individual who was not a professing Christian, this time with the additional data to the effect that he was desperately ill with a terminal disease. And I remember this visit, too. We arrived at the appointed room on the designated floor. As Dr. Allison and I walked into the room, I recall seeing this long, emaciated skeletal frame of a man stretched out on the bed. He looked like death warmed over as he was watching a television program. I recall it was a shoot-em-up because here came a posse in hot pursuit of the bad guys. This was one of the older westerns because the bad guys were still wearing black hats, and the good guys were wearing white hats.

By the way, parenthetically, to me this is the major concern on television; it's not just violence, but the confusion of the good and the evil in men. Be that as it may, we tried to get in between the firing of the rifles and the pistols to carry on something of a conversation. And I tried to be gentle and discreet, and yet I attempted to make an entree into his attention.

I said, "I know that you're having a tough time. I'm aware of the fact that you're a pretty sick fella. It occurred to me that Dr. Allison might be able to be of some help to you. Would you like for this man, who is a specialist in these affairs, to read a little bit from God's word for you and to talk with you a little bit about your relationship to him?"

Now, what I was saying in interpretation was, I know you are dying and I'm aware of the fact that you know you're dying. Would you like for this man to tell you how you can make your peace with God?

You know what that fella said? He said, "No, I don't think so."

I said, "You don't?"

"No," he said, "everything's all right," with one eye still cocked upon the posse. So, we left.

That was about 5:30 in the afternoon. By six o'clock the following morning, the ink on that man's death certificate was dry. He was within hours of eternity, and yet he was too preoccupied with a western adventure movie on television to talk about his need of God. No man, however, is going to be saved until he recognizes his need.

But notice something else in the experience of Jacob. There is no technical word to suggest it here, but I think it's unmistakably obvious. With one last futile, spasmodic effort to do something to salvage the situation himself, Jacob now turns to God for help. That shift is reflected in a technical word in the New Testament, in the Greek expression that means to have a change of mind, change of attitude, and is translated "repentance."

Sin is not the violation of certain church rules or canonical creed. The very core of sin is our effort to turn our backs upon God and to live our lives as we please. Totally independent of divine governance. From the beginning, it has been so. We have said, along with our federal ancestors, Adam and Eve, "You are not going to tell me what to do. I will be captain of my own fate. I will be master of my own destiny. I will call the shots. I will be my own God."

Beloved, that is the essence of sin. But before sin can be resolved or forgiven, we must be prepared to turn away from the futile, vain effort to successfully regulate our lives. And that's exactly what Jacob did for the first time. He is finally willing to say, "I cannot do it myself. I need help." And so, he turns to the Lord.

Following that shift, a shadowy adversary materializes in the night, and Jacob finds himself literally attacked. They began to thrash and to wrestle and to paw the ground as they attempt to gain advantage over each other. And in the course of that nocturnal encounter, as the break of dawn is heralded in the eastern sky, this unidentified opponent says, "Let me go." Apparently, there's been no communication between them up until now. Just a controversy. Just a contest.

But now Jacob says, "No, I will not let you go except you bless me." Evidently, Jacob has already begun to sense, or at least to suspect, who his opponent really is, and so he communicates directly and very emphatically. "I will not let you go unless you bless me."

To be sure, we understand that his opponent was the angel of the Lord. With that bit of information available to us, we might assume that this is a rather presumptuous, not even petition, but demand on the part of Jacob. Or, if you please, a presumptuous prayer. Jacob was not above praying a presumptuous prayer.

As a matter of fact, there is such a prayer recorded, in my judgment, in the 28th Chapter of Genesis. The context there is the vision of the ladder with the angels ascending and descending, upon the spot that is ultimately to be called by him Bethel, or the house of God. Following that vision in Verse 20 of Chapter 28, "Jacob vowed a vow, saying if God will be with me, and will keep me in this way that I go, and will give me bread to eat and raiment to put on, so that I come again to my father's house in peace, then shall the Lord be my God."

There is his presumptuous prayer.

How so? Well don't you see? Here is Jacob negotiating a contract with God. If you will guarantee me enough food and enough clothing and shelter, if you will ensure my fortunes, *then* I will give you the exalted privilege of being my God. As if he were doing the Lord a monumental favor. Can you beat that? If that is not the very essence of presumption! What's sad to say, though, is that attitude is not altogether dead in our day.

I remember talking to a young lady who had made some sort of an external act of devotion in a church up in New England. I asked her if she really had committed her heart to Jesus, and she said, "Oh, I didn't really do that sort of thing." She said, "I just joined the church because, well, it was such a pitiful little church and they needed members so desperately, so I just joined."

Well, bless her heart. It may be true that, in a given situation, a specific congregation may have to close its doors and disband its meetings because of a lack of financial or participation response. But may I remind you that the Church is the only divine-ordained institution within history, and it will survive as long as God pleases for it to. He does not have to have any one of us to keep his program in operation on the Earth. And we may have erroneously communicated in our appeals, we preachers, to the hearts of some the impression that God really cannot quite get along without us. So, at some point in time, when we have exhausted all of our own personal designs and ambitions, we will repent and we will give God the privilege of saving us and functioning as our Lord, because he really can hardly manage without us.

Beloved, you remember this well: While God does

care, and while his heart hurts for our lostness, let us never forget that God, and God alone, is self-contained from eternity to eternity, and he can function forever and beyond without any one of us, but we in turn cannot function forever without him. And when we come, we do not come to negotiate. We do not come to call the shots. If we ever come, we come on his terms at the moment of his choosing in absolute, unconditional surrender or we don't come at all. That's exactly what our Lord was driving at when he said, "No man can come to me except the father which hath sent me draw him."

But now Jacob is praying earnestly, desperately, almost viciously. Not asking for this or that but calling out of great, earnest desperation. "Unless you bless me, I cannot turn you loose."

God said, "You'll find me when you search for me with all your heart." When you're through playing games and you really, desperately need me, I am available.

So, Jacob prays to express that earnest desire. In response to that, notice that the angel of the Lord said, "What is your name?"

I suppose by this time that name was something of an embarrassment to Jacob. The fact is, he could not even say his name without making a tacit admission of what he was. He had to say, "Lord, you know me. I'm Jacob. I'm the heel catcher. I'm the supplanter. I'm the trickster. I'm the schemer. I'm the conniver. I'm the manipulator. Lord, you remember me? I'm Jacob." And by the very statement of his name, there is an admission of what he was and an acknowledgement of his character.

Now, Beloved, when we really, desperately feel our need of the Lord, this is the time to say it like it really is. Across these years, I've heard some people begin to pray a prayer of confession by saying, "Lord, I'm doing the best I know how." And I have the feeling that that particular prayer is aborted immediately. God's word says there is none that doeth good; not even one.

I'm reminded of the story of the farmer who went by the farmhouse of another friend, who was seated out on the front porch. He said, "Aren't you going to the lecture that the county agent's gonna give us in town?" He said, "Nope." His friend said, "Well, you ought to go. He's gonna give us a lecture on modern farming methods." The farmer who continued to rock on the front porch said, "It don't make any difference to me. I already know how to farm better than what I'm doing."

Yeah. There's not any of us doing what we know to do. It's time to tell it like it is. This is not a time to brag upon our goodness. This is a time to acknowledge what we are and what we've done. This is a time to smite our breasts, to say, "Lord, be merciful to me, a sinner," to acknowledge and to confess our rebellion and to ask forgiveness.

But notice in response to that, the angel said, "Your name is not going to be called Jacob anymore. But your name is to be called Israel; for . . . ."

In the Old Testament, when you find a name with a phrase following that begins with "for," in most instances, you're going to have an explanation of the meaning of that name, and this is so here. "For as a prince hast thou power with God and with men, and hast prevailed."

The word Israel means a prince of God. The angel of the Lord said, "I'm changing your name because it is no longer appropriate. You have prayed and a change is enacted, and I am altering you." Here is an Old Testament illustration of that modification of character and behavior reflected in that statement over in Revelation about a new name being engraved in the stone of Glory, one that gave inspiration to the gospel song, "There's a new name written down in glory, and it's mine. Oh, yes, it's mine."

In response to that confession, the Lord changed Jacob's name because he changed Jacob's heart and character. You read the story. He's no longer the same. His attitudes are different. His actions are different. His outlook is modified. He even walks differently. He walks with a cane thereafter, to be sure, but he is never the same. He has been changed by that encounter. And after it was over, "Jacob called the name of the place Peniel, for . . . ."

Remember what I just said? That name Peniel is about to be explained. ". . . for," he said, "I have seen God face to face, and my life is preserved." The name Peniel, along with the alternate spelling Penuel, means "the face of God." And when it was over, Jacob knew he had met God face to face.

Now and again, when I ask people, "Have you met the Lord? Has he come into your life?" they'll say, "Well, I hope so." Or "Gee, I think so. I'm working at it. I'm trying."

The New Testament writer said, "These things have I written unto you that believe on the name of the Son of God that ye may *know* that you have eternal life." And Beloved, when you meet him face to face and he changes you, you can come out of that encounter, not with some opinions, but with a conviction that you've met God face to face.

Yes, it's a stretch of the imagination, but I can

imagine that in later years, the family might have taken a vacation up in this particular area. Now, this is just a figment of course, but I think I could see Jacob stopping the chariot or the Rolls Royce or whatever they traveled in. Or the camel, to say to the grandchildren, "Now wait a minute. You've heard old granddad talk about that night that I wrestled 'til the break of dawn. That was the reason that I had to limp from that day forward. You've heard me tell about it, but it happened somewhere right around here. I haven't been in this place in years, but I remember there was a great big stone that we rolled up against a—There it is! Right there! This is Peniel, for it was right on this spot that I met God face to face."

About seven or eight years ago now, I was coming back from West Texas toward Dallas. As I journeyed through Fort Worth, I was looking for a place to get a bite to eat. Consequently, I left the freeway system and found myself wandering rather aimlessly around the south side of the city. I came to the corner of Sixth Avenue and Berry Street. On an impulse, I turned to the right, went down past the 3100 block, and I moved in front of a house that had 3116 on it. That was a familiar image that I viewed.

I went down to the end of the block, turned around, came back, and drove up into the driveway. I got out and as

I started up the sidewalk toward the porch, suddenly memories out of the past came tumbling in upon me. I recall the first time I strapped on roller skates and tried to negotiate that concrete walk and splattered all over the pavement.

I got up on the steps, knocked on the door, and again, I reflected upon the experience of sitting out there in the early '30s waiting for the ice wagon to come by so I could find a sliver of ice. I see some heads nodding up and down. I really feel sorry for our kids. They've eaten these Slurpees and juicies until their taste buds are just jaded and seared over. They don't have any idea how good a piece of cold ice all by itself in a completely un-air-conditioned world is.

But in a moment, the door opened. I said to that lady, little old lady and her husband by that time had made his appearance, I said, "Madam, I have a rather strange story to tell." I said, "I was born in this house."

She said, "Are you Corky Farris?"

Well, I hated to lie to her. So, I said, "Yes, ma'am, I guess I am."

She explained that a neighbor lady who continued to abide in that particular community, whom I had seen at a wedding or something, had told her that I wanted to come visit that house sometime. She said, "I've been looking for you to come for a matter of months now."

And I said, "Well, would it be all right if I just came in and walked through your home?"

They said, "Oh, yes, please come in."

I walked into that living room and fresh memories came crashing in upon me. That was the parlor back when I was a youngster; the only room in the house that had overstuffed furniture. We were never permitted to go into that room unless we had company. Or unless mother and dad both left, and my brother and I could go in there and wrestle on the couch. Confession is good for the soul, you know?

Then we walked into the front bedroom as I made the tour. I said, "You know, they tell me that about 10 o'clock in the morning of July the fourth, 1927"—man, that'll almost give my age away, won't it? — "I was born right here in this very room." For you younger people, I was born before you had to go to the hospital to get babies. "But I was born right here in this room." I said that in case they ever wanted to put up a monument or a marker, so they'd know right where to put it.

But then we walked into the back room. I walked up to a spot, and I circled a place on the floor with a tip of my cane, and I said, "It was right here that I was born again."

Oh, yes. So many years ago. But that was my Peniel: 3116 Sixth Avenue, Fort Worth, Texas, in the back bedroom. And I met God face to face just like Jacob did, and he changed my heart, too.

Have you met God face to face? Have you come to recognize your need of him? Are you prepared to abandon your futile effort to make things fit together? Are you ready and willing to call upon his name and to confess your failure and to ask his forgiveness? If you are, then I promise you, on the authority of God's word, that he is prepared to hear and answer your request and to change your life.

Transitional Narrative: *The Lake Lavon Four*

Although I spent some of my most enjoyable "growing up" days at GABC in Dallas, it wasn't all fun and games. Not many of my adult friends may know of my dark and sordid past as a member of the notorious Lake Lavon Four (LL4) in my youth, but it's time to go public. The tale of the LL4 occurred in the summer of 1971, just prior to the start of the school year as I was going into my junior year at Woodrow Wilson High School. The other "3 of the 4" were Steve Gates (going into his senior year at Woodrow Wilson), John Murray (going into his senior year at North Mesquite High School) and Steve Paramore (going into his junior year at Dallas's Thomas Jefferson High School). The four of us, along with others in the youth group at GABC, attended a week-long youth camp on the shores of Lake Lavon, about 30 miles northeast of Dallas. I was actually planning to go home early, on Wednesday, because two-a-day football practices at Woodrow started on Thursday, so my stay was always going to be short-lived—but not as short-lived as it ended up being.

As you might expect at a Baptist camp, the boys and girls were housed, not just in separate bunkrooms, but in separate cabins. In those days, Baptists always separated the boys and girls, even with segregated swim times in the pool. I think they were afraid we might dance. We used to joke that, if we went to the coast, we'd have to swim in separate oceans. Our youth group did, in fact, later take a trip to the Texas Gulf Coast, but both genders were permitted in the same Gulf of Mexico. At the same time, even.

Charlie Price, our youth director, roomed adjacent to the girls' cabin with his wife (an advantage of being married), a fair distance away from the boys' cabin, which housed the LL4 and two others who can only be described as—fairly, I believe—misfits. After all, if they had been as "cool" as the LL4, it would have been the LL6.

But I digress.

Our counselor in the boys' cabin was a guy named Dan, who had recently been discharged from the Army after having served in combat in Vietnam (which, I believe, explained some things), and he was currently in school at Dallas Theological Seminary. After lights-out on Tuesday night (before I was scheduled to go home the following day), the LL4 engaged in a bit of horseplay (as boys will do) that could in no way be characterized as a pillow fight. Nevertheless, Counselor Dan (not to be confused with *Forest Gump*'s Lieutenant Dan) turned on the lights and read us the riot act for not quieting down and going to sleep. (It might have been his second or third warning; I'm not sure, though some might consider that to be relevant). He told us he would send anyone home who defied his instructions to shut up and go to sleep. In retrospect, I guess he was concerned that the noise would alert the Viet Cong to our whereabouts.

Well, after the lights went back off, some member of the LL4 on an upper bunk (Steve P., if memory serves me correctly) delivered a well-placed blow with a pillow to the head of Steve G. in a lower bunk. When Steve G. yanked the pillow out of his assailant's hands, he was seen, even in the darkness but courtesy of the moon shining in the windows, by Counselor Dan. Again, on the lookout for VC.

"I guess you didn't believe me, Steve," said Counselor Dan. We then heard considerable rustling around, including jangling of coins, as Counselor Dan apparently tried to slip on his britches in the darkness. After what seemed like minutes, but was, I'm sure, seconds, he admitted defeat and stormed out of our cabin in T-shirt and boxer shorts to retrieve Charlie, the commandant of the camp.

Once Counselor Dan left the cabin for the girls'

quarters in his boxers (which, Steve G. later pointed out, made him a more deserving candidate for getting kicked out of camp than a mere bit of pillow horseplay), the LL4 made a solidarity pact. If Youth Director Charlie really intended to send Steve G. home, then we would all volunteer to go, since we had all been involved in defying Counselor Dan. Besides, no way would Charlie kick all four of us out of camp, leaving behind only the misfits— who, I suppose, were starting to feel glad that they weren't as cool as the LL4. Besides, I was the pastor's son. That was sorta like diplomatic immunity—pastoral immunity, I guess.

A few minutes later, we heard Charlie's angry voice as he burst into our cabin and flipped on the lights. "Do you guys think you're a bunch of prima donnas?"

I digress, again, to point out that the technical definition of "prima donna" is the chief female singer in an opera. Not sure how that applied. There is a secondary meaning, though, which I assume Charlie was using, which means one with an overinflated view of his or her importance. Utilizing that secondary meaning, I must admit that all four of us believed the answer to be, "Yes, we are prima donnas." After all, as I said before, I was the pastor's son. And, collectively, we were the LL4, not the misfits.

Fortunately, we recognized the question for what it was: rhetorical, meant solely to make a point. So, we kept our mouths shut.

Except to volunteer that, if Steve G. was going home, we all were. Got your back, Jack! Calling Charlie's bluff. To our shock, surprise, and amazement, Charlie called ours right back. "All four of you, get dressed and get packed."

And so, in a monumental exercise of poor judgment, Charlie packed four teenage boys (three 16-year-olds and one 17-year-old) into Steve P.'s red Chevy Vega (barely room for two with camping equipment, much less for the LL4 with camping equipment and deflated egos) and sent us off into the darkness.

I felt another type of darkness descend on me as we drove. I knew vaguely, but not with any specificity, that Corky had been dealing with a few church leaders at GABC who believed it was their God-given right to keep a pastor under their thumbs and to control every aspect of his ministry. They had run off at least one pastor in the past, maybe more, and I knew that Corky chafed at their interference. Now I was going to have to go home, ring the doorbell in the middle of the night (since I didn't have a key) and wake up the rest of the household, to confess to the troubled pastor that his son had been kicked out of his own church's youth camp. Ahh, dark was the night.

Steve G. understood that I was worried, even though he didn't know the full extent of my worries. "I'll explain it to your dad," he said. "I'll let him know it was my fault, and you didn't do anything wrong. You won't get in any trouble."

That sounded good. Got your back, Jack! Although I had already seen one example of how poorly that worked out.

We dropped off John M. first, in Mesquite, then headed to east Dallas to drop me off, then Steve G., before Steve P. could go home to north Dallas. When we reached my house, the loyal Steve G. got out of the car and followed me. I walked up the steps to the front door, while he remained at the foot of the steps. I rang the doorbell.

After a moment, Corky answered the door. He clearly had been awakened, hair mussed and wearing pajamas. He seemed surprised to see me. "I thought you weren't coming home until tomorrow," he said.

"We got sent home."

There was a moment of silence. Strangely, it seemed as if Steve G. had been struck mute. I mean absolutely dumbstruck. I kept waiting for his impassioned defense on my behalf.

Crickets, as they say.

"I was afraid something like this would happen," Corky said.

Really? He really thought I'd get kicked out of camp? I wisely, however, chose not to verbalize the question. Then he added, "I'm real proud of you boys." Even now, I can hear the sarcasm in his voice, ringing in my memory.

Still, Steve G. remained speechless. Bless his heart. I know for a fact he has spoken since, but not that night.

Without another word, I went inside and closed the door. To face my fate.

The upshot of the story is that, believe it or not, Charlie relented the next day and allowed the outcasts back to camp to join the misfits. At that point, of course, I was already supposed to be home, anyway, so reversal of the judgment had no impact on me.

What did have an impact on me was that thereafter, other than for football practice, school, and church, I was grounded for life. Corky's problems with the church leaders came to a head a few months later, resulting in his resignation, as reflected in the *Dallas Morning News* article I quoted from earlier. But that's a whole 'nother story.

Fortunately, he later relented and rescinded the grounding so that I could get married and become a lawyer . . . you know, have a life.

And there you have the saga of the Lake Lavon Four. Learn from it what you may.

Transitional Narrative:
The Floating Dice Game

At its inception, Forest Meadow Baptist Church (FMBC) was almost like a floating dice game, meeting for a time in the basement of Ross Avenue State Bank in east Dallas and then sharing space with St. Stephen United Methodist Church in Mesquite, before later holding services in the band hall at Forest Meadow Junior High School. After a couple of years, it finally built a building of its own.

While at FMBC, Corky continued a pattern he had started at GABC of using music and drama as part of his sermons, which was way ahead of its time in the early 1970s. It's interesting to see his notes and drafts of scripts for some of his sermons using audio/visual aspects. He structured a Creative Preaching workshop for local Dallas pastors, and he wrote or co-wrote two full-length dramas, which were performed multiple times at churches in Dallas. One of those dramas, called *Doomstar*, was about the Second Coming of Christ. The other, called *The Golgotha Affair*, was inspired by the Watergate hearings and depicted an investigation by the Roman Senate into the circumstances surrounding, and leading up to, the crucifixion of Jesus.

The following sermons were first preached at FMBC and reflect, I think, the sweet spirit of the congregation.

Sermon: *More Evidence of the Spirit: Joy*[9]

[Special music ends]

You see what I'm talking about? You know that when you praise Jesus like that, who needs preaching? And you're thinking, "Yeah, we're probably not gonna get any either." But we're gonna give it a whirl. But you know, when you sing like that, you don't really need any preaching. If there's anything that turns a spigot on in a preacher's heart, it's music that warms the soul and spirit like that. And Tom [Bledsoe], I've still got some sawdust in my trouser leg cuff—you know, back when you used to have cuffs—from preaching in a tent at the church down in Baton Rouge that we helped start, and we met for nearly a year in a tent. And one of these days, the good Lord willing, let's just throw us up a tent over there on Church Street and let's have us an outdoor meeting.

Would you like to do that? Okay. All right. We'll be thinking about that and praying about that, and let's see what we can do. I'll remind you, then, that you said yes.

Now, to continue our series dealing with spiritual gifts and the work of the Spirit in our lives, we've been

---

[9] Preached at Forest Meadow Baptist Church in Dallas on September 10, 1972.

addressing ourselves to the subject for a period of some weeks, indeed some months now. And to be perfectly frank, when I first began, I just wondered if I'd be able to find enough material to preach anything that would be worthy of the name series. And I'm beginning to wonder now whether we'll ever run out. I mean, every time I think, well, we'll turn it off at the end of this, I find something else, and man, I get excited about it. Just can't stop on it. So, it seemed appropriate to me that we give at least some attention, not only to the gifts of the spirit, but to the fruit of the Spirit.

And it just may be that in some critical areas of our Christian performance, the fruits of the Spirit may be much more important and significant than any high-powered, charismatic gift that might be very scintillating and very exciting. And yet, if there's not that evidence of the sweet presence of God's Spirit in our lives that gives evidence to it in terms of these marks of his fruitage, then there's something surely suspicious and suspect about whatever gifts may be present.

"The fruit of the Spirit," says Paul, "is love. And it's joy."

I remember when I was about half the size of my younger son here that I had a little hound dog. Now, boys like pups, you know, and this was a little pup. And he likes dogs. Our next-door neighbor has a little pooch that he's real fond of, just about the size of Lion. We call him Lion because . . . well, that's his name.

And this was one of those Hines dogs. You know, has 57 varieties? But the most pronounced trait was the fact that, somewhere in there, it had some of that "dash-hound" in it. You know, was built close to the ground, strung out, but it really wasn't a dachshund, but it was built sort of like that. But man, I thought that was the cutest thing I had ever seen in my life, and I did love that pooch. And one night, boy, an old cold blue norther blew through. Anyway, it got cold, it just got bitter cold. And I got to thinking about my poor old pooch out there that was going to freeze to death. Man, I couldn't stand it.

I knew better than to ask mother and dad if it'd be all right to do what I was thinking about doing. And so I thought, well, there's just no point in upsetting them, and I'll just go ahead and handle this thing myself and won't create any problem. So, I went out there and got that pooch and I smuggled him back into the house and got him into my bedroom without making too much noise—I thought— and got in the bed and got him under the covers. I thought I was doing a pretty good job with it, but about that time, boy, the light flipped back on.

My mother stood there. She said, "Son, what's that?"

"What's that, Mommy?"

"Well, what's that mound under the covers there?"

"What mound is that?"

And then that doggone mound began to move around.

"That one right there. Have you got that dog in the bed with you?"

"Dog in the bed with me!"

Man, it was back out into the cold with him.

But you know, I found out from that experience that it's pretty hard to hide a dog under the covers in the bed with you. You know, it's just real hard. And you know, I believe it's just real hard for the Holy Spirit to be in control of a person's heart and life and personality, and to not show. It just has a way of somehow showing through. And I think this is exactly what Paul is talking about when he speaks of the fruits of the Spirit. These characteristics or these attributes of life, they're the ones that bear testimony to the presence and the power of the Lord's Spirit in our lives. Because where he is, there will be love. And there will be joy.

I think the word "joy" here is the antithesis to sorrow and to grief and anguish. I remember as I think about this, the song we used to sing in camp. You remember? *The more we get together, together, together. The more we get together, the happier we'll be.* And the more we get together with the Spirit, the happier we become.

I believe that's a standard rule of thumb. As I have anticipated this opportunity in the message tonight, I've ticked off, in my memory, the great spiritual impact of people in my life across the years and, hands down, the most committed, dedicated Christians I have known, without a single exception to my memory, have been at the same time the happiest people I've known. I think that makes sense. That's the way it ought to be. Where the Spirit is in control, we're not going to be long-faced and moping around. We're going to be happy.

I think there are two distortions of this truth. There's one category that feels like you've got to have sort of what I call a Christian gloom to really be spiritual. You know, if you're going to really be committed and if you're going be dedicated and if you're going to be saintly and godly, and if you are really gonna be all sold out to the Lord, it ought to hurt. I can remember as a young person—

and it's why I responded so favorably to the young people singing tonight—but I can remember when I was the age of most of the youngsters up here tonight, the devil had sorta pulled the wool over my eyes. I had the distinct impression that anybody who was a genuine Christian, and was truly committed to the Lord, was just a little bit unhappy all the time.

And you had to wear a black suit and black shoes and a black tie. I got to thinking about it this afternoon, but that's exactly what I had on this morning: a black suit, black shoes, and a black tie. And here I've even got a black shirt on tonight. But I hope it doesn't look too drab.

But my impression was that, behind all of that façade of black and gray, that you had to have a face long enough to eat ice cream out of a churn. And that was just the way to be saintly. But I kind of had built into me the desire to want to have a good time and to enjoy life, and I was determined I was going to do it.

Really, it's a shame because for a long, long time, I did not seriously entertain the prospect of making Jesus the master of my life because I just didn't feel like I could quite hack it to be so sad and dismal and dreary. I guess this is one of the reasons it was a little bit hard for me to do some things and make some commitments. The Lord first called me into, I thought, evangelistic music, and finally he said, "I want you to preach." I guess if he'd tried to get me to preach, directly, I'd have just given him a flat "no" because I knew I didn't fit into that particular kind of a mold.

Boy, I'll tell you what, I showed up on seminary campus, walking out across there, and I just happened to meet some guys when I first got there who were regular guys. You could call them Bill and Harry. But I hadn't been there five minutes until I met the first one—and I don't mean to be critical, but this is the way it came across to me: "Ahhhh, Brother Farris."

You know what he was saying? It really wasn't so much that he just didn't want to call me Corky. He thought that was a little bit beneath the dignity of a preacher's name, I'm sure. But the reason he called me "Brother Farris" was he wanted me to call him "Brother Snodgrass." And I just refused to do that. I called him by his first name anyway. I had to admit that kind of gritted on me a little bit. Sometimes you could slip up on the back of a group and, and if you got to talking anything about the Lord, there'd be somebody who would say, "Ay-mon!"

Now, I have to say "amen" once in a while, but when it comes out "ay-mon," I don't know. That turns me off. I declare it does. But some people feel like if you are really dedicated to the Lord, it ought to put some strain on your face, and you ought to just kind of, well . . . you get the impression that they've had it tougher than anybody, and they're out there suffering for Jesus.

Now, let me tell you what. Once in a while it comes to that. But the people I've seen who have really put all their chips on the table, if you'll pardon the expression, and who have laid everything on the line, and maybe by your standard and mine they're out there suffering for Jesus, they'd be surprised to death if you told that to them. It never crossed their mind that they're suffering for Jesus. But the ol' boy with the wrinkled brow and a little halo that lights up every time he talks about what a tremendous cross he's bearing—there's something missing in his life. Because where the Spirit is in control, there's some joy. There's some real happiness.

There are some who—it's not because they think it's spiritual to be worried, but they just come like that. I don't quite understand this, but I encounter some Christian people that it looks to me like they have just absolutely over-magnified their problems. You know what I mean? There are some folks who, if they don't have something to worry about, that worries them. If everything's going great, there must be something wrong somewhere. Every now and again, you run into a dear brother or sister and say, "How you doing this morning?" and 20 minutes later, you're sorry you asked. They just throw it all on you. Man, they got nothing but misery and problems and heartache and grief and disappointment, tragedy and sorrow.

That reminds me of the story, you may have heard it somewhere, about the person who came up on this girl who was crying, and he said, "What's the matter?" And she said, "Well, I just got to thinking, suppose I were to meet a handsome young man, and we were to get married, and we were to have a child, and suppose the little child was playing out in the front yard and just suppose that a truck came along and ran over and killed it. Oh, how sad that would be." And boo hoo hoo.

Now those things might happen well on down the road, but I've seen people just about like that. People like our fair-haired, young hero Chicken Little. Peanut fell on his head and man, the sky is falling in. Just let the least little thing happen and boy, everything has come unwound and absolutely God has abdicated his throne and everything's caving in on us. And man, this is terrible, running around the world with nothing but difficulty, nothing but problems. There are some of us that, all we see is the hole in the donut.

And there are some people, like a friend of mine, and he's a dear friend and he's a great guy, but he just kind of comes in a negative vein. If he were to find a five-dollar bill, the first thing he'd say is, "Man, look at that. That's a five-dollar bill. Now why wasn't that a ten-dollar bill?"

You know the type I'm talking about. Man, just no way to come out on top.

I think of two people I know. I think of one person I've known in the past who has a wonderful family, a good job, good responsibility, has good security, but that person, all they can find is difficulties until they are just absolutely under an oppressive burden all the time.

And then I think in contrast to that of a little woman who was a member of the mission that I pastored, or attempted to pastor, down in Waco. Little Ms. Golden. She lived in a little cracker box of a house that I just promise you nobody ever even accidentally put any paint on it. It was just one room. I used to go see her because she had no regular income. And that was back before it was quite as financially prosperous to be poor. I mean, she just didn't have anything. I can remember that I'd knock on the door, she'd come the door, and I'd say, "Ms. Golden, how you doing?"

She'd say, "Oh, Brother Corky, come in and sit

down. Let me tell you about it." I'd sit down and she would begin to tell me about what a wonderful time she was having in the Lord, and she'd sit there and talk about Jesus and how sweet he is and how he provides, how he cared for her, how she's looking forward to seeing him at his coming. I would just get absolutely carried away. Here I had come to see if I could help her out a little bit and she just absolutely picked me up and put me on Cloud Nine, bragging about Jesus.

When I'd leave, I'd start pulling the door, then I'd stop and say, "By the way, Ms. Golden, what did you have for lunch?"

"Oh, well, uh, I'm doing pretty good."

Walk in there to that little nook in the corner called a kitchen, open a cabinet, and there wouldn't be a thing in there.

"Ms. Golden, when was the last time you ate?"

"Well, think it was day before yesterday."

Now, that's not an exaggeration. I'm telling you the gospel truth. But where the Spirit is, there's joy.

Now, I think there's another distortion of this truth, though, and that's on the other side of the coin. There are these Christian folks—and man, I don't mean to be critical, and I don't want to offend or grieve the Spirit—but there are these people on the other side of the coin that look like they're trying to say cheese all time. You know, man, you talk about being happy in Jesus? I'm just so happy, I can just hardly stand it. I call this a false Christian gaiety. Just nobody could be that happy. You've got to have some problems every once in a while, and if you haven't got some problems, you surely must be faking it. But there are those folks that are just too happy to be real.

I remember I was in a meeting over the southeast one time, and there was a preacher's wife. Bless her heart, I found out a little bit later she was nutty as a fruitcake, really. But I met her and the next day I was at the church, and I said, "Well, hello there, Miss Preacher, how you doing today?"

And she said, "Oh, bless-ed day, bless-ed day!"

Suddenly I felt like ol' mopey. I didn't realize it was all that great, but I tell you what, she just about "bless-ed dayed" us out of there. By the time she got through, there wasn't anything blessed about it. There was an artificiality and there was a false manufactured tone to her voice as she tried to talk about the excitement of the Lord. The people who look only at that side of the coin just get it completely out of balance.

And, boy, I just got to tell this. One time when I

was about the age of my boy back there, a little older, it was on a Sunday morning in Fred Swank's church, and in the middle of the song service, the fellow who was leading the music—he was not a full-time song leader—but anyway, he started off in the song service, looked out there in the audience, and there was a fellow that he knew. He said, "Brother so-and-so, why don't you come up here and sing something for us?"

Well, I thought that was a little bit odd. I mean, it looked like the least they could have done would have been to get together in advance. You know how boys kind of get tickled at all sorts of odd things, and that kind of hit my funny bone. There were about 10 or 15 of us on that back row back there, and we kind of giggled and nudged each other.

Well, the guy got up there and said, "I'm gonna sing a certain, certain song—" I don't remember what it was, and he asked the lady at the piano. She knew it and so she played the introduction, and he started to sing. It reminded me a little bit about, up there at the seminary this past week, this meeting in a chapel service and Dr. Allison's wife, who is a very accomplished musician, was gracious enough to ask me to sing with her. Some comments were made in the hall, and I'll not say what they were. But I said,

"Well, I would but I took a few voice lessons from a hog caller, and I can't sing in Arkansas. If I do, man, they come from miles round. When I get through singing in Arkansas, I'd have hogs all up and down."

But anyway, this old boy sang like that was the kind of lessons he'd had. He just bellowed. You know, if it's loud it's got to be good. But anyway, he got about halfway through the first stanza, and he stopped, and he said, "I'd give anything in the world to know the words to that song."

Well, my soul, I thought, "Yeah, I would, too. I'd give anything in the world if he knew."

He said, "Well, I've got to find a certain book." Man, it was just awkward, and everybody was embarrassed for him. He left the platform and rambled around out there, and he had the lady at the piano looking in the stool. Finally, somewhere out there in the back, someone found a book that had it. He rustled around through it and finally said, "Oh, yeah, here it is."

Then he tucked it under his arm and sang three verses of it, never did look at it again. Well, by that time, the service had lost a little bit of its spiritual impact for some of us.

I'm just now leading up to the point. There was a rolling step that came off of that elevated area beside the pulpit, and it was supposed to be hooked. Whoever had put it back the last time that they had done some work on the stage just overlooked that little item. That dear brother started off over there and he hit that rolling step—

I was sitting back there and all I could see was his head, and in a minute his head disappeared and there were his feet. It looked to me like he just hung suspended there for about five minutes, and then . . . *badoom*.

I want you to know that it was still as death out there in that audience for a minute. Then he came up, his tie was over on one side and glasses hanging down there, and he looked out at us and he said, "Well, praise the Lord!"

Yeah, there are some people that are just a little bit too happy for it to be real. And I've seen some folks that, in a conversation, even if they don't say ay-mon, they say amen at the wrong time. It just gets to be a little game, gets to be a little charade.

By the way, I found out years later, for what it's worth, it was Brother Swank's custom in those days, and I presume it still is, that he'd go into the living room and lie down and take a nap on Sunday afternoons. Elizabeth said that about every 15 or 20 minutes, she'd hear terrible noise in there, in the living room, and she'd go in there and there would be Fred. She said, "I found him in there on the floor, rolling and laughing."

The conversation these days sometimes gives the impression that you give your heart to Jesus, and it is just one very big, exciting, far out, funny trip the rest of your life. Now, I think a Christian ought to be happy, but that doesn't mean you have to be delirious. And that doesn't mean you have to fake or try to pretend a joy that you don't really feel. When I think about the kind of peace I believe he gives, and the kind of joy that he imparts, reminds me of that line in the old ballad, *It had to be you, wonderful you. Even glad just to be sad thinking of you.*

Now, the tears come. And they're supposed to. And there are times when disappointment is unavoidable and it stings, and it's supposed to. But I believe where the Spirit rules and reigns and controls our minds and our hearts and our emotions, there will be an inner natural sense of sustained delight in our Lord.

You know when I first saw that? It was a singer. During my days of deep rebellion, I'd been singing in a barbershop quartet in high school. That was back before they had the organization [Society for the Preservation and Encouragement of Barbershop Quartet Singing in America, Inc.], and we just sang and sang up a storm. When we graduated, at least some of them did, it tore up our barbershop quartet. And here I was without anybody to sing with.

In those days, I was singing a fake necktie tenor, falsetto, and they needed a first tenor in a church quartet. I went up there just because I wanted to sing. I really didn't care anything about the Lord, about church; I just wanted to sing. So, they put me in that quartet, and the lead, the second tenor, was the choir director of that church. Here I was frantically trying to have a good time, to get all my kicks and all my thrills and all my excitement out of life. And here was this cotton-picking song leader, and he was having more fun than I was. He wasn't having to force it, and he wasn't having to fake it, and he wasn't having to pretend it.

It was real. Yes, it was real. And God used the joy of his Spirit in that man's life that caused me to stop, to ponder, to consider for the first time that there really might be something to it after all. It was out of that that God did a work of grace in my life.

Now this and I am through tonight. I know there are a lot of translations that are out these days and a lot of paraphrases and a lot of expanded and compounded versions of the Bible, but in light of what I've said, would you permit me to paraphrase just one verse from the 84th

Psalm. I don't know whether you're familiar with it or not, but this is one of my favorite psalms and has been since the days when I was in jump school.

It begins, "How amiable are thy tabernacles, O LORD of hosts." But the verse that I'm thinking about that means so much to me is the 10th Verse of the 84th Psalm: "For a day"—*a day*— "in thy courts is better than a thousand. I had rather be a doorkeeper in the house of my God than to dwell in the tents of wickedness."

You know what I think the Psalmist is saying? He's saying, "Man, I've tried it out there without the Lord. In the words of the recent song, I did it my way and I came up empty-handed. Now I'm trying it God's way. As I make a comparison, I wouldn't trade away the real kicks of life for all the pleasure of the world at any price. I'm in God's house. I'm in God's way. And man . . . I like it."

Because the fruit of the Spirit is real joy.

Transitional Narrative: *The Great TCU Contact Lens Caper*

As you can probably tell from the preceding sermon on "joy," Corky had a wonderful sense of humor. But I learned that I shouldn't necessarily assume that "joy" greets every circumstance. The saga of the Lake Lavon Four was a prime example. Funny writing about it now, more than 50 years later, but it wasn't so funny standing on the front porch in the middle of the night. The lesson I learned is that some cliches, trite though they may be, are true: discretion *is* the better part of valor. Here is an example of my applying that lesson when dealing with Corky.

I started my freshman year of college at TCU in the fall of 1973, where I played football. Our team in high school at Dallas's Woodrow Wilson was relatively small, especially when compared to some of the behemoths playing high school football today. I played fullback and linebacker at Woodrow, weighing 170 pounds dripping wet. I worked for a landscaper the summer before starting at TCU, sweating every day in brutal Dallas heat, which melted 10 pounds off of me. Bad news for playing either of my preferred positions at TCU. Even before I lost that weight, I was too small anyway, by at least 25 to 30 pounds, to play either fullback or linebacker at a Southwest

Conference School, especially no faster than I was. As could have been said about me: "He may be little, but he's slow."

Back then, colleges still ran a freshman schedule, with freshman teams playing other freshman teams. Making freshmen eligible to play varsity football was new, instituted by the NCAA in 1972, and we had a few players at TCU who moved up to the varsity before the 1973 season ended, but for the most part, all were part of the freshman team. At 160 pounds, my choice was clear, even for the freshman team: Either switch to wide receiver or give it up.

I chose the former, although that presented problems of its own. My eyesight was not, and is not, the greatest. Not like Mr. Magoo, mind you (those of you of a certain age surely remember the cartoon character Mr. J. Quincy Magoo, who was voiced by actor Jim Backus, Thurston Howell, III, on *Gilligan's Island*), but I started wearing glasses in early elementary school. I wore them playing baseball but never wore them playing football.

Of course, poor eyesight is not such a big problem for a fullback. After all, at that position, the quarterback typically just hands the ball to you. But a receiver actually has to look back down the field and pick up the ball as it leaves the quarterback's hand, or at least while it's in flight, then watch it approach until it lands in your hands—or bounces off, as the case may be. Catching a football was never my best skill as a football player. As might have been said about me, "If he can catch it, he can touch it." (If you missed that one, think about it for a second.) But I did okay if you just gave it to me and I could run straight ahead.

My summer weight loss sealed my fate and, sure enough, the coaches at TCU slotted me as a wide receiver, specifically flankerback. Those of you of a certain age will remember when such a position existed. If you're a Dallas Cowboys fan from the era of the '60s and '70s, think Lance Rentzel or Lance Alworth.

To help me see the ball, Corky insisted that I get contact lenses, which I had resisted before because I didn't like the idea of sticking foreign objects into my eyes on purpose. I had been happy up until my senior year of high school to wear brown plastic-frame glasses. As I look back on it now, though, I see I shouldn't have been happy, but that's another story. Then I got more fashionable wire-frame glasses before my senior year at Woodrow, which made me look like a groovy guy. Maybe. In my opinion. Or at least better than the crooked plastic frames.

But I acquiesced to Corky's suggestion (especially

since he was going to pay for them) and got contact lenses shortly after the start of the season. Wearing them during practice, I was amazed to learn that I could actually see the quarterback as he threw the ball, which I could watch in flight. Could even look it right into my hands. I found that it helped me catch the ball. My horizons had broadened, and my future seemed rosy.

Until the first game after getting contacts. We played it at home, at Amon Carter Stadium in Fort Worth against the Baylor Cubs. Freshman teams were the babies of whatever the varsity was, so the Baylor Bears became the Baylor Cubs; the TCU Horned Frogs became the TCU Polywogs. Strikes fear into your heart, doesn't it?

I was on special teams, including the kickoff coverage team. Early in the first half, we kicked off following a score and I charged downfield as fast as my 160 pounds could propel me. I drew a bead on the kick returner as I approached, oh, must have been about the 25- or 20-yard line, when I noticed in my peripheral vision (something I really hadn't appreciated before I got those great new contact lenses) a freight train bearing down on me, painted green and gold. I later learned, based on jersey number, that it wasn't a freight train but was an offensive guard on Baylor's kick return team who weighed about 230 pounds.

Before I could brace myself, he made contact. Laws of physics took over as he literally knocked me up into the air, way off my feet, and into a landing that must have resembled a rock rolling downhill. I'm still not sure how many times I rolled. When I got to my feet, I realized that something was wrong with my vision. I could see just fine out of one eye, but everything was blurry out of the other. You guessed it, in my first game I was wearing my brand-new contact lenses and one of them had been knocked out. I spent the rest of the game in a sort of daze, and I probably looked like Popeye, squinting one eye. It felt like I kept running in a semi-circle, following the vision of my dominant eye, but of course that wasn't really the case.

The next day, watching the game film during a team meeting, I got to see at least the first part of what had happened. I was in the side of the frame running downfield when the Baylor player hit me. And then suddenly I disappeared from the frame. I almost felt sorry for the Baylor player. He must have thought he'd killed me.

When I told Corky the next week that a contact had been knocked out, somewhere between the 20- and 30-yard lines, between the hashmark and the sideline, on the green artificial turf at Amon Carter Stadium, he said what all good fathers would have said: "Go down there and look for it."

A brief aside about artificial turf, which was sorta like a carpet designed to create burns on your elbows every time you hit the ground. I never wore elbow pads and a friend who once came to watch a practice scrimmage at Woodrow told me that, since we didn't wear numbers at practice, he couldn't tell which one I was until he realized he could recognize me from the blood flowing down my forearms. That artificial turf at Amon Carter Stadium did the same thing to me as the hard dirt field did at Woodrow, but maybe even worse.

But I digress. My actual point about the turf was that it was just perfect for disguising a tiny speck of clear plastic resting atop it. Well, my eighteen years of life experience told me that it would be a waste of my time to go look for the lens. So, I didn't. I later told Corky I couldn't find it. You know, discretion is the better part of valor and all that. Of course, what I said was true. I couldn't find it. I didn't tell him I didn't look; not sure if maybe I told him that I did look—memory is conveniently hazy—but we might be encroaching on the grounds of another lesson for another day.

Anyway, the next week, the freshman team was

practicing on the turf at Amon Carter instead of our usual grass practice field. I'm not sure if the varsity had already left town for an away game, but for whatever reason, we got to use the field the big boys practiced on. We were in the process of running plays against the defense down on the end of the field where the train had hit me the week before. Another wide receiver had just gotten into his stance when he suddenly called out.

"Hold it. Nobody move."

We all watched as he gingerly reached down and picked up . . . a contact lens. It was dried out, a little shrunken from the drying, but unbroken.

"Anybody lose a contact lens?" he asked.

No one, including me, spoke up. There was no point, as I saw it. It was unwearable so why bother? I'll never know for sure if it was mine, but my gut tells me there were not *beaucoup* (derived from French, meaning "many") contact lenses lost that week between the 20- and 30-yard lines on that end of the field, between the hashmark and the sideline. It was probably mine, though unwearable at that point.

The lesson here is Biblical: Seek, and ye shall find. The corollary is: Don't seek, and ye won't find. At least not until whatever you should have been searching for is dried out and worthless to you. In modern vernacular: If you don't at least try, failure is assured. I guess at least one other possible lesson is to obey your parents, but that's a story for another time.

And by the way, I never told Corky the full narrative about the great contact lens caper. I feared it might test the "joy" principle. And I never wore contact lenses again playing football. The possible trauma of losing another seemed too great a risk.

SERMON: *Sin in the Life of the Believer*[10]

If you have your Bibles tonight, let's turn to the 51st Psalm and then let's pause together for just a breath of prayer, shall we? Lord, grant that tonight your spirit would help us perceive how serious is our disobedience to you. In Jesus's name, amen.

The reader of the Old Testament is hardly prepared for the vicious and the brutal things that David is destined to commit. There's nothing in his background, there's nothing in his ancestry to suggest that he could even remotely be capable of such acts and such deeds. He had unusual spiritual perception and insight as a lad. And when he was still just an obscure shepherd boy, the Lord laid his hand upon him and anointed him to become the captain over the host of Israel. During the critical days of his apprenticeship, God permitted him to watch the tragic spiritual disintegration of Saul, his immediate predecessor on the throne of Israel. And during those formative years, God granted unusual evidence of his blessing and power in David's life, such as his fantastic conquest of Goliath, that massive gladiator.

---

[10] Preached at Forest Meadow Baptist Church in Dallas on April 1, 1973.

There is just nothing to suggest that David could ever stoop so low. And yet, one day King David, in a moment of idle leisure, looked upon the wife of another man and he lusted after her in his heart. He dispatched his servants and had her brought to his own quarters, and there in the royal suite, in the capital city of Jerusalem in the midst of God's people of Israel, noble King David, in what can be nothing more nor less described than a trashy, sordid little episode, forced himself upon the woman. Once his appetite had been satisfied, he sent her back to her own quarters. The deed was done, and no one would know about it.

Can you imagine, then, the consternation and the shock to King David when he learns that, as a result of his indiscretion, the woman, Bathsheba, is expecting a child. If that child should be born under these circumstances, some very ugly questions are apt to be raised because her husband, one of the field commanders of the armies of Israel, was currently a part of the battle assignment against an enemy stronghold to which the armies of Israel had laid siege. If the child should be born during his extended absence, someone might wonder. Probing questions might be raised.

So, David came to what appeared to be a very

happy solution to his dilemma. I suppose he did the equivalent of telegraphing the front and instructing Field Marshal Joab, the commander-in-chief of the armies of Israel, to have Colonel Uriah sent back to the capital city of Jerusalem on an R&R leave. He was sure that, once he returned to his home and to his wife, that when the child was born, no one would be the wiser as to its ancestry.

So, David did that, and Uriah returned to Jerusalem. But, to David's shock and chagrin, instead of returning to his family and to his wife, Uriah insisted upon sleeping at the gate to the palace with all of his battle gear and armor. As if he were still upon the scene of battle, as if he were still in bivouac with the armies of Israel.

When this information is communicated to King David, he has Colonel Uriah brought before him. When he remonstrated, this is Uriah's reply. "And Uriah said unto David, 'The ark and Israel and Judah abide in tents; and my lord Joab, and the servants of my lord, are encamped in the open fields. Shall I then go into my house to eat and to drink and to lie with my wife? As thou livest, and as thy soul liveth, I will not do this thing.'"

I find a real ring of irony in that because, you see, Uriah is identified as "the Hittite." He was not of Hebrew stock in origin. He was an alien. He was a foreigner, and in all probability, as was frequently the vocation of his countrymen, probably he was a military mercenary. In other words, his military expertise and genius had gone for bid on the open market, and he had been purchased in competitive opposition to others who might like to have his power. And he came to be one of the field commanders of the armies of Israel.

But the irony is to be found in the fact that, quite obviously, Uriah had given King David more than his sword and his shield. He had given him the devotion and the allegiance of his heart and spirit—to the man who committed adultery with his wife.

David decided that something else would have to be attempted. And so noble King David—can you believe this?—invited Colonel Uriah to his quarters, plied him with alcohol on the assumption that, in a drunken stupor, his dedication and his devotion to David and the military of Israel would not be quite so zealous. And in his drunken condition, he would surely return to his wife. But David did not bargain for Uriah's discipline. Even in his drunken stupor, Uriah insisted on sleeping at the gate to the palace.

David found himself crowded into a corner and he took an awful, awful exit. He wrote a little document with his own hand and sealed it with his own signet. In that little missive, he instructed Joab to assign Uriah to a hazardous post in a frontal assault upon the enemy stronghold. Without alerting him to the battle plan, the Israelite troops were to fall back, leaving Uriah in an exposed position, in the hopes that he would be killed by the enemy in battle. Then, could you believe it? He had the audacity to give that death certificate to Uriah, knowing that it would be delivered sealed, unexamined. And that's exactly what happened. Field Marshal Joab did just exactly as David instructed him, and Uriah was killed in action.

David waited for what was, in his judgment, a discrete period of time, then he had the sorrowing widow brought to his quarters again and he made her one of his wives. And it was all over. The episode was ended. No one was the wiser. No one knew just exactly all that had taken place except David. Bathsheba probably only knew parts of it. I suspect she was not aware, at least not immediately, of the fact that David was responsible for Uriah's death. Joab knew only what had taken place upon the scene of battle. But apart from the fragmentary information that these people had, no one was the wiser. No one knew except David.

Oh, yes. There was one other who knew. The Lord knew. He always does.

A baby boy was born, a little child, and everything was smooth. But then one day the preacher came to the court, and he addressed the king with a request for permission to tell a story. And the king said, "Now preacher, we always like to hear you. You're an enchanting spinner of yarns, teller of tales. You tell us your story."

So, the preacher said, "Well, Your Majesty, here in this city there's a man who is very poor. About all he has in his possession worthy of the name is a little lamb. It's hardly a possession. It's almost like a member of the family. The children love it, and it's just like a part of the immediate family.

"And nearby there lives a very wealthy man who has multiple herds and flocks. But, My Lord, recently this wealthy man had a guest from out of the city, and he wanted to prepare a special feast for him. But instead of having one of his own animals slaughtered, he had his servants go and steal that little lamb from the poor man. He had it killed, and he had it prepared for a feast, for a banquet for his guest, and they ate, and they dined sumptuously at the expense of the man who had only just this one little animal.

"Now, tell me Your Majesty. What do you think of that kind of act?"

Trembling in a rage of righteous indignation, David slowly came to his feet. Trembling with a fury of the injustice of the story that he just heard. Finally, it came blurting out. "Preacher, who is that man? I demand to know. Who is that man? He deserves to die."

And then Nathan leveled his finger in the face of his king, and he said, "Sir, you are that man. You are that man."

And in a tidal wave of contrition and bitter remorse, David penned the unforgettable words to the 51st Psalm. Did you notice the superscription? "To the chief Musician, A Psalm of David, when Nathan the prophet came unto him, after he had gone into Bath-sheba." And David, alerted to the fact that his God knew of all that he had done, wrote this great expression of repentance.

"Have mercy upon me, O God, according to thy lovingkindness; according unto the multitude of thy tender mercies blot out my transgressions. Wash me thoroughly from mine iniquity, and cleanse me from my sin. For I acknowledge my transgressions; and my sin is ever before me. Against thee, thee only, have I sinned and done this evil in thy sight; that thou mightest be justified when thou speakest, and be clear when thou judgest. Behold, I was shapen in iniquity and in sin did my mother conceive me.

Behold, thou desirest truth in the inward parts; and in the hidden part thou shalt make me to know wisdom.

"Purge me with hyssop, and I shall be clean; wash me, and I shall be whiter than snow. Make me to hear joy and gladness, that the bones which thou has broken may rejoice. Hide thy face from my sins and blot out all my iniquities. Create in me a clean heart, O God, and renew a right spirit within me.

"Cast me not away from thy presence and take not thy holy spirit from me. Restore unto me the joy of thy salvation and uphold me with thy free spirit. Then will I teach transgressors thy ways, and sinners shall be converted unto thee. Deliver me from bloodguiltiness, O God, thou God of my salvation, and my tongue shall sing aloud of thy righteousness.

"O Lord, open thou my lips and my mouth shall shew forth thy praise. For thou desirest not sacrifice, else would I give it. Thou delightest not in burnt offering. The sacrifices of God are a broken spirit; a broken and contrite heart, O God, thou wilt not despise. Do good in thy pleasure unto Zion; build thou the walls of Jerusalem. Then shalt thou be pleased with the sacrifices of righteousness, with burnt offering and whole burnt offering; then shall they offer bullocks upon thine altar."

Sin is monstrous in the life of the unbeliever. It ultimately will torture and twist and doom the unregenerate heart. It is eternal separation from God. But I am convinced, as these words make unmistakably clear, sin that continues to be hidden, disguised, unacknowledged and renounced, festers in the heart of the child of God, and it brings some awful, damaging residue of disturbance and turmoil in his spirit.

May I simply call your attention to some of the things that the Psalm of David indicates sin will do in the heart of a believer? First of all, notice what he said: "Against thee, thee only have I sinned." That's very strange on the surface, isn't it? Because you see, as we study what had taken place, we find that David is a classic illustration of the fact that sin somehow demands company. It's extremely difficult to sin in total isolation. Either we have to have somebody to sin with, or at the bare minimum, we need somebody to sin against.

Now, as we examine the events of his indiscretion, surely no one can argue the statement that there were some others against whom David had sinned. For example, the woman in the case. There is nothing to suggest that she welcomed the advances of King David. She may have been very unhappy at the beginning. We just do not know. But in any event, David had sinned against her in that he had disturbed, and ultimately destroyed, the tranquility and the very existence of her home. And so, as I read this situation, I'm convinced that David sinned against Bathsheba.

And surely there can be no question but that he sinned against Uriah. First of all, he took the man's wife and then he compounded that mistake by taking the man's life. Because, you see, ultimately David was just as guilty of the assassination of Uriah as if it had been his hand that plunged the lance into his body that took his life. David was his murderer by remote control. There could be no question that he sinned against Uriah.

I suspect he also sinned against Joab. It may have been with considerable conflict of conscience that Joab executed the orders that David had sent to him. Now, to be sure, Joab, himself, was not above court intrigue and conspiracy, but Uriah obviously was one of his more capable field commanders. I'm sure that there was considerable conflict of interest in the heart of Joab as he executed the orders that David had given him. And Joab became a pawn in this murder plot. So surely David sinned against Joab.

All of the populace in Israel looked to Jerusalem not only as the center of religious worship, but they also looked there for rule and for leadership, and they looked upon David as the divine representative of the rule of Jehovah in their midst. They were looking to him to be the example and the paragon of virtue and dedication and commitment to the cause and the purposes of the Lord. And I submit for your consideration the deep conviction that, when David did what he did with Bathsheba and against Uriah, he violated the confidence and the trust of every man, woman, boy, and girl in the entire kingdom of Israel.

I don't think there was anyone in all of Hebrew life that David had not already sinned against. How then could he so glibly say, "Against thee, thee only have I sinned"? Well, as we shall presently see, even as David, himself, acknowledges that "my sin is ever before me," he was already aware of the fact that he had sinned against these others. The disturbing guilt of it gnawed in his conscience. It haunted his reverie. It flickered through his nightmarish dreams. It hounded his every waking moment until his eyes sank deep in their sockets as he prowled the corridors of the palace in the middle of the night, hounded and haunted by the guilt of what he had done against all of these toward whom he had been unfaithful.

Now, he was aware of what he'd done, and it ate his sack lunch, but it was not until Nathan, the prophet, came and disclosed the awful sordid details of his secret crime that David was suddenly aware of the fact that he had sinned against his God, and his God knew all about it. And it was then that David became aware of the fact that, as he sinned against Bathsheba and against Uriah and against Joab and against all of the Kingdom, ultimately, as if there were no middleman, he had supremely sinned against the God whom he still loved. It was that fact and that awareness that broke his heart. Against thee and thee only have I sinned. You see, in a very special and a very unique way, when a child of God is disobedient and betrays the trust and confidence of his Lord, he sins against him who bought our forgiveness with his blood on the cross.

I think we have the picture of that in the description of the trial of our Lord as it is recorded in the gospel of John. "The high priest then asked Jesus of his disciples and of his doctrine. Jesus answered Him, 'I spake openly to the world. I ever taught in the synagogue and in the temple, whither the Jews always resort, and in secret have I said nothing. Why askest thou me? Ask them which heard me what I have said unto them. Behold, they know what I said.'" [John 18:19-21]

Able to make an immediate defense of his doctrine, he offered no apology, no embarrassment over his teaching.

But how could he justify what Simon Peter was at that very moment doing out there, bathing the name of his Lord with his vile profanity and swearing, "I never knew him."

Let me tell you something. When I, as a Christian, sin, I sully his name; I bring his cause and his person and his reputation into question. And when I sin as the child of God, I put him to open disgrace and to public shame, and he is embarrassed, and he is hurt. I'll tell you what, if that be so, if what I'm saying has even a remote element of truth in it, it is utterly unthinkable that I could, as a Christian, commit any kind of a sin that could be interpreted as unimportant or trivial. Anytime I do anything that is displeasing to him, I sin against him as if no one else were involved.

But there is something else about the nature of sin in the life of the believer. David said, "Restore unto me the joy of thy salvation." Some have been quick to notice, and I think this is correct, that he did not say restore the *salvation*, but he did say restore the *joy* of it. Because while God's grace is able to endure our disobedience as his children, and we still have that salvation relationship to him, and while that is not severed, at the same time there is no question but that the joy of the salvation is shattered when we sin knowingly, willingly, deliberately, and we try to hide it, and we don't confess it, and we don't forsake it.

Now, that was a real tragedy in the case of David because, you see, David had experienced the joy of his salvation as I suppose few men had ever known. It was David, who in his spiritual ecstasy, could say, "Bless the Lord, O my soul, and all that is within me, bless his holy name. Bless the Lord, O my soul, and forget not all his benefits." It was that same David who wrote those memorable lines, "The heavens declare the glory of God, and the firmament sheweth his handiwork. Day unto day uttereth speech, and night unto night sheweth knowledge. There is no speech nor language where their voice is not heard."

It was David who wrote the words to the shepherd's Psalm. "The Lord is my shepherd, I shall not want. He maketh me to lie down in green pastures. He leadeth me beside the still waters."

But it was that same David, almost demented in the raging turbulence of his spirit as he attempts to struggle with the awful burden of his guilt, that same David, who reflected upon that inner conflict in the 32nd Psalm when he said, before he acknowledged and before he openly confessed his sin, "When I kept silence, my bones waxed old through my roaring all the day long. For day and night thy hand was heavy upon me. My moisture is turned into the drought of summer."

I'll tell you what, if we could have found David somewhere in the midnight hours pacing his restless little route up and down the corridors of the palace, if we could have found him there like some haunted wraith of a man, if we could have come upon him to say, "David, why do you not now exalt: Bless the Lord, oh my soul and all that is within me, bless his holy name?" David would've turned upon us like some caged animal, and he would've said, "I don't know what you're talking about. There is war raging in my spirit. I don't know what you're talking about."

We might have needled him. "David, what about the tranquil waters?" And David would've had to confess that all of the moisture is evaporated. "I'm out in a parched, arid desert, and I'm dying of spiritual thirst."

You can mark it down. When we deliberately sin, that is going to destroy the capability to know and to experience all of the thrill and all of the fullness and all of the delight that is our rightful heritage in a relationship to God. Once in a while, I go to preach in a revival meeting, and I talk about the fullness of God, and I talk about the joy of service, and I talk about the love of Christian fellowship. And I see some people out there blinking like a calf looking at a new gate. They don't even know what I'm talking about because they've not experienced it, not even as blood-bought, redeemed individuals. Because sin has found a resting place in their hearts. They've tried to hide it and they've tried to disguise it and they've tried to pretend it isn't there. They just don't know that joy like that could be experienced.

And I promise you this one thing, they're not ever gonna be happy. That's one of the reasons that some people look like they just took a dose of medicine when they go to church. They just can't have a good time, because it hurts too much to be around where God's people are.

David said, "Restore unto me the joy of my salvation. If you'll uphold me with your free spirit, if you'll purge me with hyssop, and if you'll wash me, make me clean, then will I teach transgressors thy ways."

Well, David, why don't you go out there and tell 'em anyway, while that awful, ugly sin continues to eat like some awful canker sore down into your spirit? Why don't you go out there and brag about the forgiveness of the Lord, and why don't you go out there and extoll his mercy and his grace? Boy, it sure is hard to talk about forgiveness when you know there's something in your life that hasn't been forgiven.

I heard a story about a deacon working on the job and one of his co-laborers was seriously injured. According to the story, as the workman lay there, mortally injured, on the floor of the big plant, his companions stood around him in an awkward circle. The man looked up at them and he said, "Men, I don't think I'm gonna make it. But I'm not ready to go. I'm not prepared to die. Is there any one of you that can tell me how I can make my peace with God and become a Christian?"

All the men stood around awkwardly. No one said anything. No one offered any counsel. The ambulance arrived and they picked the man up. They took him to the hospital, but he was dead on arrival. The story of that, as you would expect, got back to the pastor of that deacon. And according to the story as I heard it, the preacher searched out that deacon and he said, "I don't know if what I've heard is so." He repeated the story essentially as I have related it to you, and the deacon stood there for a moment, then hung his head. The tears began to scroll down his cheeks, and he said, "Pastor, that's right. That's exactly the way it happened."

And the preacher said, "But my dear brother, I don't understand that. You've heard me preach the gospel Sunday after Sunday. I know, I just know, you have to understand how a man can become a Christian. Why in God's name did you not tell him how to be saved?"

Through his sobs, that deacon said, "Pastor, I would have. But my life sealed my lips."

You know, as I talk about that, on the screen of my memory, some faces right now are flashing. I could tick off their names. Some young men that I knew in high school classrooms. I went to a lot of the dives and a lot of the nightclubs in Fort Worth, Texas, with them. I shared in all sorts of skullduggery and all sorts of ungodly conduct with them, and because of the compromise of my testimony, I couldn't say anything about Jesus. I think of one of those boys killed in an automobile wreck just soon after graduation, while on leave from the Merchant Marine. I think of another young man who was killed in the Battle of the Bulge in Europe. I think of another young man who, at the co-pilot controls of a B-24, was shot down over Tokyo. I couldn't tell them anything about this because of my unconfessed sin. And when that happens, there goes with it the awful burden of bloodguiltiness.

"Deliver me from bloodguiltiness, oh God thou God of my salvation." And when we can't tell people about the Lord, then we are responsible for them.

This final word. David had a lot of good common

sense, even in the midst of his indiscretion. He came to understand that, in light of what he had done, there was no sacrifice that he could offer. There was no offering that he could give. There was no incense he could burn. There was no office in the church that he could take. There was no contribution to the budget that he could make that would buy God's favor in his life. Isn't it amazing how we get things all out of whack when we do things we know are not right? We want to compensate for them by doing something over here at the other end of the line that will sort of make up for it. But that's not the way it works. David hit the nail right on the head when he said, "Thou desirest not sacrifice else would I give it. Thou delightest not in burnt offering."

Boy, he would've been prepared to have slaughtered all of the animals in Israel and to burn all of the cedars of Lebanon, if that would've done anything to cover the awful guilt and the stain of his sin. But it wouldn't, and he knew it. And here it is, the one sacrifice and the one offering that's acceptable: "The sacrifices of God are a broken spirit; a broken and a contrite heart, O God, thou wilt not despise."

You know, I'm persuaded that our Lord lurks in the wings of many churches tonight across our land. As the time comes for an offering to be made, I think he stands by many a communion table, many an altar, many a prayer rail, and I think he's not looking for dollar bills in the basket. I understand we need some. But that's not what he's looking for. He's looking for the penitent tears as God's people come to the altar and pour out their hearts, confessing their sin just like David did, and asking his mercy and his forgiveness. It doesn't have to be the awful combination of adultery and murder to hurt and to embarrass and to disgrace our Lord.

Any sin, any disobedience, is against him and him alone.

SERMON: *Dramatic Monologue on Hosea*[11]

The lights come up on Hosea listening to sounds from another part of the house, then he addresses the congregation.

She's still asleep. But that will give me time to tell our story. It all began—

I beg your pardon. Forgive my rudeness. *Shalom aleichem.*

But to the story. It all began many years ago. It was the Feast of Tabernacles. Of course, the city had turned out and all of the countryside was there. And we were having such an exciting and a wonderful time. It was then, I guess, that I saw her for the very first time. Well, I may have seen her before, but her family lived in the country, and I lived in the city. If I had seen her, I had only seen her as a child. But that particular day, I really saw her for the first time.

She was beautiful beyond description. Gomer. That name sounded like music to me. Oh, she was absolutely captivating. I wish you could have seen her then. Her teeth

---

[11] At heart, Corky was a frustrated actor. He often used drama and music in his sermons, including appearing in character to tell the story of Naaman, the military leader, that mighty man of valor with the caveat "but he was a leper." In this sermon, Corky appeared in costume and in character as Hosea at Forest Meadow Baptist Church in Dallas on February 8, 1976.

sparkled like the snows of Lebanon, and when she laughed, there was the echo of angel voices. Her hair, it was as black as midnight. And her eyes, oh her eyes, they just sparkled with her beauty, and they brimmed with the vitality of her youth. There was just the hint of mischief. And even then, there was just a shadow of wickedness.

But she was beautiful. She was so beautiful. Gomer. She was all I could think about all night long. She was in all my dreams, and I just hung on the fragrance of her memory for days. Then I saw her again at the market in the gate of the city. This time I had been practicing for this moment, this time I got close enough to speak. Well, almost to speak. I suddenly just turned to gelatin on the inside. I'll never forget how it came out.

Gomer.

There. I had said it. I had said her name. I had spoken to her, and somehow, I was sure in the mystery of her glance that she returned my affection and that there was a tenderness in her heart for me, as well as that devotion I felt for her.

It was then that I began to pray. Oh, I really began to pray. I talked to Adonai, the God of our fathers. I asked for his leadership. I asked for his guidance. I tried to pray beautifully and obediently, but after a while, I found myself just praying, "Lord, will it be all right for me to marry this woman? I love her so sincerely and so completely." Imagine my thrill when the Lord said, "Yes, my son. Indeed, it is my will for you to marry her."

Now, in Israelite culture, that's really only the beginning. I approached my family, which in turn approached hers. It took all the due process of time, the provision of the dowry, and then of course we had to build a little house that would constitute our home. And we had to wait for a while. But then at last, at last, the wonderful day of the wedding came. I'll never forget it, as long as I live. All of our friends making the wedding procession down this street and that, finally to arrive at the house that was to be our home. They toasted us with their laughter, with their singing. And then we were left together, the two of us.

Gomer. Gomer.

Our little house is not much, but I felt like the king of all Israel. Happiness is hardly a word to describe the utter exhilaration that I felt. I could hardly wait to come home in the evening. The meal would be prepared, and we would sit and talk about the things of the day, and she would laugh at my stories and my jokes. Oh, it was great. It was just great.

And then, after the evening meal, we would go up onto the roof and we would sit there to catch a breeze at twilight time. The glow of the sun there behind the purple hills with the peaceful panorama of the valley before us. I would hold her hand and we would talk about the things that we would do together, the family that would come, all of our dreams and all of our aspirations. But strange, when I would talk about Adonai, she would seem to be very silent. Almost solemn.

But those were glorious days. Those were glorious days. Then one day I came home—speak of happiness—I came home to the glorious, thrilling announcement that we were expecting our first child, a child of our very own.

And the days of waiting. Full of excitement and anticipation. At last, the glorious, wonderful day came. A manchild was delivered. I was the father of a son. An Israelite father of a son. I prayed to Adonai, "What shall we name the child, my Lord?" And he said, "Name the child Jezreel." Then the word of the Lord came very deep to my heart, for he said, "I will visit the blood of Jezreel upon the house of Jehu and I will destroy the house of Israel from before me."

Ah, but never mind. Manchild, my own son. My chest nearly burst with pride as I cradled the lad in my arms the very first time friends and relatives came by to say, "Oh, he looks exactly like his father." And I would just nod. My very own, Jezreel, my son and child.

But it was soon after that that the problem began. I don't know exactly how to describe it, but the sweetness of our home began to turn sour. There were those meaningless little arguments, those quarrels. I could not exactly understand why they began, but they were just, well, they just seemed to erupt spontaneously. I know what you're thinking. The Hebrew husband is to be the master in his own house, and I tried to be, but she could be so contentious.

I guess it was when Jezreel was about a year and a half of age that I had to make a long trip down into Judah. I was gone for well over three months. I thought about Gomer every night. I prayed for her, prayed for my family, and I thought to myself that when I returned, the quarrels will evaporate. Our love will blossom as it did at the beginning, and all will be well again. That's what I prayed, and God knows that's what I hoped. But it didn't work out like that.

When I got back, it was worse. Instead of warmth, it was cold. We could scarcely seem to talk at all without anger being expressed. Then she told me we were expecting another child, and I thought perhaps, just perhaps, this will somehow revive our love again. When the time came for the child to be delivered, I was very anxious because, since I had been away, quite obviously the child was not going to be full term. It would be premature, and I was apprehensive about its very life, and I was concerned about Gomer and her health.

But then the child was born. She was not premature. She was full term. I could not believe that she was my own. I prayed to the Lord, "What shall we name this daughter, this child?" As I meditated and as I sought somehow the consolation of the Lord, he said to me, "Name her Lo-ruhamah." Lo-ruhamah. No mercy. "For," said the Lord, "I will no more have mercy upon Israel. I will punish her for all her sin." Lo-ruhamah.

That was the name we gave the child. As I cradled her in my arms and friends and relatives came by, no one suggested that she looked like her father. After that, the cycle of quarrels. So many times, I would return in the evening and Gomer would be gone. I can only imagine where she would be. And another child was conceived. As I prayed for the name of this child, the Lord said name him Lo-ammi. And when this infant was delivered, I named him Lo-ammi, for God said you are to call him that for he represents the fact that Israel is no longer my people. Not my people. As I held that little child in my arms, I was haunted by the fact that it was not my child. Lo-ammi.

Well, you can imagine what finally happened. I suppose it was inevitable. I came home one evening. The children were in front of the house, but when I came inside, still silent. She would return sometime in the course of the night, I thought. But I waited on top of the house all night long. And she did not return. She was gone. Gone. Gomer. Gomer.

The shame of it, the embarrassment, the hurt. But there were those who were gracious and understanding. Now and again, I would get some report as to her whereabouts. It was always awkward to hear the news. I heard that the man for whom she had abandoned me had turned her away. I thought perhaps she would come back now. But I waited in vain.

Then came the report, that ugly report. Someone said she's gone to north Israel, to the city of Dan. They said she's joined a pagan temple. They said she serves in that temple as a prostitute. I wanted to say it's not so. So, well, maybe she's gone, but she still loves me. She still loves our children, and she will come to her senses, and she will return, and that it was all a dream, that couldn't be so. But the words would choke in my throat because I knew it was so. Gomer, my beloved, enchanting Gomer, giving herself to others and to a foreign God.

Well, years slowly begin to blend together. Five. Ten. Fifteen. I heard nothing. Then I made a trip to another town. I had barely completed my business when I went to the market—and it happened. It happened there. I saw the slave market. The people who were on auction were standing there, their hands laced with leather thongs. As I glanced in the direction of the slaves, it happened. My heart skipped a beat. I saw her. At first, I could not be sure. The beauty was faded. The black raven tresses were now a dirty, yellowish gray. Her skin was laced with wrinkles. Her gaze was toward the earth. She never once looked up, but as I came close to her, I knew it was she, my Gomer.

Well, I ran, blinded by tears, back to my quarters. I didn't know how to react. I expected all of the bitterness and all of the hurt suddenly to just gush to the surface, but somehow it didn't. Instead, as I remembered how she looked there in the marketplace, I continued to see that beautiful Jewish lass that Gomer once had been. And I found myself still loving her.

I went back to the market the next day. She was still there. Still on auction. Yes, I did love her. I did. I didn't want to, but I did. So, I went back to my quarters, and I prayed. I really didn't know how to pray this time. "Oh, Lord, our God, how could it be? I'm ashamed to love a woman like this, but I love her."

Then I heard the voice of God, deep in my heart, as he seemed to say to me, "Oh, my son, my son, just as you continue to love this harlot, so do I continue to love unfaithful Israel. I love her with an abiding, enduring love that cannot be denied."

Then I realized that was right. All of the rebellion of my people, all of their ugly, licentious ways with the gods of Canaan and all of their disobedience was like the unfaithfulness of a wife to a husband who loved God. And the hurt and the ache in my own heart was but a dim reflection of a grave, grave heartache our Lord felt for Israel. I dared to pray, "Lord, is it all right for me to love her?" And he said to me, "Yes, go ahead. Love her. Love her. Love her."

I made the arrangements with my friend. The price, fifteen shekels of silver, an homer and a half of barley. It was all I could scrape together, but it was enough to buy a slave. My friend consummated the transaction. I stood out on the edge of the crowd. Not once had Gomer looked up. Not one time had she seen my presence. After the purchase had been completed, my friend grabbed her by the leash and led her over to stand right in front of me. Her gaze was still toward the ground. She had not looked up.

Until I took my knife, and I cut those straps. Yes, Gomer. It is I, your husband. I have bought you back unto myself. Now you belong to me.

I took her by the hand and led her to my quarters. All of the provisions for the return journey were completed. I helped her aboard the camel. We journeyed all the way back without a word passing between us. At last, we arrived here at home and then I said to her, "Gomer, you are to belong to no other. You are mine. I will keep you apart. I will keep myself for you. You are to remain here with me until you learn to love me again."

She's not really a prisoner in there. I mean, not really. But you see, I intend to court her all over again. I intend to woo her as at the very beginning. I'm going to love her, gently and patiently, until at last she learns to love me once more.

I believe she's awake now. You see, she will love me again someday. I just know she will.

Gomer, is that you? Are you awake? Are you awake?

The lights go down.

Transitional Narrative: *I'm going to Graceland*

After a few years, Corky left FMBC and returned to Mid-America Seminary, which by then had relocated to Memphis, Tennessee. He spent the last 17 years of his life there as chairman of the Old Testament and Hebrew Department, teaching courses not only in Hebrew and Old Testament, but also creating and teaching a course in creative preaching. During that time, he co-wrote, co-produced, and starred in two half-hour television specials that aired locally. One told the story of Job, from the Old Testament, while the other told the story of Naaman, the Syrian commander in the Old Testament who was afflicted with leprosy.

While at Mid-America, he preached during chapel services at the seminary and hearkening back to his days as an evangelist with the Baptist Convention of Texas, also often preached weekends at various churches in the area. He even served as interim pastor for an extended while at First Baptist Church of Batesville, Mississippi. These next two sermons are from his tenure at Mid-America.

SERMON: *What's In a Name?*[12]

Turn with me now, if you will, to the first Chapter of the Gospel of Matthew. I encourage you to keep this place marked, because we will return to it at the end of the message. But let's begin there as well. Verse 18.

"Now the birth of Jesus Christ was on this wise: When as his mother, Mary, was espoused to Joseph, before they came together, she was found with child of the Holy Ghost. Then Joseph, her husband, being a just man and not willing to make her a public example, was minded to put her away privily.

"But while he thought on these things, behold the angel of the Lord appeared unto him in a dream saying, 'Joseph thou son of David, fear not to take unto thee Mary thy wife, for that which is conceived in her is of the Holy Ghost. And she shall bring forth a son, and thou shall call his name Jesus, for he shall save his people from their sins.'"

When we read that particular statement by the angel concerning the selection of the name of the child to be born to Mary, the virgin, I think it's more than a little puzzling. We gain a distinct impression that the angel was attempting

---

[12] He preached this sermon several places, including in Dallas, but the cassette recording is from April 7, 1988; location unknown.

to explain why that particular name had been chosen. Obviously, there were other Hebrew names which might have been selected. Perfectly good names like Solomon. Or for that matter Benjamin. All kinds of names which could have been selected. But the angel said his name is to be called Jesus, and then there follows a causal clause that apparently is attempting to communicate to Joseph why that particular name has been selected.

Now the fact is, that's exactly the function of that causal clause, to explain why that name was chosen, because, as we will see before the message is completed, the name has a meaning. I mean it has an individual, independent meaning all its own. We're not accustomed to that in our culture, our society. We have names like Bill and Joe and Susie and Tom, *et cetera*. And for the most part, those names really have no independent meaning. They only conjure up reactions if we associate the name with a given personality or individual.

The truth is, even in our own generation, in other parts of the world, however, names do have private, individual meanings. For example, the little girl who is our sort of adopted daughter has, as her first name in Japanese, Katsuko, which means "child of victory." That's a beautiful name for a girl. But, in the ancient Near East in general, and in the context of the Old Testament in particular, names really did have a very special significance in many instances. It is in that context, then, that the angel explained to Joseph why the name Jesus had been chosen.

I would like for us to unravel that little puzzle this morning, if we may. To do so, though, let me begin by alerting you to the fact that the name Jesus represents a compound expression that has two elements. One of the elements represents an abbreviation of the personal name of the God of creation, the God of the Old Testament, the God and Father of our Lord Jesus Christ.

If we are fully to understand and appreciate the meaning of the name Jesus, we must get some sort of orientation as to the meaning of the name of the God of the Old Testament. Accordingly, while you put the tip of your tie or a business card or something in Matthew 1, let's turn over to the third Chapter of the Book of Exodus. In the interest of time, we will plunge immediately into the center of our interest. We're in the context of Moses's commission to return to Egypt in order to secure the liberation of his people. Israel. And in Verse 13:

"Moses said unto God, 'Behold, when I come into the children of Israel and shalt say unto them the God of your fathers has sent me unto you, and they shalt say to me,

"What is his name?" what shall I say unto them?' And God said unto Moses 'I AM THAT I AM.' And he said, 'Thus shalt thou say to the children of Israel, I AM has sent me unto you.'

"And God said moreover unto Moses, 'Thus shalt thou say to the children of Israel, The LORD God of your fathers, the God of Abraham, the God of Isaac, and the God of Jacob, has sent me unto you. This is my name forever and this is my memorial unto all generations.'"

I submit for your consideration that that was a perfectly legitimate question for Moses to raise. Suppose he said, "I returned down to Egypt, and I presented myself to the Hebrew elders, and I say, 'I've seen the God of your fathers out in the desert.' Inevitably, they're going to ask me, 'What is his name and what shall I tell them?'"

That seems to me a perfectly valid question on the part of Moses. How is it, then, that no answer is given in the first place? In Verse 14, we seem to have a little bit of grammatical or syntactical or linguistic gobbledy-gook. And then in Verse 15, the Lord concludes that verse by saying, "This is my name forever. This is my memorial unto all generations," and bless my soul, no name has even been provided in Verse 15.

Or so it would seem.

But now look at it closely. I call your attention to the word for Lord in Verse 15 in all block capital letters. We very sketchily went over this last Sunday morning, but let's look at it a little bit more closely. I indicated to you then that when the word Lord is written in all block capital letters, it stands for the personal name of God, which is provided behind the translation.

You ask the question, "Why is the word Lord there? If that stands for the name, why isn't the name there?"

To understand the puzzle of the problem, we need to be aware of the fact that when the Old Testament scriptures were originally recorded or written in the Hebrew language, they were written without the benefit of vowel sounds or letters as we know it. This would, of course, present a real problem to us, but it created no great confusion to them because they were very familiar with their own language. And I suppose their procedure then was somewhat akin to the principle of speed writing in our own language in which vowel letters may be left out and, for the most part, the script is abbreviated by simply using the consonants.

That worked great. They had no problem with that. And for generations it continued. However, with the overthrow of the Jewish state in 70 A.D. and the dispersion of the Hebrew-speaking peoples—who, by this time, were likely speaking not a pure biblical Hebrew, but more probably a mutation form that we call Aramaic; it was very close to biblical Hebrew, but still different—gradually that language of the Old Testament began to sort of die out. Those who were charged with the responsibility of preserving the text of the Old Testament from generation to generation, those scribes were increasingly concerned that the pronunciation might be forgotten altogether. By this point in time, they had what is called a consonantal text. They had all of the consonants of the Old Testament preserved intact, but they had learned by rote memory, from parent to child, from parent to child, the pronunciation of those words. Accordingly, there was a written track and, frozen in the text, there was a soundtrack floating around in their memories.

And so down well into the Christian era, somewhere around the Seventh or the Eighth Century A.D., a group of these scribes came up with a system of dots and dashes designed to preserve the pronunciation of these ancient Hebrew words.

And by the way, those dots and dashes have been the curse and bane of Hebrew students ever since. It's really unfortunate that Hebrew students fight those dots and dashes because they are really the key to sound and sense.

But in any event, it worked beautifully, and they were able to preserve the pronunciation patterns which they had learned—until they came to the personal name of God. And they were puzzled because none of them had ever heard it pronounced. It had been the custom for generations when encountering that name in the written text, or even referring to the covenant deity of the Hebrews, rather than speaking the name, which they construed as a pollution of that sacred utterance, to simply use the expression in the Hebrew language, *Adonai*. By the way, that's the pattern of our Jewish brethren even today.

Consequently, these men did not know how to pronounce it, and they did not know what vowel letters to superimpose upon the consonants of the text. They hit upon a solution by taking the vowel sounds of *Adonai* and writing them over the consonants of the personal name. And they produced, in essence, a hybrid word, which is transliterated about four times in the King James by the expression "Jehovah." Now that's half one thing and half another. It's the consonants of the personal name, and it's the vowel sounds of the expression "My Lord."

In order for you to see that the name is there in the remainder of the message, I'll use the word "Jehovah" because it's a term with which perhaps we're more familiar than other pronunciations might be.

It is obvious, then, that the name is given in Verse 15, though it is obscured in the translation. But it is not just the name, rather it is the meaning of the name that is important. Now, again, just a word of review. You remember last Sunday morning we indicated that the name is built upon the Hebrew verb "to be." And by the way, as we'll see in just a moment, that explains the rather strange little formula "I am that I am," or at least gives us a key to it, in Verse 14.

It also explains the play upon the name that begin back in Verse 12, "Certainly I will be with thee." It is built upon that Hebrew verb "to be." It may mean the one who is, or the one who exists. It may have a causative form or flavor to it—the one who causes to be, or the one who causes to exist. It may also have a recurrent or repetitive flavor—the one who always exists or the one who always causes to be, or the one who perpetually causes to exist. Bottom line: The name means, in essence, the source of all being; the fountainhead of all life.

The source of all life! All life! Of all living creatures! Of all generations! Of all time! Without him, there would have been no life of any character or of any kind. So, that tells us upfront that the name Jehovah is a life-giving name.

Having determined that, then, let's go back and see if we can unravel the little paradigm "I am that I am." I used to wonder what that meant. Maybe you never thought about it. Well, when I got to seminary, I enrolled in a class that I thought was Introductory Religious Education and stayed until it was too late to drop the course, only to discover that it was Introduction to Biblical Hebrew. I just stayed in there.

Now, that's not really the way it happened, I guess, but that's about as good an explanation as I can give. But anyway, I found myself in this Hebrew class, and I just kinda hung around and tried to pick up a little bit here and a little bit there. And in the due process of time, we began to translate out of the Hebrew Old Testament, and would you believe it, we moved into the third Chapter of the Book of Exodus. Ultimately, we arrived at Verse 14. And you know what that said in the Hebrew of the Old Testament text?

It said, *'ehyeh'asher'ehyeh.* Now, how does that grab you? Well, that didn't mean any more to me than it does to you.

For the interpretation of the force of those words, I am indebted to Dr. J. Wash Watts, who is now in the presence of the great I Am and who had lived with the Old Testament scriptures in Hebrew in such an intimate fashion that he had not only a knowledge of the meaning of the text, but he had a very sweet, intimate relationship to the author of the text.

He called our attention to the fact that the Hebrew verb system, strictly speaking, does not have time or tense as we know it in English. It's hard to conjugate a verb in English without doing it in either past, present, or future. But that's not the case with the Hebrew verb system, so there is some flexibility. There are some options available to us. And he recommended that we take the first form of the verb and recognize the possibility of recurrence or frequency, to use the technical terminology, and put it in the future. Take the second verb and maintain that same concept of recurrence or frequency but cast it in the past. And it would be quite meaningful.

Now remember, he was about to identify himself in Verse 15 as the "God of your fathers, the God of Abraham, Isaac, and Jacob." Dr. Watts's translation would read like this: "God said unto Moses, 'I will continue to be what I have always been.'"

And suddenly it makes sense. The God of Abraham, Isaac, and Jacob . . . I will be, in your experience, I will be in your lifetime, what I've always been for them. I was a covenant-keeping, promise-honoring God, and I will continue to do just exactly what I promised. I am the same yesterday, today, and forever.

And by the way, that same little pattern or formula for translation will unravel some other mysteries in some other parts of the Old Testament. But time will not permit us that extravagance.

But that tells us, then, that this is a dependable, a faithful name. I will continue to be what I've always been, and faithfulness is the hallmark of his conduct and of his character.

I think, then, that we're ready for a return to Verse 15 briefly. At the end of the verse, the Lord said, or Jehovah said, "This is my name forever. This is my memorial unto all generations." Now, that may have sounded a little hollow to Moses. I'm not sure that we fully understand the irony of this claim. Because you see, at the time of this event, when these words were originally uttered, there was already a name that was a synonym for permanence, for power, for preeminence, and Moses knew that name. Only too well. Actually, it was a title. *Par'oh.* Pharaoh. That was the name that spoke of the authority of the ruling dynasty, of its permanence.

To hear a voice from a flaming bush in a remote region of the Sinai Peninsula, a study in desolation, to say "this is my name, and it will last forever" might sound hollow. For you see, by the time that happened, the great pyramid had been a sentinel on the horizon of Egypt—are you ready for this?—for at least one thousand years. By the time of the birth of Moses, the great pyramid was already a thousand years old, and for a thousand years already, the name Pharaoh had been the name that brought allegiance and submission.

What a wild, extravagant claim you say, and yet I remind you. Theirs was a mighty kingdom, no question about that. Just a year ago, some of the magnificent artifacts from the era of the rule of Ramses were on exhibition in our very city. Impressive. Almost overwhelming. Awe-inspiring, perhaps.

But may I remind you that the speaker from the flame is still in charge of the nations of Earth today. And the specimens that once marked the grandeur of the ancient Pharaohs are now on display in far-off exhibitions and in museums to be gawked at by the idly curious, and the Pharaohs themselves have their mummies frozen in death. But the one who spoke to Moses is still King of Kings and Lord of Lords, and his name, and his name alone, will endure throughout the endless ages of eternity. And the sands of time and infinity will overtake all of the other monarchs.

And so, we learn, then, that his is an everlasting name.

Now, very quickly, please flip over to Exodus 34 for another insight into the significance of that name. In this context, it is Moses and the Lord again, Jehovah, if you please. This time, Moses had requested to see the glory of Jehovah. Jehovah had responded by saying, "No man can see my glory and live. However, I will hide you in a cleft of the rock, and I will pass by and show you my backward parts."

And it is in that context then that, in Chapter 34, Verses six and seven are recorded. "And Jehovah passed by before him and proclaimed 'Jehovah! Jehovah! A God of mercy and grace. Longsuffering and abundant in goodness and truth. Keeping mercy for thousands, forgiving iniquity and transgression and sin. And that will by no means clear the guilty."

Now I modified the King James translation just a bit in order for you to see the word Lord, that there is a repetition of the personal name Jehovah. And then we have the term for God followed by some descriptive terms. The expression translated "merciful" in Verse six is not at all associated or connected with the noun that is translated "mercy" in Verse seven.

But that expression "merciful" in Verse six comes from a word that is rather fascinating. It seems to be a term that has the idea of emotional tenderness. It's difficult to know exactly where some of these concepts may have originated, but in one of its modifications, it is used to describe a mother's womb. Some of the other languages similar to biblical Hebrew, to which biblical Hebrew is related, will translate the word to mean to have pity or compassion. It is even used in one context with a verb that means to weep and another that means to cry. Bottom line, it obviously is a word that describes deep, emotional feeling of tenderness or pity. Mercy, perhaps, is not bad, but I don't think it's quite broad enough.

We really pick up on the thrust of the use of that term, I think, in the Old Testament. We observe it in the 103rd Psalm. Verse 13 says "Like as a father," and there the King James has it, "pitieth his children, so the Lord" or so Jehovah "pitieth those who fear him." But the word that has been translated pity there is basically the same word. They're from the same root. It's the same essential context or idea of meaning. "Like as a father has compassion on his children." I think the word compassion is much closer to it because, you see, compassion means to suffer with. That is what is in a father's heart or a mother's heart. Everyone else may sympathize, but a parent *suffers with* a child.

Again, I spoke last week of my youngest, second son, third child, and my own personal family and the problems related to him that developed following his birth at the Baptist Hospital in Kyoto, Japan. But back into the context of that anxiety and that distress and trauma, when we finally observed that he was not keeping his formula down as he should have, we also noticed that he was not only not gaining weight but was actually losing it. Finally, we called one of the missionary doctors down in Kyoto, described the symptoms, and he encouraged us to take the child to a Japanese pediatrician as quickly as we could. Accordingly, we bundled him up. It was about four o'clock in the afternoon, but it was wintertime. And in that part of Japan, the sun sets around three o'clock in the afternoon.

And so, we braced ourselves against the darkness and the blowing snow, and got in the automobile, drove across the city of Sapporo to a hospital, and there anxiously placed him in the hands of a Japanese doctor. I suppose it was not until then that I really came to understand the extremity of the situation. When the doctor unfolded those blankets to expose the body of my baby, he looked like a little skeleton. The doctor went over an examination rather quickly, and then he explained to me in Japanese that the child was suffering from advanced malnutrition.

My baby was starving to death!

Then he gave an instruction to a Japanese nurse that I couldn't understand, and she left the examination room. In a little while, she came back with a tray, carrying an instrument that I had known all of my life doctors kept somewhere. It was the most vicious, vile, wicked-looking hypodermic needle and syringe that I've ever seen in my life. The shaft of it was as big as the shaft of that microphone. It was filled with some sort of evil-looking green fluid. And there was a needle—so help me, I'm not exaggerating—it was about that long. And then the doctor took that syringe, gave the nurse the instruction to hold the baby's hands, and he turned to me and said in Japanese, "Father, hold his ankles."

I reached out and grabbed hold of those little bony ankles in my hands. And he said, "Don't let him move."

And then I watched in utter horror as the doctor plunged that needle into the thigh of my baby and pushed the handle down, and a pone ballooned on his little thigh, and he began to scream as if he had been impaled through his tummy on a lance. By the time that procedure was over, despite the chill of the night, I was bathed in sweat, but I held him there so he couldn't move.

Now, why did I do that? "Oh," you say, "you didn't care. You didn't love your boy. Didn't hurt you. No skin off your nose. You were just insensitive to his pain. That's the reason you held him so securely."

Well, dear friend, if you think that's the reason, you can't even spell love, much less understand it. I did it because he needed it! And now more than 20 years later, it still wrenches my insides even to think about it.

That's the way God feels for us in our hurt and in our pain. Like as a father has compassion upon his children, that's the way the God of compassion feels for us. He is not aloof, detached, distant, remote, impervious, unconcerned, untouched with feeling for our infirmities. He feels and hurts with us and for us.

And so, we learn, then, that the God of the Old Testament has a name that is a compassionate name.

But look at the next expression, the word for grace. Someone has suggested that, at least in the pages of the Old Testament, grace is used to describe a kindly act on the part of a superior with regard to an inferior in a situation in which there is no agreement, no promise, no covenant, no pledge, no obligation on the part of the superior to do anything for the inferior at all. That's a beautiful description of grace. Remember God in the Garden warned our federal ancestors concerning the consequence of rebellion, "In the day you eat thereof, you will surely die," but they disregarded it. They went ahead and took of the forbidden fruit. And let me tell you that from that moment forward, God owed mankind nothing. Absolutely nothing.

He could have indeed done exactly as the deists accused him. He could have turned man free and let him run his own hellish course, but He didn't. And every day of charity and every day of postponement is a demonstration of grace on the part of a superior who owes us nothing. And the supreme exhibition is in the disclosure of the fact that in the person of His Son, He died in our place when He was under contract to provide nothing. Nothing. That is grace.

And so it is that his name is a gracious name.

But notice also in the text, he is a God who is longsuffering. This expression hides a little idiom in the Hebrew language that says literally "long of nostrils." Now, please, I don't think that means that God has a Bob Hope silhouette, but apparently the ancient Semitics, or Hebrews anyway, associated a flaring of the nostrils and a snorting with rage or anger. Consequently, the expression "long of nostrils" means it's a long time until God becomes angry.

Now, you know, we've built a little theoretical scenario that really doesn't exist. That God loves us, but He hates or He's angry with our sin. And so, we really have no problem with it because God loves us. But now wait just a minute. The truth is, you can't have sin without a sinner. Oh, you may have thought about that philosophically, speculatively. You may discuss it theologically as a concept. But you're not gonna have a sin without a sinner any more than you could possibly have murder without a murderer.

And God is unhappy with our sin, but He is angry with sinners. You say that's not what the New Testament teaches. Look at John 3:36: "The wrath of God abides" not only on his deeds, but it abides "upon him"—the sinner.

You say, "Well, I thought God loves us. He couldn't love us and be angry at us at the same time." You obviously don't have any children.

But coming out of that, we've had the idea that, you know, God is just going to be a soft touch. Not so. "God is not slack concerning His promise as some men count slackness, but He's longsuffering to us." According to the New Testament, God is "not willing that any should perish, but that all should come to repentance."

But while His name is a patient name, it also has another dimension. Look with me, if you will, in Verse seven. It's a patient name, all right, but notice down in Verse seven: "I will by no means clear the guilty." Now this expression, in essence, means that there are not going to be any acquittals, there will be no plea bargaining, no probated sentences. And I recognize that we're living in a highly permissive age, and we are under the impression that we can just do anything we please, and when we get down to the end of the road, we will, in the language of the song, meet my friend or the man upstairs. And we somehow have projected God as a grandfatherly, indulgent, Santa Claus-type figure who, despite our ungodliness and our degenerate ways, when we get down to the end of the road, He will scoop us up in His arms, put us on His knee, chuck us under the chin, and say, "Oh, I know you really didn't mean all of that, friend."

Nothing could be more alien to the depiction of God in scripture. He said, "I will by no means acquit the guilty," and when we stand before the Divine Tribunal, rest assured punishment will be meted out for our sin without exception. And that tells us, then, that His is a holy name.

But how can we reconcile all of this and put it back

together? Well, in the first part of Verse seven, he described himself as a God who would be keeping mercy for thousands. But notice this, "forgiving iniquity and transgression and sin." Now, how can He forgive if He's not going to acquit? On the one hand, to forgive our sin problem would seem to be in essence to say, "Well, we'll just let you go free."

But if we look behind the word translated "forgive," I think we'll pick up on something. This is really not primarily a theological term, but it is an action verb. It is a word that means to lift, to pick up, to carry. It is the word that is employed in the Book of Genesis to describe the action of the waters that picked up the ark and made it float. The same word is employed to describe what the pagan seamen did when they picked up Jonah to throw him over the side of the vessel. It means to lift up, to pick up, to carry.

It is also the word that is used in that haunting 16th Chapter of Leviticus, the ceremony of the great day of atonement, in which there were two animals for the people. One was the so-called sin offering, and his blood would be taken into the Holy of Holies and sprinkled upon the mercy seat. But the other animal, the so-called scapegoat, according to the description in Leviticus 16, the high priest would place his hands upon the head of that animal and symbolically, not literally, but symbolically, place his hands upon the head of that animal and transfer the guilt of the sin of the whole congregation. And according to the text there, the animal would be led away into the wilderness carrying or bearing—same word—the iniquity of Israel.

And by the way, it's the same word used in the 53rd Chapter of Isaiah, "Surely he will bear our sin and carry our sorrow." And so, the word means to lift up, to pick up, and to carry. And if it was not the identical word, it was surely the concept in the mind of the baptizing prophet preacher beside the Jordan River when as he saw that carpenter from Nazareth, pointed in his direction and said, "Behold the lamb of God, who carries away the sin of the world."

He does not ignore, He does not acquit, He does not forget our sin. Instead, He bore that sin and consequence Himself. And so that tells us that the name Jehovah is not only a compassionate name, a gracious name, a patient name, a holy name, but it's also a redeeming name.

Now let's go back to Matthew, Chapter One. "Thou shall call his name Jesus, for he shall save his people from their sins."

The name Jesus in English is really our writing out

in English letters the Greek word for Jesus—*Lēsous* (yeh-sus). In English letters, the name Jesus doesn't mean anything by itself. In Greek, the word *Lēsous* in Greek letters doesn't mean anything by itself. But *Lēsous* is the writing out in Greek letters of a Hebrew name, and the Hebrew name is *Yehoshua*. And that means something.

It means Jehovah, or the source of life, and the verb to save. The source of life who saves. "Thou shall call His name the source of life who saves, for He shall save his people from their sins." What a name.

It's a life-giving name. It's a faithful name. It's an everlasting name. It's a compassionate name, a gracious name, a patient name. A holy name.

But, praise God, a redeeming name.

SERMON: *Come to the Water*[13]

I forgot to warn you that when you introduce a guest speaker as a professor of Old Testament and Hebrew, a third of the audience goes to sleep immediately. I have been working on a revision that might begin, "Our speaker this morning is a former teenage werewolf." But my conscience won't quite let me do that.

So, anyway, it is a real delight to be here this morning. I've known your pastor for many, many years. We were at Baylor together, and it's been my privilege to speak for him on other occasions, in other situations, but it's a privilege to be here today.

Turn with me, if you will, to the 54th Chapter of the book of Isaiah. In the interest of time, I will not read the whole passage. However, I will attempt to draw my remarks from selected Verses in Chapters 54, 55, 56, and the message won't necessarily be any longer just because of the three chapters. But if you'll locate that and just keep your Bible open there, it will make it easier for me.

His face is lined with sadness. His shoulders sag under the heavy burden of defeat. Now he stands as a study in total, dismal despair. The place: the pitcher's mound.

---

[13] He preached this at Trinity Baptist Church in Richmond, Virginia, on July 25, 1982.

The personality: our little round-headed friend Charlie Brown, at the end of another debacle. About this time, juvenile psychologist Lucy walks across the infield and she hollers at Charlie Brown. "Don't be discouraged, Charlie Brown. You win a few and you lose a few," and she moves out of sight.

Charlie Brown reflects on that for a minute. And then his face breaks into a wreath of smiles, and he looks out at the reader to say, "Gee, wouldn't that be great?"

Poor Charlie Brown. The truth is, in light of the statistics that I've kept, I think win one and Charlie Brown would go into orbit. I suppose we really identify with Charlie Brown because he is kind of the personification of the Born Loser, just as each one of us fears we are, behind a façade of self-assurance. Where we live and hide, we're all haunted by the nagging question: "Am I a born loser, too?"

I suppose it's because of that identity, then, that we can understand and be sympathetic with the spiritual pilgrimage of ancient Judah in the days of Isaiah, because, man, they were having a tough time. And in Chapters 49 through 59, we find reflected, again and again, evidences of the defeat and the despair of Judah because of their sin.

Obviously, it was not enough to be the physical

descendants of Abraham, Isaac, and Jacob. They could still know all of the consternation because of sin that others might know. And so, in Chapter 49, the first problem is a problem of failure. And the Lord, through the prophet Isaiah, speaks to that issue.

The second problem is the problem of a sense of abandonment. Not that Jehovah had abandoned them, but they felt as if he had. The Lord, through the prophet, speaks to that particular dilemma as well. The third problem is a sense of being separated from God, or alienation. The fourth problem is a problem of weariness.

When we get to Chapter 54, the sin problem manifests itself in a slightly different aura or flavor. To use the language of the text . . . well, let's read that first Verse of Chapter 54, and I think we'll find the key to the problem. "Sing, O barren, that thou didst not bear; break forth into singing and cry aloud, thou that didst not prevail with child: for more are the children of the desolate than the children of the married wife, saith the Lord."

I picked the word from the text for the manifestation of the sin problem of Judah at this stage by the word "desolate." Ancient Judah, because of its sin, was plagued by the problem of a sense of desolation. Well, what do we mean by being desolate? To use the jargon of the day, by being wiped out? The text spells it out in some very graphic specifics. Look again at that opening line of Verse one. "Sing, oh barren, that thou didst not bear . . . ."

The desolation, then, is like barrenness or childlessness—but not in the abstract. Instead, it is like barrenness to an ancient Hebrew wife. Today, that probably does not say a great deal, but to the ancient Jewish wife, to be without a child was a real difficulty. It was a problem of monumental proportion. Not just the danger of the family line or the family name being cut out of the annals of Israel, nor the social stigma that was attached in that particular culture.

But the ancient Hebrew wife understood that a part of the purpose of her being was that she was designed and programmed by God, not only to be a companion to her husband, but to bear children in his name and to rear them and to nurture them in the admonition and the instruction of the Lord. That explains the anguish of Abram's wife, Sarah. That also indicates the depth of despair and distress in the heart of Hannah. For a Hebrew wife to have no children was to come very close to having life be totally meaningless. In other words, it would mean that she might miss the ultimate purpose for which she was designed, planned, and created.

Now, we may not understand what it means to be childless like an ancient Hebrew wife. But we can lay that down in our own schedule of values and priorities, and we can identify with a confusion and a dilemma that causes us to wonder whether or not we have gone through this terrible rat race for nothing. Nothing concrete, nothing tangible, nothing permanent, nothing eternal to show for our trip through the Veil of Tears.

I'm reminded of the story I heard about the commuter up in the Northeast who went one morning to catch a train to the city. While he was walking around in the little train station, he saw a new machine there in the lobby. And he looked at the printing on the front of it, and the printing said that this machine will give you your name, your age, your weight, and tell you what you're doing.

Talk about a computer. Fantastic! How could that be? He decided he'd check it out, so he pulled a coin from his pocket, got on the scales, and put it into the slot. Lights began to flash. Bells began to ring. The wheels begin to roll, and after a little while, this piece of paper fell into the little slot.

He picked it up. It said, "Your name is Bill Spivens. You're 30 years of age. You weigh 166 pounds. You're waiting for the 8:15."

Incredible! Absolutely accurate. How could that be? Well, he fished another coin out of his pocket, got back on the scales, and tried it again. Lights begin to flash. The bells begin to ring. The wheels rolled and out came that little piece of paper.

He picked it up. It said, "Your name is Bill Spivens. You're 30 years of age. You weigh 166 pounds. You're waiting for the 8:15."

I mean, how could a machine know that? So, he went over to the newspaper stand. He bought a paper, some sunglasses and put them on, turned up his coat collar, pulled the brim of his hat down, opened up the newspaper, and, with a coin between thumb and index finger, he just sort of backed up to that machine. And then quick as a flash, he wheeled around, leaped onto the scales, dropped the coin in the slot. The lights begin to flash. The bells begin to ring. The wheels begin to roll.

Here came the card. He picked it up and looked at it. It said, "Your name is Bill Spivens. You're 30 years of age. You weigh 166 pounds. And you just fooled around and missed the 8:15."

We don't even have to miss a train to begin to feel that inner sense of uneasiness. Am I in the process of missing the real reason for my existence? Who am I? Why am I here? Where am I going? What is it all about? These are questions almost chronically asked by young people today, with a total lack of a definitive answer. Well, that may be one of the reasons for the expanding problem for teenagers these days of suicide.

But now, notice yet again, if you will, that desolation is not only like barrenness to a Hebrew wife, but let's look at the text in Verse four of Chapter 54. "Fear not, for thou shalt not be ashamed. Neither be thou confounded, for thou shalt not be put to shame. For thou shalt forget the shame of thy youth and shall not remember the reproach of thy widowhood anymore."

For the ancient Hebrew wife to be left alone was to find life hollow. That's still a problem for widows in our own generation. I can remember the loneliness of my own mother when she was left a widow. I really cannot particularly identify with that. I suppose it is conceivable that my wife, who is in the audience here this morning, could speak more eloquently to this particular question or problem than I. She was left a widow with two daughters.

And while I cannot speak to the emptiness of a woman without a husband and the responsibility of rearing two daughters, I can identify with the problems of being a widower, because the five children that we have are really three of mine and two of hers, making a happy bundle of five. But I can remember what it was like to have my companion of 30 years taken as a victim to a malignancy.

The emptiness, the best way I can describe it, is to say that my days were like this until I met Sue. I'd get up in the morning and I would shower and shave and sprinkle some cologne and put on my Sunday best and walk out the front door only to find that the house was in the middle of a desert. And I had the feeling that, as far as I could see in all directions, there was nothing but parched, arid, still, lifeless, meaningless, desert, empty and hollow. No one to share the joys with, no one to share the sorrows with. A desolation that leaves one empty and alone. It was that desolation that is characterized in Verse 11 by the expression "afflicted." "Oh, thou afflicted." Desolation that is equal to affliction.

But, my stars, what is affliction? Once more, the prophet has been very precise under Holy Spirit guidance. Notice in Verse 11: "tossed with tempest." That expression, those three words— "tossed with tempest"—really reflect a single Hebrew word in the original text. It means, in essence, storm-tossed. Do you know what it means to be storm-tossed?

I had the experience of booking passage on a

freighter from Japan to the United States a number of years ago. A violent typhoon had raged across the South Pacific. It had already passed, but when our vessel moved out into the open sea, the huge swells that came in from the side created quite a problem. The vessel was very lightly loaded. It had taken a cargo out to the Orient, and it was coming back high in the water. According to the seamen, those swells were 30 feet high, and our vessel just bobbed from side to side. Every once in a while, the propeller would come completely up out of the water for about three or four revolutions, and then it would shudder back into the sea.

And I'll tell you what, you talk about an experience. You had to eat a meal as it went by, back and forth. All of the drawers and all of the furniture in our stateroom had to be jammed. And when we got ready to go to bed at night, we had to take life preservers and put them under the edge of the mattress.

I'd try to sleep on my back, and I had the sensation that my body was filled with wet cement. You know, when the ship would go to one side, I just kind of slushed over to that side and then I just kind of slushed back over to the other side. We'd have to get on our stomachs and just kind of cling to the mattress to get still enough to try to rest. And

I can remember thinking after about the third day, man, if I could just get to someplace where everything would be still for a little while.

Storm-tossed.

The prophet spelled it out pointedly in Chapter 57, Verse 20, when he said, "The wicked are like the troubled sea, when it cannot rest, whose waters cast up mire and dirt. There is no peace, saith my God to the wicked." No stability. No sense of completion. No tranquility. Things always restless, turbulent, churning. That kind of desolation.

Yeah, we can identify with that, can't we? We can identify with a life that seems to have no purpose. We can identify with a sense of being abandoned and forsaken, with life being empty. And also, lonely. And we can identify with a life that is turbulent and storm-tossed. Oh, to be sure we may have all of the externals programmed to create fulfillment and satisfaction. But somehow it just really doesn't work.

I remember reading several years ago a magazine article about Ol' Blue Eyes. The chairman of the board, Frank Sinatra. The article said that he was plagued with chronic insomnia, and in the article, he is quoted as having said, "I don't care what it is, whether it's booze or broads or prayer, anything to get me through the night, I'm for it."

"There is no peace, saith God to the wicked." You may have money, you may have fame, you may have talent, you may have a great hoard of things, but there is no peace to the wicked. So, the problem of Judah, a sin-caused problem, left for them life as meaningless, as empty, as troubled. And the Lord said, "I have a solution."

Look, if you will, very quickly in Chapter 55. Down in Verse three: "Incline your ear and come unto to me: hear and your soul shall live; and I will make an everlasting covenant with you, even the sure mercies of David."

May we lift up from the text the "sure mercies of David" and build the solution from scripture around that? But someone says, "Now wait a minute. If I check my Bible chronology, it seems to me that David was dead by this time." That's true. He'd been in his tomb for 200 years. So, what kind of a promise is this: the "sure mercies of David"?

Obviously, the prophet here, along with other prophets of the Old Testament, when they speak of the marvelous, marvelous scene of restoration that unfolds in the pages of Old Testament prophecy, they are not talking about the cadaver of the ancient king of a combined Israel. Rather, they are talking about a coming David. A second

David. An ideal David. A complete David. A perfect David, of whom the original David was simply a symbol or a type. The prophet is looking forward to that one who would be addressed again and again in the cities of Galilee, "Thou son of David." He is looking toward the coming redeemer, the Messiah. So, the solution, then, is interwoven with the promises and the pictures and the predictions of the coming Messiah.

But now let's look at that solution, then. Yes, first of all, it will be a solution that features a true satisfaction. Look in Verse 1 of Chapter 55: "Ho! everyone that thirsteth, come ye to the waters. And he that hath no money, come ye, buy and eat. Come buy wine and milk without money and without price. Wherefore do ye spend money for that which is not bread? And your labor for that which satisfieth not?"

Why are you spinning your wheels? Or as a later spokesman would say, why take your wages and put them into a bag with holes? In Second David, there is a true satisfaction that is like finding the solution to the problem of hunger or the raging monster of thirst.

I carry this cane because, when I first came to the Evangelism Division in the State of Texas, I was involved in a plane crash down in the Big Thicket, in the southeastern part of our state. The crash took place on Tuesday night. They did not find the body of my companion—the pilot—and me until Thursday afternoon. And during that period of time, with a broken back, I was trying to drag myself. I couldn't even get on hands and knees. You could hardly call it a crawl then, but I was sort of worming my way toward a highway, I thought in hopes of getting help. But of all the things that are burned indelibly in my memory—would you believe it? —is not the shadow of pain, but it is the recollection of thirst.

Oh, thirst. Do you know what it's like to be truly thirsty? It can lead to all kinds of demented conduct. I remember on that second day as I was moving along in that fashion, I came to an indention beneath a tree that had an exposed root with a slash of white paint on it. And somehow in my particular condition, it was just as clear to me as if someone had written me a note that that white paint was on the root to mark the location of an ancient spring of water that the Indians had once used.

And, with that fevered imagination impulse, I began to claw in that indention. As I got down into the soil, I got into some moist sand, and I clawed, and I clawed until I got this arm as far down into that hole as it would go. And I got a fist full of moist sand. And I recall putting it in my handkerchief and twisting it as tightly as I could, in the hope of extracting just one drop of moisture.

Isn't that ridiculous? Isn't that absurd? But I'll tell you, my dear friends, I have observed others doing things just as ridiculous and just as irrational, clawing into the dry sand of the pleasures and the escapes of this world, trying to find something to satisfy the burning, raging thirst of the spirit. You will never find the moisture you seek. But in Second David, there is satisfaction.

There was a man out on the West Coast several years ago who, as he looked toward his future, sensed that there was something missing in his life. And he thought, "The thing I need to do now in order to find fulfillment and completion is to make my fortune." He was a talented, dedicated young man, and it was not long until he had amassed a considerable fortune.

But, after having reached a certain financial plateau, he took stock again. He looked down inside and the emptiness was still there. So, he said, "I decided that the thing I needed to do was impress people with my affluence and my importance." According to the testimony of others, he later said, "I realized it was a ridiculous thing to do," but he went down to the car dealer and bought six brand new Cadillacs and paid cash. He had them brought to his place of business and parked one behind the other, out in front. And he went out front and swaggered back and forth so that everybody would know that he was the owner of the establishment and that those Cadillac automobiles were his.

But even while he swaggered back and forth, he took an inward look and realized that that had not satisfied the longing. Well, he decided he needed to get married and settle down. And so, in the process of time he met a lovely young lady. They got married and had two precious children. But after the second child was born, he again took spiritual inventory and, again, there was still something missing.

What he needed now was a home that was worthy of his family and a man of his status and position. So, he built a palatial mansion on the hills overlooking the Bay area of Oakland, California. I had the experience of going into his home one evening with 15 or 20 guests, and I got lost from the guests and anyone else in the house.

But just as he came to the conclusion of the building of that house, he stood in that spacious living room and looked out through the window at the Bay and took stock once more. And he found himself coming up short. He finally concluded that a person spent his entire life looking for something but never finding it.

But then one night, he stopped at a neighborhood church out in East Oakland on MacArthur Boulevard, and he heard a gospel message. The invitation was extended. In response to that appeal, he came, not to the altar, but he was ushered into a prayer room. It was their custom at that church to take those who had responded to the appeal into a prayer room, and they got on their knees to pray through the decision.

According to the testimony of those who were in that prayer room that night, as that man poured out his confession of sin and asked Jesus to come into his heart, as he concluded his prayer, he paused there for a moment and then, in barely a whisper he said, "That's it."

As he started to blink the tears away, he got a little louder. "That's it."

As he slowly came to his feet, he began to repeat it with an increasing volume. "That's it. That's it! That's what I've been looking for all my life."

Now, you can hang any kind of label you want to on it but, my dear friends, ultimately the satisfaction you seek, you will find exclusively in Jesus.

But I notice something else: that solution includes the "everlasting covenant." It is described in 54:10 as a covenant of peace. In Verse 3, entering into that covenant, there is the promise of life. So, it is an everlasting covenant of peace and life. A resting place, a harbor. A place where there is tranquility and assurance.

Notice also there is built into that solution an abundant pardon. Look, in 55:7, our God will have mercy upon those who seek him, and he will abundantly pardon. But observe that it is an abundant pardon that is conditioned on a timely response. "Seek ye the Lord while he may be found; call ye upon him while he is near." Not in the moment of our convenience, not in the moment of our selection, but when the Spirit of God draws near and there is that inner drawing, there is that inner stimulus. There is that inner urge that only God can initiate.

It is then that we must react, and we must receive him. But it must also be conditioned on true repentance. "Let the wicked forsake his way and the unrighteous man his thoughts." We cannot continue to embrace our rebellion and our ungodliness and expect to find forgiveness and peace.

But now also observe very quickly that it is a solution that is based upon God's guaranteed performance. Look at the marvel of his ways. "For my thoughts are not your thoughts, neither are your ways, my ways." And when we slip into God's frame of reference, all bets are off. We are at an entirely different level of operation when God begins to work in our lives.

Notice also it is based upon the miracle of his Word. "For as the rain cometh down, and the snow from heaven, and returneth not thither, but watereth the earth," God said, "so shall my word be that goeth out of my mouth. It shall not return unto me void, but it shall accomplish that which I please, and it shall prosper in the thing whereto I sent it."

And that is the very Word, my dear friend, that we are attempting under God to preach in your ears today.

But notice this, too. Full acceptance in Chapter 56, Verse three. "Neither let the son of the stranger, that hath joined himself to the Lord, speak saying, 'The Lord hath utterly separated me from his people;' neither let the eunuch say, 'Behold, I am a dry tree.'"

Earlier in the Old Testament, an outsider to Judaism could participate in the worship of Jehovah, but he could not be thoroughly incorporated into the Commonwealth of Israel. And so, too, those who were physically mutilated or maimed could not be completely accepted into the family of God. But now the prophet says it doesn't matter who you are or what you are. You now become a member of the family of the Redeemed, and you are made whole in

Christ—that Second David.

It is not without notice, then, that the first convert to the Gospel of Christ reported in the pages of the New Testament was an Ethiopian eunuch. As God said, once and forevermore, from anywhere and from everywhere: All who will may come and find access to my salvation.

And so, this morning we conclude the message with an appeal, putting together the great universal invitations of scripture on the basis of the problem. A problem that is human, that is timeless, that is universal because of the total experience of sin in man's life. A desolation is the result, that makes life pointless, empty, and troubled. On the basis of the problem, we extend the invitation, but more supremely on the basis of the solution. Second David offers a true satisfaction, a covenant of peace, life abundant, pardon, and full and complete acceptance.

Did you see it in Chapter 55? "Ho, everyone that thirsteth, come ye to the waters." Earlier, Isaiah said, "Come now and let us reason together, said the Lord. Though your sins be as scarlet, they shall be as white as snow. Though they be red like crimson, they shall be as wool." Once more he spoke for the Lord: "Look unto me and be saved, all the ends of the earth."

And when that marvelous, incomparable ideal,

Second David made his appearance in history, he said, "Come unto me, all ye that labor and are heavy laden, and I will give you rest. If any man thirst, let him come unto me and drink."

And the final invitation of God's word. "And the Spirit and the Bride say, 'Come.' And let him that heareth say 'Come.' And let him that is athirst, come. And whosever will, let him take the water of life freely."

You say, "Preacher, how do I do it?" It's so simple, a child can understand. I know I understood as a child the futility, the vanity, and the pointlessness of life with only your own ingenuity and human devices. You turn to the Lord Jesus and say, "Lord, I can't quite pull it off. By faith, I receive you as my Lord, and I open my heart to you and trust you as my savior. Right now, I invite you to come into my life and to save me and make me a part of the family of God."

Transitional Narrative: *Corky and Juanita: A Romance for the Ages*

As part of their "autobiographies" that Corky and Juanita wrote for their application to be appointed Southern Baptist missionaries to Japan, they both offered rare insights into their personal histories, some of which I never knew before. It's particularly interesting to read about their courtship in 1945-1947. I have put together this narrative using both of their "autobiographies." Some of it may be repetitive of the opening bio of Corky, but I have repeated it here to establish some context.

As I noted before, when Corky tried to drop out of SMU in order to join the military, his parents only agreed to let him leave school in exchange for a promise to start going to church again, which he did at Polytechnic Baptist Church in east Fort Worth. It was there that he first became acquainted with music director Dallas Alford, who got him involved in a men's quartet. It was also at Poly Baptist that he first met my mother, Juanita Peacock, who sang in a women's sextet at the church, though he knew of her from having played football at Poly High with some of her brothers.

He writes: "I . . . was immediately attracted by her vivacious, Christian personality and charming beauty. She was the older sister of three boys with whom I had played football in high school, although I had not met her until I came to the Baptist church in Poly. Juanita was nearly five years my senior so that our relationship was strictly a brother-sister affair. After a time, however, I began to realize that my admiration for her was rapidly becoming something more than that. I was certain that it was entirely preposterous for me to hope that there could ever be anything serious between us, so I tried to hide my feelings about the matter."

Juanita also initially shared his opinion that nothing would come of their relationship. She writes: "I had heard of him through my brothers with whom he played football and had seen him play and seen him in the senior play and operetta at the high school that year. I never dreamed that anything would ever come of it."

Over the course of the next year, they became quite close, though Juanita also characterized it as a "brother-sister thing." "I was five years older than he was. His mother was my Sunday School teacher, and I worked close with her and, of course, saw him quite often." But then she was in a car accident in which she was thrown into the windshield. Following the accident, Corky visited her regularly. "My face was cut up rather badly," Juanita wrote, "and I was put to bed for the next three weeks. It was during this time that I began to suspect that Corky cared for me more than just a brother relationship."

Corky joined the Army in April of 1945 after two of his closest friends joined. He felt that military service was inevitable, but he "also felt that I could more readily recover from my infatuation with Juanita by getting away from her for a while." As noted before, for basic training, he was sent first to Fort Sam Houston in Texas, then to Camp Hood (now Fort Cavazos) in Killeen, Texas, only 150 miles away from home. "[M]uch to my chagrin, I had wanted to get away from Juanita, but instead found myself going home every weekend and more certain of my love for her."

After basic training, he was assigned to Camp Hood. He found that he was "certain of my love for Juanita despite my youth. I knew that it was silly for me to feel that way. I had never even had a real 'date' with the girl and, besides, she already had a boyfriend in the Coast Guard." Desperate to get far away, he re-enlisted and asked to be reassigned overseas. While waiting for his re-enlistment to be processed, he went home to Fort Worth to "tell Juanita I loved her, despite the futility of it."

But Juanita rejected him, confirming his view that it was futile. She wrote: "I didn't see how it could work. I had a lot of respect for him, and we had lots of fun together in our group of young people at the church. I was quite confused about the whole situation and just didn't know what to do."

Back at camp, Corky was told he had to take a two-week furlough in connection with his re-enlistment. He asked to be excused from it, but he was told it was mandatory. At first, he was reluctant to go home to Fort Worth because he was "too embarrassed to see Juanita, but then I decided I would use those two weeks to my advantage and determined to press my case." By the time he left Fort Worth again, "It seemed that I might stand a chance after all."

Corky was reassigned to Fort Oglethorpe, Georgia, to the Adjutant General's School where he spent six weeks in administrative training. "While I was there, I received a letter from Juanita which indicated that the Army had won out over the Coast Guard." As Juanita put it, after much prayer, thought, and consideration, "I came to the conclusion that I did love Corky. When I finally settled the question, all confusion and turmoil which I had in my heart and mind just seemed to drop away."

After receiving that letter from Juanita, Corky was ready to return home, "but the Army had other plans," assigning him overseas to Japan as part of the Army of Occupation. Before leaving, though, he had a chance to take one last trip home in July of 1946. "I was in Fort Worth long enough . . . to ask the right question, get the right answer from Juanita, and buy the right ring for the right finger of her left hand."

The wedding would have to wait, though, for almost another year, but they were married on June 27, 1947.

Here are the self-assessments each gave in their autobiographies:

Corky:

> In my opinion, I have a free and open disposition. I like people and enjoy working with others. I have a good sense of humor, I think, and can always see the lighter side of a situation. As a result of this, I believe that I am able to get along with others with a minimum of difficulty.
>
> I believe that I am dependable, for I feel a sense of obligation in any task that is assigned to me. At times, this area of my make-up has actually been a source of difficulty. I am extremely reluctant to quit a job before it is finished, though there are times when to do so may be more discreet. In making decisions, I try to keep this part

of my character in mind. Accordingly, I am not accustomed to pursue a given course of action unless I am prepared to do my best.

Juanita:

I am rather quiet and let others do most of the talking. I do a good deal of listening, though, and know what is going on around me. I like people and like to meet new people, and I enjoy working with them. I feel that the Lord has given me the ability to get along with almost anyone. I am conscientious about my work and like to finish what I have started. I feel that I can be depended upon, for if I tell someone I will do something, I will do it if at all possible.

I find it hard to say no when asked to do a lot of things and sometimes find myself loaded down with too many jobs to do. I love my home and love to work in it and keep it up. I thoroughly enjoy my children, although I become impatient with them at times, as most mothers do, I suppose. I love my church work and enjoy doing anything I can to help. I have a good sense of humor and can usually see the funny side of things . . . . I feel that I can learn anything I set my mind to and am willing to learn.

Juanita died of breast cancer on September 3, 1978, after slightly more than thirty-one years of marriage. The following month, Corky first addressed her passing from the pulpit at a chapel service at Mid-America Baptist Theological Seminary.

SERMON: *Psalm 23*[14]

First of all, I need to thank all of you for praying for me in recent days. I am indebted to you individually and collectively. I hope you'll continue to pray for me because, as I guess you will presently see, the experience is not completed yet.

One would think that out of the time such as this, anyone would learn some very deep, profound, and important lessons. I was more than a little distressed when one of you came to me yesterday to speak of concern regarding a dear loved one, plagued by a very serious, potentially life-threating illness, to ask the question, "What do you do to try to take care of your loved ones in a time like this?"

I pondered that for just a moment. Would you listen to the profound answer? You comfort your loved one and you hurt. You say, "Man, I already knew that." I did, too. But if there's a better answer than that, I don't know what it is.

But, still, the Lord does reveal some things to us in his Word. One morning, just about the beginning of school, I picked up my Hebrew Old Testament. Some of my

---

[14] Preached at Mid-America Baptist Theological Seminary on October 12, 1978.

students have asked, "What will the language do for your preaching?" I can't say for sure, but I'll tell you what, now and again, it'll do something for the preacher, and that's much more important.

And I began a pilgrimage down a very familiar road, but it was in an entirely different context. That particular morning, I understood for the first time the distress of Job as he expressed it in the Third Chapter of his book, when he literally exploded with his grief, "Let the day perish wherein I was born." My soul, I wish I had never seen the light of day and that I'd never drawn breath! And I understood how he felt that particular morning.

And as that despair intensified in his spirit, he continued later, "Why died I not in the womb?" If I had to be born, why couldn't I have at least died in infancy? I would've been spared all of the grief and all the trauma. And then he finally comes to say, "Wherefore is light given to him that is in misery and life unto the bitter in soul, which long for death . . . but it cometh not."

Some of you have said, "Dr. Farris, we appreciate your faith and your courage." I hope I do not betray that confidence, but I'm being honest with you. I reminded some of my students before all of this crumbled in upon me that faith that is sterile, vacuum-packed, uncontaminated by fear and doubt is not worthy of the name, any more than courage that is unplagued by fear. Anyone can play the role of a John Wayne so long as he knows that all of the Indians are Hollywood extras, and he knows that the script calls for the arrival of the cavalry on time.

But when the conflict is real and when the wounds hurt and when the injuries are sustained in great trauma and you're not real sure about the end of it, there's where you find what courage and faith are really all about. The despair of life on that particular pilgrimage, or the stages of it, are first the *willingness* to *suffer* for a loved one. That enlarges to a *desire* to *suffer* for a loved one, and then that intensifies to a *willingness* to *die* for a loved one, and then the *deep burning hunger* to die *instead of* the loved one, or to die *along with* the loved one. Now, when you find those emotions, remember they're not alien to the human heart.

But it was in that context that I began to look in the 23rd Psalm. Familiar lines, "Jehovah is my shepherd, I shall not want." And when I read that, I heard a voice, a very familiar voice. A voice that whined in Eden, "Yay, hath God said you shall not eat of every tree of the garden?" The same voice that dripped with venom as it hissed, "Doth Job fear God for naught? He just serves you because you bless him. Take away your blessings and he'll curse you to your face. You'll see."

That voice! Recognize it? "Jehovah is your shepherd, you shall not want? Man, look at you! He promised an abundant life and what do you have? Nothing but poverty. He guaranteed victory and you wallow in the deepest of defeat."

One of the reasons I don't like Satan is he's so accurate sometimes.

Well, praise the Lord for verb forms.

I'm aware of the fact that we language teachers, now and again, squeeze a whole lot more flavor and nuance out of a verb form than the writer or the Holy Spirit or the originators of the language ever conceived. But I tell you what, every once in a while, there's something great there. I got to looking at that thing again in light of what the tempter and the accuser had said. "I shall not want." It didn't say I will never be in need. And it didn't say I will not want at some time. A frequentative imperfect. I will not be *accustomed* to want.

Well, that sent me scurrying over to some other verses that I had found and been sort of pondering, over in the 34th Psalm, the 11th Verse. In the Hebrew text, "Young lions are in need, and they are hungry."

You've seen him. Behind bars, pacing back and

forth in a study of fluid muscular motion. Despite the cage of concrete and steel, there is the aura of his beastly, regal splendor in every movement. When he roars, even from his prison, it rattles the tops of the trees, and it strikes fear even into the spectator's heart. Incarcerated by the two-legged animal, but unconquered. Take him out of that dungeon and release him in his native plain, and once again, he will prowl, and he will prey upon his victims.

But water holes dry up. Game can become scarce; quarry can become elusive. And even young lions, with all of their strength and with all of their power, they need, and they grow hungry until their old boney frames punch outlines through their leathery hides. But the seekers of Jehovah will not be *accustomed* to lack any good.

Lord, can I claim that promise? I'm seeking you. There's the principle. I'm the contradiction. There's the rule. I am the present miserable exception.

And then I looked over in that 37th Psalm. Yeah, there's a line over there that says something about it. The King James has it, "Delight thyself also in the Lord, and he shall give thee the desires of thy heart." In talking with people across the years, I have warned and cautioned that the text does not say "delight thyself also in the Lord *that* he may give the desires of the heart." It's not an I'll-scratch-your-back-if-you'll-scratch-mine or a grandiose trade out. So, I thought maybe I ought to look over there at that and just see how all of that was put together. And bless my soul, you know what it said? It said, "Delight thyself in Jehovah *that* he may give me the desires of my heart." The very thing I'd said it didn't say, it said.

Well, how am I gonna deal with that? Obviously, it had to do with that verb to "delight thyself." That word has the idea of softness or delicacy, and when it's used in this reflexive form of the verb, it means to delight one's self exquisitely. Or, if I may coin the verb that I would use, it means to "luxuriate" in the Lord.

And how do you do that? Well, it's amazing how much light God's Word can throw on God's Word . . . and clear up some of the commentaries.

In the 58th Chapter of Isaiah, "If thou turn away thy foot from the sabbath, from doing thy pleasure on my holy day and call the sabbath a delight, the holy of the Lord, honorable. . ." Now listen to this. ". . . and shalt honor him not doing thine own ways, not finding thine own pleasure, nor speaking thine own words, then shalt thou delight thyself in the Lord."

So, it's still not an out-of-hand trade out. What he is saying is that, when you honor him, not seeking your own plans, not pursuing your own designs, not searching after your own pleasure, not speaking your own words, and when he occupies, not a prominent place, but the *preeminent* place in your heart, then you cannot help but delight in him. And how can God not bless and meet the needs of our lives and give the desires of the heart to us when the heart's supreme desire is to honor him? Well, I began to work with that, and I'm still working with it.

But the psalmist continued, "In meadows of grass he will make me to stretch out. Along the waters of peace and tranquility, he will lead me." In this particular word "lead," the emphasis is upon destination. It means to bring me to the desired haven. He will lead me to those waters of peace.

But as I read those words, I remembered those long nights walking back and forth after my loved one, in the wee hours until finally utterly exhausted, I would fall on the couch. And watch her. She would continue to pace like that caged lion but, in her situation, incarcerated in the dungeon of pain. And I would want to cry out, "Lord, where are the waters of peace? If only she could stretch out and lie down, and if I could do so, too. Where are the waters of peace?"

But then one morning, in the wee hours again, He

soothed her troubled, pain-racked body, and He lifted her from that bed of suffering, and He stretched her out in the green meadows of the Everlasting Dominion. And now she walks up and down the rivers of life. No wonder then the psalmist could say, "He restoreth my soul."

"He guides me into the tracks of righteousness for the sake of his name." This word means not a path that footmen might wear out, but it's a path that wheels have cut. When I was a boy, we used to visit our kinfolks up in Hunt County. We didn't have relatives, we had kinfolks. There's a difference, if you didn't know. I was grown before I found out that my Aunt Irmie spelled her name I-R-M-A. That's kinfolks.

But out in that black land of Hunt County, when the rains came, you had a problem. You either had to get back to the paved surface of the highway before the rains came, or you had to wait, because in those primitive days, there were deep ditches on either side. And when you started out across that slippery surface, you were prone to slide into the ditch and you'd have to wait until some old boy with a team of mules and a wagon would come along and cut some grooves in that slippery gumbo. And then maybe a truck or two to come along behind until finally the tracks were cut. He leads us in the *tracks* of righteousness to keep us from slipping off into the ditches of despair and total defeat within.

But then notice, as the King James has it, "I walk through the valley of the shadow of death." I still insist that there's a twist here that is grammatically undesirable as well as logically incompatible. The emphasis would seem to suggest this may not happen to me. But the truth of it is, it does. It will. I would offer the translation, "Moreover, *when* . . . ." Because you see, Beloved, we somehow have the feeling that we've been plunged into a pit of despair by accident or mistake because God has abandoned us. But that's the name of the game. "Moreover, *when* . . . ." Every one of us, if the Lord delays his coming, will walk into that valley, either with a loved one or we'll walk into it ourselves. Not ninety-nine percent of us, but all of us. "Moreover, *when* I walk in the valley of *tsalemaveth*"—the death shadow— "I will fear no evil."

You remember the story about the young lady weeping uncontrollably and a friend said, "What's wrong?" She said, "Well, I was just thinking, what if I were to meet a young man, and we were to fall in love and what if we were to get married and have a little baby boy and he would grow up to be about nine or ten, and he were to crawl up on this house and fall off and break his leg. And I'm crying because he might break his leg someday."

The truth of it is most of our fears are just like that. They're groundless. They never become reality. But at the same time, Beloved, I must also tell you that my experience has indicated that in the dark valley there are some pits I didn't know existed. And some of us in that valley will learn new ways to hurt that we didn't know could occur. Nightmares undreamed will materialize. Fears that are not some flickering shadow on the periphery of our imagination, but monstrous, brutal, concrete, inescapable realities. They're in that valley. But in the midst of the darkness, there's a hand. It holds on to you. And now and again, if you pardon the indelicate expression, there will be that pain that will reach out with a gut-wrenching yank at your soul. And you clutch hard on that hand. And in the palm of it, there's a scar. The man of sorrows, the one whose vision pierces every shadow. He is there. So, I fear no evil.

Once more, it's that frequentity. It doesn't mean I won't have some fears, but I will not be *accustomed* to fear evil. Why? Because thou art with me.

Well, I wish there were other things we could say here, but I must hurry for time is fleeting. In that context, in Verse five, "You set before me a table right out in front of all of my adversaries." All the folks that vex me. Now, can you imagine that in that dark valley, surrounded by my adversaries, be they external or internal, may they be opponents who resist the work of God in my life or whether they simply be my own doubts, my own despair, my own discouragement, my own defeat, my own lust, my own greed, my own ambition. But the same one who girded himself with a towel and bathed the feet of the twelve, including Judas Iscariot, he sets a table before me right out in front of all my enemies in the valley.

And the text says, "You make fat, with oil, my head." I hope that's not the origin of the expression "fat head." I don't think it is. But what he is saying is, man, you have literally inundated me with blessing. My cup sloshes over. Surely that ought to rivet our attention on what follows: Unmistakably, unquestionably, *surely* goodness— that goodness I've been searching for, that good thing that I have been seeking after—that goodness and mercy shall follow me.

Well, more than that. This is our golden word of the Old Testament. The Hebrew word *hesed*, a covenant-related word that speaks of loyalty and fidelity to covenant promises and pledges. It is the basis upon which one who has entered into a redemptive relationship with a covenant-keeping God can be assured of his blessings and his mercy and his sustaining grace in every situation. His goodness and his loyalty.

David used this word in some other places. He used it one time with King Saul, and in that particular case he said, essentially, "Why do you hunt me like a man hunts a partridge?" Not just follow, but to pursue, to hound, to hunt. Surely goodness and his covenant loyalty will incessantly pursue after me all the days of my life. You know, the sad thing about that is, so many times we stretch the outer limits of his pursuit capabilities, don't we?

"And I shall dwell in the house of Jehovah forever." This is not the conventional word for eternity or expression for eternity. It simply says, "length of days." And so, we ask the question then, is this speaking of eternal life? I think eternal life is talked about very clearly elsewhere in scripture. But I'd like to say something about another Psalm. In the 84th Psalm, the text says, "A day"—*a* day— "in thy courts is better than a thousand." I choose, literally, to be a doorkeeper at the entrance to God's house as over against dwelling in the tents of wickedness. I would rather spend my life with his goodness and his loyalty in hot pursuit after me to end up with only one day in his presence as to live ten thousand years in this life.

One day with him.

Folks, I'm still in the valley, but I really would rather walk here with him than to walk alone on the heights. The Lord, in deep water experiences, gives a verse, a passage, and sometimes a song. I conclude with this. It's a verse from an old hymn that's been taken out of most of our books, and yet, I guess it kind of summarizes where I am.

There are so many hills to climb upward,
I often am longing for rest.
But He who appoints me my pathway
Knows just what is needful and best.
I know in His word He hath promised
That my strength, it shall be as my day.
And the toils of the road will seem nothing,
When I get to the end of the way.

SERMON: *The Big Thicket*[15]

I, across the years, have not shared the experiences that I'm going to share with you this morning, really for several different reasons, I suppose. Usually when people ask for me to share a word of testimony, they're suggesting they'd like me to talk about the plane crash. And I guess that's not a common experience for an average individual, but I have been hesitant to do so for two or three different reasons.

It's not that the memory of the events is painful, but there are some things about this that are not always easy to reflect on without creating some distress, I guess, of spirit. But more pertinent, I'm hesitant many times because, if we're not careful, when you try to share something that's out of the ordinary or unusual, it can be very easily construed as flamboyant. And I shy away from the concept of a testimony that begins, you know, I was a teenage werewolf or something along that line. That creates the impression that if you've not had some weird, bizarre, far out, unreal kind of an experience, that you don't have a testimony. And the truth of it is, the level of testimony that

---

[15] To students at Mid-America Baptist Theological Seminary in Memphis, Tennessee, on December 12, 1990, discussing the January 1965 plane crash that left him dependent upon a cane to walk.

is most precious to my heart, to be honest with you, comes at some other levels than this. But I realize that there are some things that perhaps can be of value.

Another reason that I have been hesitant to share the testimony is, if you're not careful in trying to communicate some of these things, they get a little bit out of perspective. It's easy for people to concentrate on the events and the unusual circumstances and so forth.

Another reason is the fact that, if we're not careful, when we begin to share a testimony, the focus of interest gets locked in on the singer rather than the song, if you understand what I mean. It's the Lord of grace and faithfulness that needs to be the center of focus and that needs to be magnified.

But having said that, let me plunge right on into it and try to share the events. Then I'd like to back up and talk with you about some particulars and the implications of those particulars. If you have questions along the way, I'd be happy to try to answer them if I can.

The circumstance occurred soon after my joining the staff of the Evangelism Division over in the State of Texas. In fact, I had been working there for only about three months, and I had responsibility for an associational evangelism conference down in the southeastern part of the state. I needed to make, as a part of my job responsibility, a trip up to the Panhandle the day before. Well, that's a long distance to travel, and so we had worked out the possibility of such an arrangement in advance. It all fit together in this particular situation with a gentleman whom I had met during the New Life Movement in Japan, who was a deacon, a member of First Baptist Church of Dallas, and was a builder and developer in the little community of Duncanville on the southwest corner of Dallas County. We'd worked out an arrangement for him to fly me to a couple of assignments, and so we flew to the Panhandle on the day preceding the evangelism conference, came back, had lunch at his home going through Dallas, and then we flew down to the little community of Evadale down in southeast Texas.

We landed at a landing strip owned by a paper mill company—it was a private little runway. When we arrived there, first of all we had some difficulty because the phone at the little shed at the end of the runway was out of commission, so we had to walk to the highway and toward town until we came to a house. We used the phone there and contacted the church. They came and picked us up, and we went ahead and met the assignment. We were there for the meetings that night.

Now, we had originally planned to spend the night in Evadale, in a motel. Well, I'm sure you've all heard of Evadale, a thriving, bustling metropolitan area. But unfortunately, they did not have, and probably to this good day it does not have, a motel. And so, we were going to have to stay in the pastor's home and it was not going to be altogether convenient for him. So, we talked about it and my deacon friend suggested that perhaps we ought to fly on back to Dallas that night.

He'd been flying for nearly 20 years, but he was reluctant to fly at night unless he could land at his own home base, which was Redbird Airport out in southwest Dallas County, near Duncanville. When he suggested we ought to go back, that seemed like a good idea to me. But, anyway, he called the weather station at Beaumont, and if I remember correctly, I think it was after the meeting that he made the telephone call. But, and again, if I recall, I think we were still sort of iffy about what we would do.

After he contacted them, he said, "Well, we really better go on tonight. They've indicated that, in the morning, there will be a low ceiling at about 800 feet." And he said that was pretty low. But the ceiling at Redbird was 13,000 feet. And so, he said probably it would be good if we left.

Well, as I said, that sounded like a pretty good

option to me. Accordingly, after the meeting, we went on out to the landing strip—folks from the church took us out there. The landing lights for the runway were manually operated. We turned them on. The pilot, his name was Len Rogers, instructed the people that after we got up and circled the field, that they were to turn the lights off and we'd go on. Well, we got in the plane and took off, circled the field, and I remember seeing the lights extinguished.

Just about the time they turned the lights off, we hit the cloud cover. Now, he had been reluctant to fly with a ceiling of 800 feet in the daytime. That's one of the reasons we left that evening. But here it was nighttime, and we hit the ceiling at about 750 feet. When we got up in that heavy soup, I had the distinct impression that the right wing dropped. And I said something to him about it, and he continued to handle the controls. But in a minute, we came out underneath that overcast in the old graveyard spiral, they call it, with that wing down. So, he leveled off and we got back up in that soup. Man, we were hitting it at 750, 800 feet.

Incidentally, let me just intersperse this. I did not know until later that, although he had been flying for a number of years, he was not instrument-rated and so he was at a real disadvantage in that overcast at night without the ability to fly from his instruments.

Well, we got up in there a second time and the wing dropped again. Apparently, he was suffering from a touch of vertigo, and I could certainly sympathize with that in light of the circumstance. But, when we came out underneath that overcast again, that wing was down. This happened two or three times. He finally suggested that perhaps we ought fly underneath the overcast, expecting that it would raise as we got closer to Dallas. He reminded us that the ceiling there was 13,000 feet. That seemed like a pretty good idea after having gotten into that soup.

The last thing I remember is flying underneath that overcast, seeing the lights on the ground, and the next thing I remember is it being deathly quiet and his shaking me, saying, "Corky, get out. We've crashed."

It took a little while for the shadows and the fog to lift, the cobwebs to clear away a bit. I remember looking out through the window straight ahead, and there in front of us, closer than from here to the front row of these chairs, there was a tree. If we'd gone another six feet, we would have absolutely wrapped around that thing.

I started to get out of the craft but found that I couldn't move my legs. Anticipating that I was pinned in by wreckage, I reached out to see what it was that was holding my legs, in order to move it. When I reached out, what I felt had the sensation to my hands that this desktop has to my hands. The only thing was that what I felt was shaped like my knees. I remember thinking to myself, "Well, you've broken your back," which I had. And "You'll never walk again." I came pretty close to that, too.

Now let me just pause for a moment and sort of explain the circumstances. Flying underneath that low overcast, we had taken off almost at sea level. We were very close to the coast. The cloud cover at 800 feet was 800 feet above sea level, and we were hitting it at about 750 feet. I found out later that one of the inspectors who came out to investigate the wreckage located an elevation marker not too far from the crash site that, if I remember correctly, he said that it said 550 feet. Well, that was ground level 550 feet, which meant that from 550 feet to 750 feet elevation was only 200 feet clearance of ground level.

I also found out later that in the weather report—I'm sure Len didn't pick up on this, and I frankly have wondered since then if that ought not to be something that would be distinctively featured in giving out weather information to pilots—but there was only one degree difference between the temperature and dewpoint. And of course, when they come together, there's fog almost immediately. And I found out later that there had been heavy ground fog at the nearest town to the crash site, which was the little town of Woodville in southeast Texas.

But back to that night. In a little while, I got my head cleared enough to try to respond to his instruction, and he helped me a little bit. I literally pulled myself out of the plane just using my arms and onto the ground. And he got out and laid down next to me. This was January the 12th [1965], and even in southeast Texas on a January night, it can be cool. So, we decided we'd try to build a fire. He had some matches there and the ground was very dry, and we were afraid that we might start a fire and burn ourselves up. I remember emptying out a little overnight suitcase and we built a fire in that to get a little warm.

We burned all of the twigs, limbs, and loose pieces of wood that we could find on the ground and a few leaves. The leaves didn't burn very well. But we began to run out of fuel, and the only thing I could find around there to burn was a notebook full of sermon outlines. I finally decided I probably wasn't going to have much of a chance to preach those outlines anyway, so I just burned them. I'm inclined to think that that probably was my greatest contribution to 20th Century preaching, that was to burn those outlines.

I remember that night Len tried to recall exactly

what happened, the circumstances of the crash. He could not remember. I didn't either. That may seem a little strange, but as best I can reconstruct what happened in light of the report of the inspector who came to visit with me in the hospital room later, apparently, we were flying almost on a level line at about 170 miles per hour when we hit the tops of the trees. I found out later that we had crashed in the edge of what is called the Big Thicket, which is a virgin forest preservation in southeast Texas. If you're really out into it, you are really out into something. And I understand that people have gone hunting in there, wandered into the Big Thicket, and have never been heard from, period.

But, anyway, we hit these tall trees almost on a level flight, and the inspector said that he found two trees that were gashed between them, making it clear that the fuselage had gone between the trees. He said, "To be honest with you," he said they were so close together, "I don't see how the fuselage got through, but obviously it did." What that did, though, was to pull both wings off the plane simultaneously. That did two things. One, it kept the plane from cartwheeling, and secondly it pulled the gasoline tanks off at the same time. So, we then hit the ground and slid to a stop.

But neither one of us could remember the exact

event, and probably there was not enough time to remember anything. I imagine, as I've tried to reconstruct that particular setting in mind, there was no long fall from the heavens or anything like that. We just flew into the trees on the ground.

The next morning, I remember being able to drag myself. I couldn't get up on my hands and knees. My legs were completely paralyzed. That morning, I can remember dragging myself over to the side of the fuselage and finding a large stick. And I can remember beating out an SOS signal, hopeful that maybe someone might hear it. We were close enough to a highway that we could hear highway traffic. It was not real close, but in the stillness, we could pick up the sound of automobiles and trucks. We were close enough to civilization that we could even hear some children laughing once, in the distance.

A military plane flew over and apparently the pilot was talking to someone on the ground, but the radio to our plane was still on and we could hear his voice. Len tried to get over to the plane to see if he could maybe reach that pilot to get help, but he couldn't get there before the pilot got out of distance and the radio was no longer picking him up.

I began to notice, though, that he was really having

some problems. He was beginning to hallucinate, talking to people who were not there. So, it occurred to me that it might be the better part of valor to see if I could get to that highway. At one time he stood up, but he couldn't stay up. He had to lie back down and apparently was in some rather intense pain when he tried to stand up. But I found that by getting up on one elbow, using this left hand to kind of pull with, I could kind of drag myself. I couldn't crawl, but I could move. And so, I told Len that I was going try to get to the highway to see if I could get help.

Now, one of the old principles in an emergency in a plane crash is to stay with the wreckage until the search party can locate you. It's easier to find the wreckage than it is an individual. But still, we were so close, and he was obviously losing ground rapidly that it seemed to be the option to pursue.

Question from student: *How long after the crash did this happen?*

This was the next morning. We crashed about 10:30 on Tuesday night. This must have been about 8:30 on Wednesday morning.

Anyway, I began to crawl away from the wreckage, and I would call back to him. We carried on a conversation for just a little way. I remember the last conversation that we had, I thought I saw some evidence of someone maybe doing some work out in the forest. And I hollered that information back to him. I told him, I said, "I believe I'm gonna be able to find someone here before long." And that was the last conversation that passed.

But as I dragged myself over to where I thought there was some evidence of someone having been around, it was just wild forest. I'll talk some more about that just a bit later, but at total ground level things don't always look exactly the same as they do when you're upright or even if you're on your hands and knees. But I began to try to move in the direction of the highway. Every once in a while, I'd encounter a fallen tree or a log, and when you're crawling the way I was, you don't crawl over anything. You have to crawl around it. So, I kind of snaked my way up along through the bed of the forest. This went on until dark and I still did not reach the highway.

Incidentally, I found out later there was a hog-wire fence around that part of the forest, and even if I had gotten to the edge of the thicket, I would not have been able to get through that hog-wire fence. But of course, I didn't know that.

By this time, I was some distance from the wreckage site, or at least I thought I was. I was a lifetime away from it, nearly. I remember pausing to rest for a little while in a place that looked like it might have been a campsite for some Boy Scouts. It looked like there'd been a fire there. And just the vestige of human occupation was kind of attractive. And so, I laid there and rested for a little while.

While I was lying there, suddenly I heard a woman scream. And I mean her scream just filled the blackness in the forest. I remember thinking, "Well, boy, no wonder she's screaming. She's lost out here in this thicket and that is frightening." So, I began to call to her to let her know that there was someone out there, another human being. She screamed again. Boy, it just—talk about stereophonic sound. It just absolutely bathed me. But at the end of her second scream, there was a low growl. Then it dawned on me that that was not a woman at all. That was a panther and probably it smelled my blood. It also occurred to me that I really did not want to get the attention of the origin of that scream, so I no longer hollered. I tried to play quiet-mouse, and that was fairly easy to do.

Another event happened that night, but I want to come back to that later, if I may, because it has to do more with my interpretation of all of these events.

I'm not really sure whether I slept that night or

whether I just lost consciousness, or whether it was a little bit of both. But, anyway, the next morning I began to try to crawl some more. There were some men somewhere out in the forest cutting wood. I could hear their power saws, but of course they couldn't hear my voice over the saws. My ribcage was pretty badly battered and, by this point in time, the shock had worn off some and it was pretty painful to try to holler. But I was close enough that I can remember hearing not only the sound of children, but I remember hearing a dog barking, a rooster. And I recall thinking to myself, "So near and yet so far."

I continued to crawl, and I remember coming up to a stump. It was kind of interesting, things that—priorities that develop in a situation like that. It seemed to me that the ultimate of luxury would be to be in a bed where you could pull a cover up and be warm. And to have a glass of water and a cup of ice. Man, that'd be great. Well, thirst became a real factor. I don't ever remember being hungry, but thirst became almost an obsession. I remember crawling up to this stump and, over in the stump, there was a little liquid. I couldn't get up enough to get my face in the stump to drink from that liquid, but I remember taking a leaf and I could get just a little moisture on that leaf, and I could kind of sip it. It wasn't much, but it was kind of nice.

And then as I continued to drag myself along, I came to a tree that had an exposed root underneath it, sort of an indentation in that exposed root. There was a splash of paint on that exposed root. Now, you have to understand in a situation like this, your imagination begins to play strange tricks on you. Somehow in my imagination that indentation marked by that paint on the root was the site of a spring that the Indians used to use. I thought, "Wow!" Fantasy, but boy, that was real. And I started trying to claw a hole in the ground in that indentation, and I ultimately got the hole so deep I could just barely reach the bottom of it with my arm in it. The sandy soil down at the bottom was moist, but I don't really think it had anything to do with a spring. But I can remember taking a handkerchief and putting that sandy loam in there and trying to squeeze it tight enough to get a little moisture. But I was not successful.

Well, I continued to crawl and had to pause a little more often, and it was a little bit more difficult to get back up on the elbow each time. But the early part of the afternoon, I paused to rest, and I was just about to lie back to take a little break, when I looked off in the distance. Between me and what I was seeing was a sort of a draw. On the far side of that draw, there was a field. I remember it had—there were some pumpkins in the field and there were shocks of corn standing out in the field. There was this unpainted, crude country farmhouse and some children playing out in the yard.

I don't remember exactly why, but when I'd left the wreckage, I had grabbed one of my shirts and I would cradle my head on it when I would rest from time to time. When I saw the children at the house, I began to wave the shirt and holler as loud as I could to get their attention. But they obviously could not hear me, and I thought, well, I'll crawl in that direction. That's a good sign to get to highway traffic.

I kind of laid back to rest for just a moment and then when I got back up on my elbow and looked over there across the field, there was nothing but forest. Now, that's strange, but I can remember that scene as vividly, or more vividly, than many things that I've actually seen across the years. That was just as real as it could be.

I crawled a little bit farther and paused to rest again. By this time, I was running short of company. I was talking out loud to myself and, again, I heard the sound of that highway traffic. And I remember saying, "Boy, so near and yet so far. Now, Farris, what in the world are you going to do? Well, you're going to die out here, that's what you're going to do." I remember saying, "Well, if I'm going to die, I'll die crawling." So, I got up on my elbow and tried to crawl some more.

Let me pause parenthetically to say that the doctors who examined me later in the hospital attributed my survival to the fact that I crawled all that time. The immediate cause of death of the companion pilot that I left behind was pneumonia.

But, anyway, I crawled.

It was about three o'clock in the afternoon, and I laid back down to rest. I'm not real sure that I could have gotten up again. Getting up on one elbow doesn't seem like a big chore, but after a while, it's like trying to climb Mount Everest in a situation like that.

Unbeknownst to me, of course, no one at home had missed us because they had expected us to spend the night down in Evadale. Because we had not originally planned to return that night, the pilot did not file a flight plan, and there was no record of our having left. It was not until late the following afternoon, on Wednesday afternoon, when one of my colleagues called the house to inquire about where I was, that anyone realized that something was amiss. My wife thought that I had come back and gone on to the office, which was our original plan. So, it was about four o'clock, nearly dark, before they began to realize that something was wrong. So, the colleague, Byron Richardson, who was one of the associates on the staff, called down to Evadale, and they said, "Well, they left last night." So, it was dark on Wednesday night before they were aware that anything had gone wrong. Consequently, the search did not start until Thursday morning.

On up into the day, I'm not sure exactly the time of the day of all of these events, but a Civil Air Patrol pilot, flying around looking for us, spotted the wreckage, and a ground search party swept through the area. They found the wreckage and the body of the pilot who, according to their autopsy report, had died the previous day. He was still alive when I left him, but he had died apparently on Wednesday evening or Wednesday night. And they found me about five minutes later.

I was taken to the hospital at Woodville, and I stayed there for a month, then I was transferred to Baylor University Medical Center in Dallas, where I underwent back surgery. The doctors there didn't think I'd ever walk again, but despite their fears, the Lord was gracious, the therapy was excruciating, and everything combined to get me back on my feet. After three months in the hospital, I was finally discharged.

Now that basically is the account of the events, but it's the meaning, or it's the interpretation, it's the reading, I think, that makes it important, so far as I'm concerned. It's not just the events. Two or three things that came out of that total experience have proven to be invaluable to my mind and heart across the years. One, I was not a total stranger to tragedy or sorrow or emergency. I had lost members of my immediate family. But from Tuesday night until Thursday afternoon, some 40 hours, I had the opportunity, in this particular case, the obligation, the unavoidable occasion, to check out what I had believed and what I had been preaching for a number of years: Namely, that the Lord's grace and presence, sufficiency, are adequate for any and every circumstance.

As I look back on it, I am amazed at the calm with which things like that can be experienced. It seems, in light of the fantasizing, it seems almost irrational to speak of calm in a time like that. It's amazing. During that period of time, I think I experienced, at least for a moment, almost every range of emotion that I know anything about personally. Except one. And I am still astounded—but if I didn't say this, it would be inappropriate as well as untruthful—I experienced every emotion except fear. I don't understand that. I'm not a brave man. Make no claim to be a hero. But I just never did experience any fear.

The other thing is death was almost like a personal presence during that period of time. It was almost as if you were looking him in the eyes periodically. But there was no fear. Boy, the Lord's presence has a way of producing tranquility in the midst of a storm.

The second thing that occurred—to explain, I've got to back up a little bit. When I was a student out at New Orleans, I was working for Dr. Gray [Allison] in the field mission program, faculty mission program. He had already joined the faculty and was teaching in the area of missions evangelism. And Dr. John Abernathy, who at that point in time was a Southern Baptist missionary in Korea, after the withdrawal from China, came to the campus. When he arrived, Dr. Gray made an appointment with Dr. Abernathy to come by and talk with us in Dr. Gray's office. I had been working on a paper of some sort and had stumbled onto a little volume entitled *The Shandung Revival*. It was not the one written by Dr. Charlie Culpepper, but it was the original *Shandung Revival* written by Mary Kay Crawford, published in Shanghai.

When I read that, I had never in my life encountered anything like that. It took me an awful long time to read it because I had to read for a little while and pray for a little while and cry for a little while and go back and read some more. But it was the account of a phenomenal, astounding Holy Spirit revival up in Shandung Province in northern China that centered primarily in Southern Baptist missionaries.

We learned that Dr. Abernathy had been in that revival, and so Dr. Gray had invited him to come, and we went in and closed the door, locked it, and pulled the shade down. Dr. Abernathy sat there, and, for the first time, I heard somebody not only talk about unusual events, but who talked about the Bible as if it were really so.

Coming out of that book and that unforgettable conversation with Dr. Abernathy, there begin to develop a . . . something. I don't know what. A certain sense of appointment, for want of a better description. I've talked about this infrequently across the years but, although I have mentioned this particular aspect of it, I don't recall anyone ever reacting to it, pro or con, one way or the other, except once. But somehow this inner something began to crystallize into what, for want of a better expression, I have called a sense of destiny of some sort. And frankly, by the time I left to go to Japan, I wondered if perhaps it was a destiny that involved a revival in Japan similar to the revival that they had experienced in China.

While I was in Japan, that thought was stimulated from time to time. I remember on one occasion while I was in language school that a couple, I don't even remember their name—I believe it was Parker—were coming through on their way back to the States and they were retiring after missionary service in Korea. I found there was a little fellowship in one of the language school student homes for them, and I attended and got to visiting with him and found out that he had not only been in Korea, but he'd been in China. And I asked him if he'd been in the Shandung Province, and he said yes. I asked him if he knew anything about the revival. Boy, I'll never forget—he put his hand on my shoulder, and he said, "Yeah, I was there. I remember it." And boy, I'll never forget the challenge he gave. He said, "It would be a tragedy to go to the mission field and have to come home and never see something like that."

Well, you know, just about the time that notion or that idea would die out, something else would come along and stir it up. Like for example, I had the opportunity to go to Taiwan and met Dr. Charlie Culpepper, Sr., for the first time. And had the unforgettable experience of listening to him give a firsthand account of the Shandung Revival, my first hearing of that from him. On the side of Grass

Mountain overlooking the city of Taipei, from about one o'clock in the morning to about four. Great day!

I had already learned from Dr. Abernathy and Mr. Parker that Charlie Culpeper had been a key figure in that revival. In fact, one of them said, "Humanly speaking, Charlie Culpepper was the key man."

I was just about to get over that, you know, when a year or so later I made a trip to the Philippines. I spoke at a mission meeting there that took place in the seminary at Baguio. The active president of the seminary was Dr. Frank Lide who, it turned out, had been in China and been in the Shandung Province. I don't remember whether it's in Dr. Charlie's version of *The Shandung Revival* or not, but I do recall that it was in one of the volumes, perhaps Mary Kay Crawford's, but there was the account of one of the missionaries who, following his experience with the Holy Spirit, would laugh when he prayed. And she described his laughter as "holy laughter." Well, I thought to myself when I read that, "Holy laughter. Gee, that's kind of weird. Oxymoron terminology if I ever heard it."

But while I was there at the seminary in the Philippines, Dr. Frank invited me to come down for lunch. So, I went down and had a bite with him. He said, "Now, Brother Corky, before you go, why don't we have a word of prayer together." I said, "I think that'd be great." So, we went in his bedroom. I'll never forget, we got on opposite sides of his bed. I prayed first. If I do say so myself, it was probably one of my finer prayers. You know, I mean, I prayed around the world and back again, prayed for everything that was a worthy prayer object. Took about two, two-and-a-half minutes. Then when I got through, Dr. Lide began to pray.

Now, Dr. Lide lived down there alone . . . or so I thought. But when we got in there on our knees, I found out that someone else lived there too. And as he began to talk with a third party, he started to laugh. I've never heard anything like it. It was as if the laughter started off in a cavern somewhere. It just came rumbling, rolling out. I've never heard anything like it, before or since. Only one way to describe it: Holy laughter.

By the time I came to the end of that five-year term of service, it became quite clear to me that there was not going to be a revival like that in Japan, not while I was there. I am by disposition very optimistic in outlook, but for the first time I began to have periods of real depression. And the depression was caused by the nagging question: Is it possible that I have come to Japan, I've been at the right place at the right time for that destiny, but I have not been in the right spiritual condition, and I missed it? Now that's a terrible question to consider. Have I lived past the real purpose, the real meaning, the real point of at all?

By the time I left, that was really bothering me, and I was having some periods of real depression about it. I never mentioned it to anybody. The Lord was good, though. When we came back, we located up in Baltimore and served as the interim pastor at a church in New Jersey. God just blessed the ministry of that church, and I believe one of the most fruitful years of my life was at the First Baptist Church in Wrightstown. Man, it was fabulous. So, I kind of forgot about that.

Then I got this phone call one day just out of the blue and, when I answered it, it was Dr. C. Wade Freeman, director of the Evangelism Division back in Texas. He startled me by telling me that he wanted me to consider the possibility of coming to join his staff permanently. I said, "Dr. Freeman, I just don't see how on earth I could do that." I tried to explain to him two or three reasons why I thought that would not be appropriate. And he said, "Well, before you decide, would you and your wife let us fly you down here, and you look at the situation and talk to us about it? And if the Lord doesn't confirm, then that'll be fine." You know, that's a hard proposition to pass up.

Besides, it meant a free trip back home.

So, we took him up on it. And I'll be honest with you, I really thought more about the free trip home than I had seriously pondered the possibility of making that move. But it was just almost uncanny. From the time we got off the plane, there were just little things that began to communicate to my heart and my wife's, as well, that this is it. This is right.

I remember, as we were flying back to Baltimore, talking about it, I recall saying, "Well, we've got to be real sure. We can't afford to make a mistake here. In the first place, we've worked so hard for the language. If we don't go back to Japan—I mean, what'll happen to all of that? We've got to be real positive that this is the Lord's will. We can't jump on one side of the horse and off on the other side. And we really can't afford to make a decision and wait three years and wonder if we've made the right one." So, we prayed about it and tried to think through it, and we finally came to the conviction that the Lord was in that move. So, we made the change.

That second night in the Big Thicket—I can't remember whether it was before or after the encounter with the panther—but it was that second night, I was lying on my back trying to rest a little bit. Then I had the strangest sensation. It was almost as if I could feel strength just like it was draining out of my fingertips. Boy, I could just feel energy going. It created the impression of lying on my back in dark water. And it was as if I would sink beneath that dark water into unconsciousness. Then I'd bob back to the surface, but I always felt weaker when I came back up.

I remember thinking to myself, "What in the world is going on? What's happening?" I remember thinking, "Farris, you're dying. That's what's happening." And then I thought, "But you're too young to die." And I couldn't help but smile. I remember thinking, "Yeah, and if you were 85 years old, you'd still think you were too young to die."

Then I thought about my family. What about my family, my children? What will happen to them? Then it occurred to me that if the Lord was ready to take me, it did not mean that he would abandon them and that he would not care for them. They would be well taken care of, if that was his will.

Then I began to try to reach out for something. I didn't have to wait three years to go back over that decision. It was just three months. And I thought, "Well, is it possible that we missed the Lord's guidance here and we rebelled?" So, I went back over all of the ins and outs of that decision. And in retrospect, even in that situation, as near as I could tell, we had acted consistently with the Lord's guidance as best we could understand it.

And then I thought about, well, what about that day? Maybe the trip was out of the Lord's will. Then I recalled that when we went to that house to get the telephone to use, that while I was on the phone, my deacon friend began to talk to the man and wife in the home and asked the man, "Where do you folks belong to church?"

And the husband said, "Well, we belong to the Assembly of God." Then he went on and said, "Well, that's where my wife belongs. Tell you the truth, I don't belong anywhere. I'm not a Christian."

By the time I got off the phone, the deacon was witnessing to him and it turned out that not only was the man not a Christian, he was by his own admission an alcoholic. And he said, "You know, today's my day off. And I started to go into town, but I knew if I did I'd just get drunk." And he said, "I've just been kind of waiting around here as if I was waiting for somebody to come."

Anyway, the man was gloriously saved before we left that afternoon. So, when I reconstructed the memory of the trip that day, I came to the conclusion that if I'd ever made a trip in my life that the Lord was in, it was that trip.

Well, that, that's really good news, right? But no, it's not necessarily in a situation like that. You see, if you say, "Well, Lord, I rebelled and I shouldn't have come to the Evangelism Division and I should have stayed up there in New Jersey where you led me," then I could have said, "Lord, if you get me out of this predicament, I'll go back. I'll straighten up and fly right." Or "I made the wrong trip and I'm sorry and I repent in sackcloth and ashes." You've got the prospect of maybe getting off the hook. Kinda like the old story of the response of the mouse—forget the cheese, just let me out of this trap. If you have a deliberate rebellion, then you can repent. You know, things work out great. But if you don't have that rebellion to renounce, what do you do then?

Well, I finally, frankly, came to the conclusion that the Lord had led us back to Texas and had led me on that trip because that was the time and that was the circumstance. And so, I said, "All right, Lord, if that's the case, then that's fine. I'm ready to go."

When I said that, suddenly that something came back. I hadn't even nodded in that direction in well over a year. But it was suddenly that sense of appointment and purpose. And so, I remember saying, "Lord, if you still have something for me, even though it's taken a miracle to preserve me this far, I want you to perform another one if the destiny is still there."

When I prayed that, I began to sink beneath that dark water, and as I went under, I didn't know where I was going to come up. To be honest with you, if I had been the one to cast the deciding vote then, I'm not real sure I'd be here now. But when I woke up a little bit later and I was still hurting and it was still cold, I had the conviction that the Lord still had something for me.

And you know, man, that was 25 years ago, and I'm not sure 'til yet what the appointment was or is. But for 25 years, I've had a sense of purpose for being here that I would not have had otherwise.

Well, something else, and I'll wrap this up quickly now. There have been times when having to fool with that cane has been a real drag across the years. And limitations of mobility are really not the most difficult parts of my existence. I can pretty well live with that. But it's been a source of some frustration, I guess, occasionally. But I'll tell you what, far outweighing that has been the ability to stand next to a bedside, maybe in an intensive care unit, trying to encourage and trying to comfort. Boy, it has been great to have that cane so that people could understand that, as I talked to them about the Lord's sufficiency, they could be aware that I knew what I was talking about.

But the real crux of the whole thing, one night at the hospital—you know, I haven't talked about that hospital, but the truth of it is three months in the hospital is a lot worse than 40 hours in the Big Thicket. Much, much, much, much worse. But that helped me to understand that there are two kinds of people in hospitals: there are patients and there are prisoners. And if you don't know the difference, you've never been a prisoner in a bed. But there's a world apart, and there's a chasm beyond measure that exists between the side of a bed and being in it.

But one night in the hospital there in Dallas, I had occasion to remember a conversation that had taken place back at Baylor. One of my buddies had been reading in the Book of Job, and he reminded me of the account there of the meeting of the angels with God and Satan coming in. And the Lord's challenging Satan by saying, "Have you considered my servant Job? He's just and upright, perfect in all of his ways." And Satan's response, of course, was to accuse Job of being a cheap opportunist. "He just serves you because you bless him. Take away your blessings and he'll curse you to your face."

But then my friend had personalized it by saying, "How would you feel if you knew that right now the Lord was saying to Satan, in a comparable confrontation, 'Have you considered my servant Corky Farris?' And the accuser were to say, 'Oh, he just serves you because you bless him.' How would you feel?"

I thought about it that night in the hospital. I came to the conclusion then, and it's still my economy of the whole situation now, that the real challenge was not then, nor is it now, the ability to walk again or even to survive, but if I can prove—and this is something that cannot be measured in time; it'll have to endure to the last day, whenever, or however—if I can prove that, when he thus charges me with serving the Lord only to receive blessings, if I can prove that's a lie, that will be the victory. Not walking, not surviving.

This and I'm through. Some people have said, off and on across the years, "Well, when you get to heaven, the Lord will explain to you why you had to carry that cane." And my response has been, "Well, he may. But we have an agreement: So far as I'm concerned, he's under no obligation ever to mention it."

The glory to be revealed surely is not worthy to be compared to this present circumstance. But I have the feeling that when we get to heaven, each of us with his cane—we'll all have one. And when we get there, if the

Lord should say, "Hey, Farris, let me explain to you why you had to carry that cane all those years," I'm just almost sure that, without a single exception, our response will be, "Lord, what cane was that?"

May it be so.

Transitional Narrative:
On the Home Front

At the time of the plane crash, we lived in Duncanville, a suburb just south of Dallas. Juanita was holding down the fort, trying to keep control of three kids until Corky got home. I was nine years old, in the fourth grade; my sister Darlyne was eleven, in the sixth grade; and my brother Steve was four, in no grade.

Because the original plan had been for Corky and Len to fly home Wednesday, about mid-day, Juanita first began to worry when Corky didn't arrive home that night and she hadn't heard from him. She thought, at first, that maybe he had gone to the office, but he wasn't there when she called. At supper, we ate quietly while she fretted. Being young and stupid, I thought I'd say something to lighten the mood.

"Maybe they crashed."

To this day, I feel guilt and shame for saying that, as if my words caused the crash. The plane had already been down for close to 20 hours by then, but that didn't stop my nine-year-old brain from assuming responsibility. My adult brain still harbors guilt feelings to this day.

The next day, my fourth-grade class combined with the other fourth-grade class in our school (Merrifield

Elementary in Duncanville) to watch a film. While it was playing, the principal came over the public address system and summoned my teacher, Ms. Walraven, to the office. She came back a few minutes later, approached me where I sat, and said, "They found your daddy."

She then sent me to the office where my grandparents waited. Juanita had already left for Woodville, Texas, where Corky had been taken to a small hospital. He stayed there for about a month, then he was transferred to Baylor Hospital in Dallas for back surgery followed by rehab. While Corky was at Baylor, Juanita stayed with him, while we three kids were farmed out to friends' homes. For the next few months, I lived with the family of our pastor at First Baptist Church of Duncanville, Gene and Mary McCombs and their kids, Paula and my best friend, Terrell.

I'll never forget the night a couple of months later, though, when Corky was released from the hospital. His doctors had told him that he would never walk again but, though he had to wear a bulky metal-and-leather back brace, heavy leg braces, and arm-brace crutches, he walked out of the hospital under his own power. When the ambulance arrived at home, he also walked into the house under his own power. I still get teary-eyed thinking about it. Every kid who was ever threatened with "Just wait 'til your father gets home" should be so lucky. I was never happier for my father to get home.

SERMON: *The Plight of Job*[16]

Now if you have your Bible, will you turn with me please to the first Chapter of the Book of Job. Some of you are going to be somewhat perplexed. That's in the Old Testament and if it will help you any, it's Ezra, Nehemiah, Esther, Job. That's a lot of help. Well, let me see if we can simplify it for any of the rest of you who may still have difficulty. If you can find Psalms, look right back before Psalms and there it is, you know, and it's page 571.

And tonight, we're going to move into a vein of study that, on the surface—and listen very carefully now—on the surface may appear to have a negative theme. But I hope you'll stay with me in these messages because it is simply impossible to move all the way through the controversy in the life and the experience of Job, to the marvelous climax and conclusion—simply impossible to do that in one message. Really, impossible to do it in two. So, I hope you'll stay with me because the initial impression may be somewhat negative. But the sum total message of the book, I'm convinced, is positive and glorious beyond nature. So, I hope that you'll stay with me to the very end

---

[16] Corky preached this six-part series on Job at Forest Meadow Baptist Church in Dallas in June of 1974. It was heavily influenced and informed by his ordeal following the plane crash.

in our preaching in the Book of Job.

Now, by this time you found it. We'll begin reading in Chapter One, Verse one. For a focus of interest, the first twelve verses.

"There was a man in the land of Uz whose name was Job; and that man was perfect and upright, and one that feared God and eschewed evil. And there were born unto him, seven sons and three daughters. His substance also was seven thousand sheep and three thousand camels and five hundred yoke of oxen and five hundred she asses, and a very great household; so that this man was the greatest of all the men of the east. And his sons went and feasted in their houses, each on his day; and sent and called for their three sisters to eat and to drink with them.

"And it was so, when the days of their feasting were gone about, that Job sent and sanctified them, and rose up early in the morning and offered burnt offerings according to the number of them all: for Job said, it may be that my sons have sinned and cursed God in their hearts. Thus did Job continually.

"Now, there was a day when the sons of God came to present themselves before the LORD, and Satan came also among them. And the LORD said unto Satan, 'Whence comest thou?' Then Satan answered the LORD and said,

'From going to and fro on the earth and from walking up and down in it.'"

He's still busy about that particular assignment, by the way.

"And the LORD said unto Satan, 'Hast thou considered my servant Job, that there is none like him in the earth, a perfect man and an upright man, one that feareth God, and escheweth evil?'

"Then Satan answered the LORD and said, 'Doth Job fear God for nought? Hast not thou made an hedge about him and about his house and about all that he hath on every side? Thou hast blessed the work of his hands and his substance is increased in the land. But put forth thine hand now, and touch all that he hath and he will curse thee to thy face.'

"And the LORD said unto Satan, 'Behold all that he hath is in thy power; only upon himself put not forth thine hand.' So, Satan went forth from the presence of the LORD."

I'm convinced that Job was a real, true-to-life, flesh-and-blood, actual three-dimensional man. Students of the Old Testament record are divided concerning their position with regard to the historical accuracy or historicity of the book. But as I observe it, it appears to me that there must have been a man like this, or a story such as we have recorded in the Book of Job would never have been transcribed, not even in the throes of pessimism and conventional discouragement. Nor, I am persuaded, would an individual be able to deal with the thorny issues in it and be able to project the suffering and the difficulty and the bewilderment that plagued the man called Job unless he was real. I believe the very verbiage of the opening verses of the Book of Job support the contention that we're dealing with something that actually transpired in history.

"There was a man in the land of Uz." Now, this is not, for those of you who are a little bit more familiar with wizards and warlocks and witches and that sort of thing, this is not some fairy tale land of make-believe on the other side of the rainbow. This is the land of Uz. Students of the Old Testament text and geography suggest that this probably was a section of the ancient world on the southeastern corner of what we now call the land of Palestine. Back in those days, it was the land of Canaan near the region of Eden. But there is a reason to believe that this is a reference to a specific, concrete geographical location. The context of the book, the prologue—the earlier chapters that tell the story of the heavenly council and the calamities that befell Job—as well as the epilogue, for those of us who are now familiar with that particular terminology as a result of our television set. You know, the prologue and the four acts, and then the epilogue. There was an epilogue to the Book of Job long before this was a conventional television pattern. This shows you how modern the Bible is.

Anyway, that part would also support the position that whenever the book was reduced to writing, that Job likely lived in the patriarchal period. Now, that might create more confusion and raise more questions than it answers. "Patriarchs" is a term in the Biblical jargon that refers to the people that we know as Abraham, Isaac, and Jacob.

Evidently, these excruciating experiences in the life of Job occurred at least in the general time pattern of Abraham and his immediate family. This would mean, of course, that the Mosaic code that we know in terms of the first five documents of the Old Testament had not been reduced to record. And so, Job was living in a period of man's early antiquity before, so far as we are able to determine, anything had been reduced to holy writing.

But as I read this story, I find here a real flesh-and-blood man, a true three-dimensional person who is to be the central character of a very strange and a very moving and mystifying drama. I observe that he lived in a specific place. And I find some evidences to give me an insight as to what he was like. I notice he is depicted as being more literally not a perfect man, but a whole man. The word that is translated in the King James "perfect" is not a word intended to describe moral perfection. We recognize that all human personality is flawed by sin and disobedience. God's word clearly indicates that all have sinned and come short of the glory of God. Job was not a flawless man, but the word that is translated here "perfect" means a whole man or a complete man.

And it's the same meaning that we find, for example, over in the Book of Hebrews when the record says, concerning our Lord, that he was made perfect through his sufferings. Now, Jesus, of course, had no moral or spiritual flaw in his being, and it was not necessary for him to be made ethically or morally or spiritually perfect. But the record is simply saying he was made complete in terms of his humanity by the experience of suffering.

Job was a whole man. He was a godly man. He was a complete man. And he had a family. This tells us that he was a family man. And obviously there was real fellowship among these people. Apparently, the generation gap had not particularly haunted or plagued their domicile. The sons had already grown apparently into adulthood, but there seems still to have been a circle of fellowship and communication.

The record indicates that he was a very wealthy man. He had seven thousand sheep, three thousand camels, and all of his possessions are enumerated. The sum total is that he was the greatest of all the men of the east, with vast estates and apparently almost innumerable holdings. He was a man of considerable influence, and he was a man of supreme position among his peers and his contemporaries.

But these initial words also indicate that he was a very devout man. He was a religious man who, after his sons had observed their cycle of feasting, lest they might have violated the divine conscience, would pray for them. Job was a godly father who prayed for his children, and he was concerned about them.

That was Job. Everything about him was commendable.

But then the scene changes and the focus is brought to bear upon a heavenly council, the likes of which we have never been party to. Nothing but the Holy Spirit of God could reveal the fact of this strange, celestial conference. The future and the fortune of Job proved to be jeopardized by what took place in that heavenly council.

I notice two things. First, I see great pride and great pleasure and great confidence in the heart of God concerning his servant, Job. I've said to some of you while you had to walk the veil of tears, the mysterious valley of tragedy, God must have great confidence in you to let something like this take place in your life. I believe that's true. God had great confidence in the integrity and the commitment, the devotion and the dedication of Job to the extent that he was willing to jeopardize Job by alerting Satan's attention to him.

"Have you considered my servant Job?" Then Satan, the adversary, literally in the text, it is "the" Satan—the opposing one, the adversary, the opponent. Then he responds by maligning the character and the dedication and the motivation of Job's service. "Does Job serve God for nought?" It's simply because you bless him, and you protect him but withdraw your providential care and he'll curse you to your face.

Now, this is all together in keeping with the Satanic practice. You remember back in the Book of Genesis, when he appeared on the stage of history for the very first time, he was there to accuse—this time to accuse God to man. He said to the woman, "[i]n the day that you eat thereof, you shall be as gods, knowing good and evil." He was bringing under critical scrutiny the purposes of God for man, questioning his love, questioning his wisdom, questioning his design, questioning his purpose.

Now, with Job, he comes to appear in the presence of God in order to accuse man. He plays both ends against the middle. Accusing God to man, accusing man to God. That's his role, to try to set God and man against each other. Does Job fear God for nought?

But, as Satan comes to malign Job, as he spits out that question, he articulates, and he crystallizes, and he defines one of the most probing questions that any Christian ever is to ask: Whether Job served God for nought. For that matter, does any man serve God for nought? Do I serve God for nought? Do you serve God for nought?

As a result of that dialogue between God and the adversary, deep calamity strikes the experience of Job. This is expressed, first of all, in great physical loss: the loss of his possessions. In Verse 14, "There came a messenger unto Job and said, 'The oxen were plowing, and the asses feeding beside them. And the Sabeans fell upon them and took them away; yea, they have slain the servants with the edge of the sword; and I only am escaped alone to tell them.'"

So, here's a great portion of his investment, a great portion of his holdings, that has been eradicated in one fell swoop. While this man was yet speaking, "There came also another and said, 'The fire of God is fallen from heaven, and hath burned up the sheep and the servants and consumed them; and I only am escaped alone to tell thee.'"

Now, let's pause for just a moment as we move into the progression here. The man reported what he saw. It is his interpretation that the fire was originated by God. But in light of the insight, the little picture that we have in the heavenly council, we must surely be constrained to believe that it was Satan who really hurled that power bolt. To be sure, if he did it, God permitted him to do so. But he was the instigator of the calamity because he had waited for a long time for God to relax that edge of protection in order that he might afflict and persecute and beleaguer this man of God. Now, he had his time, he had his moment, and he was making the most of it.

"While he was yet speaking, there came also another and said, 'The Chaldeans made out three bands, and fell upon the camels, and have carried them away, yea, and slain the servants with the edge of the sword; and I only am escaped to tell thee.'"

So, in one memorable, miserable day, Job suffered a

monumental collapse of the market. It was a Black Monday, indeed, when all of his resources and all of his wealth and all of his possessions were in one brief instant of a day eliminated.

Some of us have our cages rattled when we lose just a portion of our resources. When just a little prized possession is touched, like an automobile or a house or a boat or a lakefront cottage, something that we are greatly concerned about. Or maybe an investment or maybe some of our stocks or some of our bonds or some of our interests—when these things suddenly undergo a reversal or they are eliminated from us, boy, it can really shake us up.

Consider then, if you can, the plight of Job when he lost everything he had. He was a man of considerable means. But we would say, attempting to make the most of a difficult situation, if we were in Job's circumstance, that at least he had his health. Or did he?

In the Second Chapter, we observe a second heavenly council. "Again, there was a day when the sons of God came to present themselves before the LORD, and Satan came also among them to present himself before the LORD. And the LORD said unto Satan, 'From whence comest thou?' And Satan answered the LORD and said,

'From going to and fro in the earth, and from walking up and down.'

"And the LORD said unto Satan, 'Hast thou considered my servant Job, that there is none like him in the earth, a perfect and an upright man, one that feareth God and escheweth evil? And still, he holdeth fast his integrity, although thou movest me against him, to destroy him without cause.'"

The Lord is able still to boast of the faithfulness and the commitment and the love and the devotion of Job because, despite the loss of his physical holdings and also the loss of his family, which we did not even refer to in the words up until now, Job responded in this fashion: "The Lord gave, and the Lord hath taken away; blessed be the name of the LORD. In all this, Job sinned not, nor charged God foolishly."

And so, the Lord had legitimate occasion to exercise this expression of confidence and pride in Job. He did not serve and honor the Lord because of the benefits and the blessings. He served the Lord because he was genuinely dedicated to him and he sincerely, from the heart, loved his God.

"And Satan answered the Lord and said, 'Skin for skin, yea, all that a man hath will he give for his life.'"

Now under this somewhat obscure formula, skin for skin, apparently the adversary was saying that man will give up almost anything to save his own hide. But you touch his body . . . "'Put forth thine hand now, and touch his bone and his flesh, and he will curse thee to thy face.' And the LORD said unto Satan, 'Behold, he is in thine hand; but save his life.' So, Satan went forth from the presence of the Lord."

I have the feeling he went forth prancing. "And he smote Job with sore boils from the sole of his foot unto his crown. And he took him a potsherd to scrape himself withal; and he sat down among the ashes."

This man who was once the most powerful, prestigious individual among all of the magnificence of the east was now reduced to a pitiable beggar in a garbage heap, scraping his open, running sores with a piece of broken pottery. Job experienced great physical loss, the loss of his health. But to consider Job's plight, we must see more than just what happened physically. Externally, I think there must have been some very deep, emotional jolt to the things that took place. Yes, we've alluded to it, but may I direct your attention specifically again to Chapter One on the very selfsame day that all of his possessions were taken from him.

"While that third messenger was yet speaking, there came also another and said 'Thy sons and thy daughters were eating and drinking wine in their eldest brother's house; and behold there came a great wind from the wilderness and smote the four corners of the house, and it fell upon the young men, and they are dead; and I only am escaped alone to tell thee.'"

As if it were not enough, the precious children that, in their infant days he had cradled in his arms, as he'd watched them in their childish play, he'd dreamed of their future, he'd envisioned the prosperity that would be theirs. He had coveted for them the fulfillment of all of the potential of life's adventure and excitement. His dreams and his hopes were wrapped up in the lives of his children. I'm convinced, though I have not experienced it personally, but there is no grief to strike the human spirit like that that accompanies the death of a child. And Job lost, not *a* child, Job lost *all* of his children.

Oh, how devastating to the spirit. How deep and how unspeakable, how unfathomable his anguish and his grief and his sorrow. But that's not all. As he has been reduced to an open running sore of physical humanity, and as he finds his shelter in the garbage heap outside the city, "Then said his wife unto him, 'Dost thou still retain thine integrity? Curse God and die.'"

That must have stung his heart like acid. Already engulfed with a tidal wave of grief, bewildered, and confused by the sudden tragedy that has just caved in upon him, and now the companion of his years, the one who knows him most intimately, the one in whom he has the greatest trust and confidence, turns her back upon him and says as she spurns him, "Why do you maintain your integrity? Curse God and die." Now, friend, if that wouldn't shake you, I don't know what would.

But as a part of that emotional jolt, we need to read deeper into the story. In response to this blasphemous curse from the lips of his wife, he said, "'Thou speakest as one of the foolish women speaketh. What? Shall we receive good at the hand of the Lord, and shall we not receive evil or calamity?' In all this did not Job sin with his lips. Now, when Job's three friends heard of all this evil that was come upon him, they came every one from his own place."

So here they are, the three comforters. "Eliphaz the Temanite, and Bildad the Shuhite and Zophar the Maamathite, for they had made an appointment together to come to mourn with him and to comfort him. And when they lifted up their eyes afar off, and knew him not, they lifted up their voice and wept; and they rent everyone his mantle, and sprinkled dust upon their heads toward heaven."

As these companions, these cherished friends, these comrades of innumerable experiences, as they came to express their grief at the tragedy that had come into Job's life, when they came within gaze of him, they saw him in the distance. So marred was his visage, so transformed was his appearance, so miserable was his countenance, that they did not even recognize him. When they ascertained that it was indeed their companion of longstanding, they began to grieve. They took their clothing in the traditional ancient fashion, and they ripped it apart, and they took the dust of the earth, and they threw it in the heavens, and they covered themselves with the dust of the earth to express their deep concern over Job. And "they sat down with him upon the ground seven days and seven nights, and none spake a word unto him; for they saw that his grief was very great."

Seven days solemn silence is the period observed in the Old Testament to mark the passing of a man. It is the death watch. They came, and for seven days and seven nights, they sat up with Job as if they were sitting up with a body. Maybe some of us are not familiar with that particular practice. In many parts of our own country today, the waking of the dead, as it is called, is still a conventional pattern. I'll never forget, I almost lost my first pulpit as a result of not being really aware of how this thing operated, serving the church over at Baton Rouge. It was a young church. Most of the people in it were young married couples, but we had a premature death, and the chairman of the deacons called me late that night after that man passed away. He said, "Preacher, the body of this individual is down at the funeral home, and we need someone to sit up with the body between the hours of two and three in the morning. Would you be willing to go down to the funeral home and sit up with the body overnight?"

I never heard of anything like that. And I said, "Well, sure, uh, I'll be glad to go down there and sit. But why?" I figured he wasn't going to get up and run away. I just never had heard anything like that. I want you to know, it was just because he had a sympathetic, understanding heart that I didn't get run out of town on arrival just for raising the question. I was not familiar with the pattern, but I understand it's a result of, in the early frontier days of our country, to protect the body of the deceased from beasts of prey, it was the custom for friends and members of the family, in their grief and sorrow, out in the country along the frontier, to sit up overnight until the body was to be interred.

And this is the picture in Job. His three friends sat for seven days and seven nights in silence to express their concerns. And then they popped him right between the eyes when they began to talk. Now, God bless their hearts, they meant well, but they had a locked-in misunderstanding about the nature of suffering. They were convinced that sin produces suffering. And that's true. That's true. Sin produces heartache. Sin produces misery. Sin, indeed, produces calamity. Sin leaves its awful residue. In the guilt of a human conscience, sin produces sorrow and heartache. No question about it. But they had come to believe that one sin produced a specific result. And where there was a specific result of suffering or calamity, there had to be a specific and an immediate sin as the cause for it. And so, they came really intending, I'm sure in their hearts, to comfort Job, but they came in effect to accuse him of sin.

Here comes Eliphaz to say this: "Remember, I pray thee, who ever perished, being innocent? Or were the righteous cut off?" In effect he was saying these things just don't happen in the lives of the Godly. It just doesn't work like that. "Even as I have seen, they that plow iniquity, and sow wickedness, reap the same." So the trusted compatriot, because of his restricted understanding of the mysteries of

God's providence in the great context of the suffering of mankind, comes now to accuse his friend of the years of some sort of violation of integrity. And to accuse him of some sort of secret, hidden sin behind the facade of poverty and righteousness. And then he brings his recommendation. Said he, "I would seek unto God, and unto God, would I commit my cause" if I were you. In effect, he's saying, "Now you just 'fess up, Job. Tell us what you did that you shouldn't have done. Acknowledge your transgression and the Lord will come along and deliver your soul, and all will be well."

Job, in response to that, was just as bewildered and baffled because, initially, he believed apparently just as they did, and he is at a total loss to explain the calamity that has come. He knows in his own heart that he has been true and faithful, and he cannot understand why God would permit such calamity to take place in the life of one who has been true. He's bewildered. He doesn't know the answer, but he protests his innocence.

Then Bildad, the second of his companions, comes to underscore the accusation. Said he, "If thou wert pure and upright"—if you're all you pretend to be, if you're all that you insist you are— "surely now he would awake for thee and make the habitation of thy righteousness prosperous." Then he comes back to underscore again. "Behold, God will not cast away a perfect man, neither will he help the evil doers."

All Job can say is, I don't understand, but I know— *I know*—in here, I have not violated my conscience, God being my helper.

Then Zophar, the third of his comforters, comes to say, "Know therefore that God exacteth of thee less than thine iniquity deserveth." The first two accuse him of some sin that they're not able to identify, and the third man comes to say, you're really getting off easier than you ought to. If God gave you your just penalty, he would be even more severe than this.

So, with the loss of his possessions and the loss of his health, the loss of his wife's trust and confidence and sympathy and understanding, he also loses his friends. Here, really, is the crux of the dilemma, the spiritual questions that are raised in his own mind and in his own heart. He believes that they're correct, that the innocent cannot suffer with the guilty. He cannot understand that the innocent could suffer like the guilty, though a distinction be observed. He is overcome, he is overwhelmed. He is overcome by the mystery of the innocent suffering, and he is hard pressed for an answer. Job was in a real difficulty.

I think I understand at least the nature of his problem. We were serving up in New Jersey when I received the telephone call from Dr. Wade Freeman, the chairman of the Evangelism Division at the Baptist General Convention of Texas. It was like a bolt out of the blue. I knew Dr. Freeman only casually, not at all certain that he even knew who I was, much less had a name and a face identified together. So, when the telephone rang, I was startled beyond measure. I didn't know why he would call me. As we got into the conversation, I began wildly to speculate "why." Why this call? Could it be that he wants me to maybe come speak to some conference or some retreat or something like that? Then when he said, "Corky, we want you to consider the possibility of being a part of our staff here at the Evangelism Division," man, I was thunderstruck.

My first response was, "Well, Dr. Freeman, I don't see how we can." There were problems there in New Jersey. There were other implications that just made it very difficult for me, even favorably, to consider the possibility. And he said, "Well, would you at least let us fly you down and talk with us about it? Don't say no until you've come. We've looked at the situation, we've talked about it, we've prayed together about it." And he asked if Juanita would come with me.

Just to be real candid about it, we accepted his invitation just about as much to get a free plane trip back to Texas and visit with the folks as we did to have any serious consideration that we might be coming to the Evangelism Division. But after we came, after we saw, after we began to pray, the growing awareness that God was, indeed, leading in this direction. And as we discussed it and as we prayed about it, I remember two or three things. I said to my wife, I said, "Now, you know, after the years that we've spent in Japan and the long time that we've invested in language study, we cannot afford to make a decision that will take us out of Japan and let all of that effort, for all practical purposes, as near as we're able to determine, go down the drain. And at our age, we cannot afford to make a decision that's like jumping on one side of the horse only to bail out on the other side. We must be real sure and must be certain that we do not make a decision now and wait three or four or five years and look back upon it and wonder if we made the right decision."

We prayed earnestly. We prayed genuinely. And we came to the conviction in our minds and hearts that, even with all of the problems and with all of the difficulties and with all the tangled threads, that God was in it. We made our decision on the basis of that conviction. We came back to Texas. We took up our residence here in Dallas. And I had been with the Division just three months when I made that fateful plane trip down to southeast Texas. The second night following that plane crash in the Big Thicket, as I lay alone in the darkness, I began, step by step, to go back over that decision. I took all the considerations out and I studied them again. I evaluated them again. I analyzed them again. Did we miss it? Were we disobedient? Were we unfaithful? Did we rebel? Did we deviate from God's purpose?

And as I studied it, I came to the conviction that if ever I had made a decision in my life that was compatible and consistent with God's leadership as I understood it, the decision to come to the Evangelism Division was that kind of a decision.

You say, "That's great." Oh no, it's not. No, it's not. If you're Jonah in the stomach of the fish, you can say, "Lord, I'll do right. I'll repent of my rebellion if you'll just get me out of here." But what do you say if, as best you know it, you have followed God's will and you have not deliberately rebelled, what do you say then? How do you explain that?

Then I begin to wonder, what about that trip that day? But as I rehearsed the events of that day, the marvelous, marvelous conversion of a man in his mid-sixties, by his own admission, an alcoholic of long years. We had just at random walked up to his home in order to use the telephone. I came to the conclusion that, if I had ever made a trip in my life that God had specifically directed and led in, it was that trip.

So now what do you do? To the best of your knowledge and understanding, you have followed his leadership, and you have been as honest with his purpose in your life as you know how to be, as Job had been, and still the calamity comes. What do you do then?

And especially when there seems to be no answer from God. What do you do? What can you do in the face of stark tragedy, in the face of illness? You pray for God's healing, and it doesn't come. What do you do then? On the threshold of death with a dear loved one and you pray for life, and it doesn't come. What do you do then? When you come to the altar of intercession and you pour out the deep, earnest petitions of your heart, but the sky is like brass and God seems to be as deaf as some idol, and there is no response to your petition, no answer to your prayer. What do you do then?

I'll tell you what you do. You prove whether Satan is right when he raises the question, "Does a man serve

God for nought?" You prove the degree of your devotion to the God you cannot seem to understand, in the valley of the shadow, or you confirm that Satan was right, you were just trying to buy the blessings of God with a superficial devotion.

SERMON: *The Plea of Job (Part 1)*

I would invite you please to locate the Book of Job in your Old Testament. For those of you who may have some difficulty, it's just before the Psalms. That was a kind way to say it, wasn't it? And for others of you, that may still create some problems. It's page 571. At least in my Bible it is.

Now, may we pause just a moment for an additional breath of prayer. Lord, give us wisdom rightly to divine the word of truth and may it speak to our hearts and may it be measured of your Spirit to deal with our needs. May we be pointed to him who is able to save to the uttermost, even Jesus, in whose name we pray. Amen.

The Bible presents Job as a historical personage who was an inhabitant of a sector of the ancient world that in all probability was on the southeast section of ancient Canaan. The central character of the book, who bears the name Job, was a very wealthy individual. He was an owner of large possessions, and he had a large family, huge holdings. Indeed, he is described by the writer of the Old Testament record as being the greatest of all the men of the east. But in one of the most strange and melancholy sequences of tragedies ever recorded in any of the world's literature, this man Job finds himself devastated by unexplained and unreasonable calamities. All of his possessions, in one day, are taken from him. He loses his children, seven sons and three daughters. And, in the course of circumstance, he loses even the prosperity of his health.

Attempting to come to grips with some of the basic human need questions that are raised by Job, we previously observed that this ancient patriarch of spiritual pilgrimage sustained a physical loss that was, in and of itself, disturbing and devastating. He lost all of his possessions worthy of the name, and then he was deprived of his health. As a compounding factor, there must have been a very deep and a very severe emotional jolt because, as we've already indicated, his children were taken from him also in a single day, and there was the travail of sorrow at the loss of his entire family.

This deep heartache surely must have been compounded by the lack of understanding on the part of his wife as he sat there in his misery, in his sorrow, in his suffering. She said unto him, "Dost thou still retain thine integrity? Curse God and die." And then, somehow, in the topping on this awful experience, three of his trusted compatriots of the years, his intimate companions, came to express their grief and their sympathy and their sorrow when they spied Job from a distance.

At first, they did not even recognize him. This man who had been so wealthy and so prosperous was now reduced to the position of a beggar sitting in the garbage heaps of the city, scraping his open, running sores with shards. A resident of despair. They came to sit for seven days and seven nights in a muted silence that gave an eloquent expression to their sense of tragedy in the life of their friend. They observed the period of mourning that one would mark for the passing, for the literal physical death of a close friend.

But then, when they began to speak, to Job's chagrin and amazement, these trusted companions of the years began their dialogue by making subtle insinuations that, because of these terrible calamities, there must be some hidden, unknown sin in the life of Job, that he must somehow be living a lie. He must be the monumental hypocrite of the ages. That there of necessity has to be some contradiction of righteousness and integrity in his life for these things to take place. And so, he is faced with perhaps the bitterest pill, the misunderstanding of his trusted friends.

Then we observed that Job came to a spiritual dilemma. Questions raised that still haunt and plague us. Questions such as, "How can it be that the innocent would suffer like the guilty?" For this is precisely what was taking place in the life of Job. And then perhaps the crowning mystery of it all. The strange, bewildering, mystifying silence of his God in the face of his heartache and his suffering. No answer, no explanation, no deliverance, no redemption, no evidence whatsoever of God's favor. Job simply could not understand the cause of the tremendous impact of this profound and complicated, complex tragedy as is recorded in the first two Chapters of the Book of Job.

In the third Chapter, we find this experience giving expression to a threefold wish on the part of the one who is being plagued by these tragedies. First, he said, "Let the day perish wherein I was born." Job wished he had never seen life. He wished he had never even been born. And then as he realized that this was a wish that could not be granted, a second question: "Why died I not from the womb?" It would've been far better, if life was mandatory, that I might have died at birth. Then an experience, or at least an emotion, that perhaps many in the audience this morning might be able to understand. He said, "Wherefore is light given to him that is in misery, and life unto the bitter in soul, which long for death, but it cometh not?"

Job was saying, "If I could have my preferences, I would prefer that I had never even drawn breath. That being denied me, I wish that I had died at birth. But that, too, being impossible, at least I desire that I would die now and be released from my suffering and my misery."

But the first two Chapters of Job also describe a most unusual event. It occurs twice, a heavenly council at which the sons of God come to present themselves before the Lord. Satan also comes among them, and they're in this strange, eternal confrontation. There is a dialogue between God and Satan that is essentially reduced to two halting questions. The first, by God himself, "Hast thou considered my servant Job, that there is none like him in the earth. A perfect and an upright man, one that feareth God and escheweth evil." God's question to Satan: Have you considered my servant Job?

The second question is the question articulated by the opponent, by the arch adversary of man and God. "Then Satan answered the Lord and said, 'Doth Job fear God for nought?'" And the suffering and the anguish, the heartache, the misery, the frustration, the expression that borders very close to blasphemy on the lips of Job himself, all of it must be understood and interpreted in light of these two monumental questions.

In the first half of the Book of Job in this dialogue, this conversation between Job and his so-called comforters—and I would put that word in quotations because it turns out that they are more his afflictors and his tormentors than they are his comforters—these so-called friends who, in the crucible of his testing, become his adversaries and his opponents. In this conversation, there is a threefold plea that comes to light in the Sixth Chapter. In Verse 24, as they come to taunt him and to accuse him, he responds by saying, in essence, "Teach me and I will hold my tongue, and cause me to understand wherein I have erred."

They have accused him of some contradiction, some breach of integrity, some hidden disparity of his testimony, that somewhere behind that facade of piety, there is a sinner lurking. There is some awful crime that he's committed, or these things could never have taken place. And so, Job responds by saying, "All right, you point it out to me, and I will then be silent. Cause me to understand wherein I have erred." And with this plea, Job, in essence, is asking some of the age-old questions that always thunder for our attention in the midst of suffering and pain and grief and anxiety.

The first question he asked, in essence is, "Why? Why is this happening? Why is this taking place?" This is a question that always rears its head for consideration, whether it be suffering, whether it be disappointment, whether it be some setback. Whether it be the dashing of our hopes, whether it be the loss of a loved one, somehow the question always leers in our face: Why? Why did something like this take place?

In the ancient classical Hebrew language, people had the capacity to ask that question with two different words, with two different nuances, or two different colorings or two different meanings. There was one word to ask the question "why" in terms of a cause or a reason. Upon what basis did these things develop or what caused all of these results that issued?

And a second question, for what purpose? To what end? For what reason or rhyme or strategy? For what goals? Job, of course, is raising, with these words, the question for what cause or upon what basis has all of this taken place. Now, Job poses this particular question, really, in the context of natural or physical calamity. And he well might have asked that same question that the philosophers have asked across the centuries, "Why is there physical evil?" For if we have lived very close to the true issues of life, we observe that behind the facade of beauty and peace and tranquility, there is a brutal and a savage and almost a vicious side to nature itself.

I remember that morning that I drove into Waco some years back. It was two or three days following a devastating tornado that had ripped through the business district of that city in the heart of Texas. The sun was shining. It seemed to be such a peaceful setting, but as I drove into the familiar surroundings, I saw the evidences of that awful event. There was the carnage of buildings as they were leveled. There were great mountains of rubble and brick. Somehow it seemed to be unreal. I had the feeling that, perhaps, this was some rerun of a newsreel report of a far-off war fought by phantom figures in a distant land. It could not be the Waco that I had known so intimately.

Many were injured and lives were taken. The beauty and the tranquility of the natural setting of the day of my entry somehow seemed to laugh at what had taken place. Why do these things occur? Why are there storms? Job might have asked about a storm such as would level a building and cause his children to be slain thereby. Why is there illness that plagues my own body? Or to branch out from it, why must there be hunger? Why must there be pain? Why must there be sorrow? Why is there despair? Why sickness?

These questions. Questions. Questions.

Now, surely, in light of the somewhat feeble answer of the sages of the ages, I could not presume to come up with all of the solutions to that particular question in one brief sentence or two. But I remember back to the third Chapter of the Book of Genesis, the story of man's disobedience, his spiritual fall, and alienation from God. Then as a part of that curse that is pronounced upon Adam, God said, "Because thou hast hearkened unto the voice of thy wife and hast eaten of the tree, of which I commanded thee, saying Thou shalt not eat of it; cursed is the ground for thy sake; in sorrow shalt thou eat of it all the days of thy life. Thorns also and thistles shall it bring forth to thee; and thou shall eat the herb of the field. In the sweat of thy face shalt thou eat bread, till thou return unto the ground; for out of it was thou taken; for dust thou art and unto dust shalt thou return."

That's part of the answer to the question. Once man chose to rebel and to disregard the edicts of God, and opted for a path of hellish rebellion, it became necessary that man be separated from God and that the seeds of death be sown in his body. And when death became mandatory, there came also with it an attendant necessity for death-dealing conditions in our environment, circumstances that would make death a possibility physically for us. Maybe calamity, maybe sickness, maybe tragedy, but something in order to activate the physical death of man. That was no longer an option, not even for God. And because of that course, because of that hellish selection, even the very creation of which we are part is under the curse.

Paul said, in writing to the church at Rome, "all of creation groans and travails" for it, too, has been subjected to decay and depravity because of our disobedience. And as if to score what it might have been like in the heavenly pattern and blueprint in the restoration scene as it is described and pictured by the prophet, we find this very strange vignette or snapshot of nature in the words of the ancient prophet: "And righteousness shall be the girdle of his loins and faithfulness the girdle of his reins. The wolf also shall dwell with the lamb; and the leopard shall lie down with the kid; and the calf and the young lion and the fatling together, and a little child shall lead them. And the cow and the bear shall feed; their young ones shall lie down together; and the lion shall eat straw like the ox."

This is the picture of the divine blueprint of the course of nature. But when man became a renegade, he set upon all of the earthly pattern the vileness and the depravity of his disobedience, and he has corrupted, by his very sin, the very nature of which we are a part.

Or to come back to condense the answer to the question, "Why must there be evil?" Because God gave man the privilege to exercise moral choice and threw open the door to the possibility of all the sins and all of the calamities and all of the sufferings that we have known across the ages in order to give man the possibility to say "yes" or "no." God could have created man entirely differently. We could have been a docile race of robots who could have had the capacity only to say "yes," with the potential of an emotion only to love, with a programmed response only of obedience that would've been a part of a universe and a setting that would've been totally alien to evil.

Why does God permit these things? By virtue of the fact that I raised the question. By virtue of the fact that I have the capacity with my mind even to question the integrity and the wisdom of God. There is the answer. It is not that God is cruel or capricious, but that he has chosen to give me the right to ask that question. And I have chosen to be a part of a human race that is a renegade from God. As a result, our whole nature and order is plagued by the curse.

Job also raised the corollary question, "Why must the innocent suffer?" Why could not this only happen to the vile and to the depraved? Now Job and his friends had since evidently—oh, this experience was in all probability before any of the Old Testament had been reduced to written record—but apparently these men had sensed the cause-and-effect relationship of sin and suffering. Indeed, one of Job's companions spells it out. He's very precise in what he says. "Even as I have seen, they that plow iniquity, and sow wickedness, reap the same."

They had observed this connection, and this is a valid connection. Indeed, God's word reinforces it in other sections of his book. "The soul that sinneth it shall die." "For the wages of sin is dead." Said Paul to the church in Galatia, "Be not deceived; God is not mocked. For whatsoever a man soweth, that shall he also reap. He that that soweth to his flesh shall of the flesh reap corruption."

They had observed a valid, legitimate process, a connection between sin and suffering, but they had assumed too much. They had assumed that that principle operated in a personal, immediate cause-and-effect relationship. If there was suffering, there had to be some immediate sin in order to explain it. When there was a sin, there must be an immediate residue. There must be an immediate aftermath. There must be an immediate expression of condemnation. And so, they came to the erroneous understanding that specific suffering is the result of specific sin, and Job himself bought that proposition.

But this was a part of his difficulty, because he could not reconcile that principle with what was taking place in his own life. As best he knew in his mind and heart and experience, he had not violated his love and his commitment to his God. How, then, to explain these awful things that had taken place. Why must the innocent suffer? I think this gives us an insight into the tragic nature of sin and disobedience and gives us some understanding as to the scope of evil. We see it illustrated over and again in the lives of people around us, perhaps right within the intimacy of our own families. There is the child of the alcoholic, who has to feel the awful bitterness and the heartache and the misery and the discomfort of the thirst of a drunkard father. The child is not guilty at all, yet he must bear the awful brunt of a parent's disobedience.

There are those innocent civilians who find their homes leveled and who find members of their families blown to smithereens as a result of the greed for power on the part of some aggressor or some militarists, and the civilian population having no participation whatsoever in the issues of whether war is to be declared or not. And yet they become innocent victims of the awful result of man's lust for power. Or the illustration of the innocent victim of a rapist pursuing gratification. We see it all around us. The innocent, unfortunately, do suffer because of the devastating process of which all of us are integral parts. How devastating sin can be!

The ancient Greek myth came awfully close to Biblical truth. In the story of the first woman, as that ancient pagan legend had it, Prometheus constructed an image and attempted to infuse life into it by stealing power from the gods. And in response to this, these capricious human-like deities reacted. The supreme god, Zeus, instructed one of his subordinates to create a woman, Pandora, and to place at her disposal a little chest or a little box. And the gods, in order to retaliate against the act by Prometheus, according to the story, put in that little box all of the ills that were ultimately to plague mankind: sorrow, pain, sickness, suffering, disappointment, despair. The box was closed, and it was placed in the hands of the first woman with the instruction that her husband was to receive this as a wedding gift. When she came to dwell among men, the brother of Prometheus married her and, despite the warnings of his brother who was apprehensive at the opening of that present, this man took that little chest and opened up Pandora's Box. And there leaped from it all of these awful patterns that haunt human experience.

That's a myth, that's a legend. But the fact is, our federal ancestors, Adam and Eve, in effect, did exactly that. When they chose to sin, they turned loose the phantoms of hell upon time and nature and history. And they continue to haunt and plague us, and they continue even to curse the innocent in the process. Oh, but isn't it easy to fault God? Isn't it easy to fault God? I am reminded of the story of a young GI mortally wounded right at the close of the Korean conflict, while the last delicate hours of combat were draining away before the ceasefires were to go into effect. And before his last breath, he is reported to have said, "Now, isn't that just like God?"

Well, perhaps our dissatisfaction might be because we understood him only as some classical creature, far beyond the scope of our suffering. One who could not sympathize, one who could not fathom, one who could not understand our suffering. But listen to the writer of Hebrews when he said, "We see Jesus who was made a little lower than the angels for the suffering of death, crowned with glory and honor; that he by the grace of God should taste death for every man. For it became him, for whom are all things and by whom are all things, in bringing many sons unto glory, to make the captain of their salvation perfect through sufferings."

So, when you raise the question, "Why must the innocent suffer for the guilty?" do not level an accusing finger in the face of God. For his son, the only guiltless one the earth has ever known, of his own choice and by his own volition, chose to walk the lonesome valley with us and chose to bear in his body our griefs and our sorrows, and chose to carry to his cross the hell of our sin and our disobedience. And he was made complete by suffering, the supreme innocent, for the infinitely guilty.

But then Job personalized that question in the way that all of us somehow wonder: Why me? Why me? Granted that physical calamity is inescapable, accepted that even the innocent must suffer, but why could I somehow not beat the rules of the game, or at least fly in the face of percentages? Why must it take place in me?

Job did not, could not, have knowledge about that heavenly council. He could not even imagine that his God had boasted of him before the adversary to say, "Have you considered my servant Job?" He could not understand that the excruciating experience through which he was passing was, in reality, a badge of God's confidence in the integrity of his love and his devotion.

Every time Job breaks a piece of that broken pottery over one of those running wounds, God surely must have paid close attention, for He continued to hear, I'm persuaded repetitiously, that haunting accusation: "Does Job serve God for nought? Take away your blessings and he will curse you to your face." So, Job could not understand the answer to the question, "Why? Why does he thus plague me? Why is this taking place?" But if he could have seen beyond the veil, he would've known that it was because of God's great confidence in, and respect for, Job that he permitted him to endure these unspeakable agonies.

And you know, I've said that to some of you, in the hospital corridors, in the mortuary waiting rooms, inside the intensive care units. God must have great confidence in you, if you are a Christian, to let you experience something like this. Because he believes you still love him, and you will still trust him even through the agony.

But you know, there's an answer to that question that Job didn't even ask here. The other side of the question, not "why" in terms of the cause, but "why" in terms of the purpose. Not the origin, but the end; not the start, but the goal. Why did he let these things take place? That's the same question that the disciples of our Lord asked as they saw that man, blind from his birth. "And his disciples asked him, saying, 'Master, who did sin, this man, or his parents, that he was born blind?' Jesus answered,

'Neither hath this man sinned nor his parents . . .'"

You could put a comma there or you could put a period there. It really doesn't matter, but perhaps it would read a little bit more intelligently to put a period there. "But that the works of God should be made manifest in him, I must work the works of him that sent me, while it is day; the night cometh when no man can work."

Calamities must come. Tragedies are ultimately unavoidable. Death cannot be permanently circumnavigated. Why do these things come? It's the name of the game. When God gave me the privilege to say "no" to him, this was a part of my heritage, and this is a part of my law and circumstance. When I asked the question "why" or "for what purpose?" here it is: That it might create an occasion in which he would work a gracious work of his love and his mercy and his compassion and his deliverance. It was so ultimately, Paul said, "We know that all things work together for good to them that love God, to them who are called according to his purpose."

Not that everything that transpires will, in and of itself, be sweet, beautiful, and gratifying. But even the tragedy and even the disappointment and even the frustration, even the confusion—he will take it if I will surrender to his will and to his design. The capacity of the mercy of God is illustrated whereby he could take even the bitter experiences of life as discordant threads and weave them together in a tapestry of mercy, compassion, and love. That's why these things happen to me if I'm a child of God.

If I speak to someone this morning who has never given their heart to Jesus, and you find yourself in the context of controversy, of disappointment, bitterness, sadness, sorrow, suffering, maybe that's the reason for the turmoil and the conflict: because God would use it to bring you to this service, to this moment, to this hour, that you turn your life over to Jesus. That's perhaps the reason why these things have not worked out on their own. That's the reason why you're disturbed and unhappy. That's the reason why, in your confusion, you have come to this service in order to let God step in and take the shambles of your life and put them back together for your good and his glory.

Would you let him do that right now? Would you yield and submit to his tender purpose in your life? However bitter the disappointment, however mystifying the defeat, how frustrating the disturbance, would you come and say "yes" to Jesus and let him take a broken life and make it over again? To be a thing of beauty. Would you do it right now?

SERMON: *The Plea of Job (Part 2)*

All right, if you have your Bibles, will you turn please to the Ninth Chapter of Job. I will not read the Verse at this particular point, but if you'll locate Job 9, Verses 32 and 33. Let me encourage you to keep your Bibles open because we will be returning to these and some other verses in Job in the course of the message.

I hope we are not insensitive to human suffering. I heard just recently, and I do not recall whether it was over the radio or whether I read it or whether I viewed it on television, I just cannot recall the circumstances, but it was an event that took place within the last two weeks, as I recall. But the gist was like this. A boy swimming in a motel swimming pool had crawled out in the midst of a thunderstorm and was struck by lightning. Amazingly enough, the lad was not killed by the thunderbolt, but he was knocked down. They had picked him up, carried him into the lobby of the motel, and covered him with a blanket. Whoever was making the report had come into that scene and his evaluation was that it was amazing to listen to the conversation going on around the stricken lad there on the floor of the motel lobby. Covered with a blanket, still stunned and still tingling, I'm sure, from the massive jolt of electricity.

All of the guests at the motel were standing around and talking where the boy could hear them. But the gist of the conversation, according to the reporter, was this: "Gee, I'm sorry I missed that. I never saw anybody struck by lightning before. I just came along just a few moments too late." The reporter was simply aghast at the total indifference and insensitivity to the traumatic experience that the lad had just gone through.

We can be pretty cold, and we can be pretty detached, can't we? I hope we're not that way about Job with all of his pain and all of his suffering, but we can be somewhat indifferent, can't we, if we're not careful? A part of our indifference, I'm sure, stems from our inveterate optimism. Someone wrote that, during World War II, the average GI was optimistic to this degree. If a platoon commander were to address his troops on the eve of battle to say, "Men, I know for a fact that after the battle tomorrow, only one of you will survive and be alive," that 95% of the platoon would look around and say to himself, each in his own personal way, "Gee, I sure am gonna miss the fellas after they're gone."

But this is the way we think. This is the way we operate. It always is something that happens to someone else. Especially, I think, we find it difficult to bridge across the centuries to certain events in the Bible and certain characters in God's word. And perhaps Job is one of the more difficult people for us really to identify with.

Until . . . our moment of suffering comes.

So I hope that, as we attempt to probe even more deeply into the heart, into the mind, and the bewilderment of Job, that we will be able to do it with the full awareness of the fact that the day will come, if it has not already arrived, for everyone in this audience, when for a matter of moments or hours or days or weeks or maybe even years, we, too, will sit in the ashes of our despair just as Job sat. Shorn of his family, robbed of his health, the confidence of his friends now forfeited, the sympathetic voice of his wife now twisted and tortured by sarcasm and the acid of indifference, and Job all the while stinging and burning and itching with the pain of sores that literally engulfed his body.

We observed last week he began to raise the question "why?" Why do things like this have to happen? Why must there be evil? Why must there be calamity? Why must there be suffering on the part of any individual? And why must the innocent suffer along with the guilty? This was that nagging question that just thundered for some sort of answer in the mind and the heart of Job.

And why me? Why me? To be sure, Job could not be aware of that conference that had taken place between his God and Job's own personal opponent and adversary, Satan. He could not know that what was taking place was a badge of confidence on the part of God, confidence in Job's integrity and genuine allegiance and surrender. Nor could he understand that the assaults that were mounted upon his body and upon his whole frame of reference were initiated by the adversary, rather than by the father God that he loved and trusted.

But now I see Job asking some other questions. I see him, as it were, making a plea. In Verses 32 and 33 of Chapter Nine, he said, "For he is not a man—" speaking of God— "as I am, that I should answer him, and we should come together in judgment. Neither is there any daysman betwixt us, that might lay his hand upon us both."

The term "daysman" that is translated in this fashion in the King James is really a word used to describe one who makes a decision or one who decides an issue. Accordingly, it can more appropriately, and perhaps more intelligibly for us, be translated as an "umpire."

Which brings me to the game last night. We lost, but it was because we had to play not only the opposing team, but also the umpires. That's awfully hard to overcome. But there has to be someone to call the shots and to make the decisions. And this, in effect, is what Job is pleading for. Someone to come and to decide the issues and to weigh the values and the events in the balance and to make some sort of verdict that would be acceptable.

As he thinks of God, he notes that God is "not man as I am, that I should answer him and that we should come together in judgment." Job is asking for an umpire, but he's asking for an umpire who can understand sympathetically the problems and the heartache that he's currently experiencing. Because to Job, as to all of us in the crucible of pain and sorrow, God at first seems to be very distant or remote. One can be tempted to feel abandoned and terribly alone in times such as these, and Job longed for someone who could share the pain and who could share the bewilderment with him.

Where was Job's God? Was his God, after all, like that deity of the prophets on the top of Carmel, who shrieked and wailed, who literally screamed and thundered at the heavens, calling upon Baal to come and to kindle a fire upon that sacrifice? Was Job's God like that? A God who was so distant and so far removed that apparently, he could not hear the pleas of his supplicants? Was he like some cold landlord in a far-off land who is totally impersonal and totally uncaring about his tenants? Was Job's God like Baal? Was Job's God like that? Or was Job's God like the deity of the Orient that our friends in Japan have identified as the Lord Buddha? A great, massive statue of metal or stone, sitting with hands folded, a faint enigmatic smile frozen upon the features of the face. Silent, lifeless, deaf, apparently totally unmoved by the anguish and the grief that may flood the hearts of those who kneeled before him to pray for deliverance. Was Job's God like that?

A God way out there who simply couldn't care less, or a God who was frozen, immobile in helplessness, who could not respond and who could not deal with the pain and the heartache of his life. Was Job's God like that? So, it seemed. So, it seemed to Job, for at least a while. But just as Job could not understand that unearthly confrontation between Satan and his God, Job did not understand the mist of antiquity, long before God's word had been reduced to written form, before all the blessings and all of the promises that can enrich our lives. He was not aware of the fact that in the divine council before the foundation of the world, there was one appointed to be slain from the foundation of the world, to bear our griefs and to carry our sorrows.

There would ultimately come an umpire, a great sympathizer. Job could not be aware of the fact that the day would come when there would be one who would be tempted in all points like as we are, and yet without sin. One who would walk the same dreary paths of misery and heartache and suffering and loneliness and anxiety, one who is the captain of our salvation, who would be made complete through suffering, just like Job. Job could not know that. But his plea for a God who would see and who would know and who would understand and who could sympathize—my friends, that prayer and that plea has been answered.

How tragic it is, then, to find people who still sit in bewilderment like Job, without a personal knowledge of this God, without any direct, intimate fellowship with this umpire who does understand. This one who is able to carry all our burdens, this one who is willing to walk the lonely valley with us. How sad for us to face the heartache and the suffering of life without that strength and without that support.

But Job is also praying for someone to mediate; someone who could lay his hand upon both of us. The chasm is too massive, the gulf is too deep, the bridge is too expansive for me to be able to reach over to him. Oh, that there was someone who could understand and someone who could bridge that great gulf between God and man. That's what he longed for. And God had already designed one who could bridge that great chasm.

You know, it's amazing. With all of our scientific skill, experience, and ingenuity, we are now able to take an earthling and implant him on the surface of the moon, at least for a designated period of time. That's amazing. That is fantastic. Almost unthinkable. Almost completely incredible. And yet, with all of our know-how and with all of our expertise, while we can place a man on the moon, there is not a rocket that has yet been designed, there is not a spacecraft that has yet been engineered, there is not a mode of travel that has yet been conceived that can take a man into the presence of God and have him meet the eternal creator.

But there is such a one, the great sympathizer who is also my great mediator. There is one God and one mediator between God and man, the man Christ Jesus, one who saves to the uttermost, able to save because of his eternal intercession and the presence of the Father. One who would say, "I am the way, the truth and the life. No man comes unto the Father except by me." One who is able, through his cross, to lift us up from the earth and to lift us into the presence of God and his blessing and his life and his strength. Job longed and yearned for that kind of an umpire and, praise God, there is one now. And as we have to walk into that crucible of sorrow, our suffering, there is one who is prepared to go in there with us and to keep the communication open with the Father, even Jesus Christ his son.

But there's another factor here, another facet of his appeal. In Chapter 13 and Verse three: "Surely, I would speak to the Almighty, and I desire to reason with God." A plea for an umpire, a plea for consideration, an opportunity to present his case. A circumstance, an occasion in which, if you please, he might argue his innocence. A desire to be personally identified with God. I'm sure he was haunted and plagued by the doubt and suspicion that perhaps God had overlooked him.

And surely, we can identify with that frustration. There are many of us who feel that way from time to time. We do not want to be just an anonymous face in a numberless throng. We do not want to be some blank computer card in some great mechanism. We do not want to be just an unidentifiable digit in a sea of statistics. We would like to think that God knows us personally, directly, and individually. Job longed for an opportunity, and I'm sure he was saying to himself, "If I could just see him, if I could just communicate with him, if I could just talk to him directly, then I would press my case and I would make my defense and I would advance my arguments and I would extend my explanation."

Job was not aware that that particular plea was going to be answered in a very dramatic fashion. Before the book is completed, Job finds himself confronted by that eternal God who speaks to him out of a whirlwind. What, then, is Job's defense? What is his plea? What is his argument? Job found himself in the same place that Thomas found himself when he confronted the Lord. Thomas, who was so sure that bodily resurrection from the grave was utterly unthinkable. Thomas was saying, in effect, I am of a modern scientific bent. Unless I can see him, unless I can take my fingers and touch the scars on his side, unless I can see the imprint of the nails in the flesh of the palms, I cannot believe that that cadaver has come back to life. I just cannot believe.

But then when he faced it, what was his response? To touch the scars? To probe the wounds? To ask for some sort of definition about bodily resurrection? To have the chemistry of rejuvenation explained? Oh, no. When he did face his God in his resurrected flesh, he fell upon his knees to say, "My Lord and my God."

And when Job finally saw God face to face and had just an inkling as to the magnificence of his providence and just a faint insight as to the gentle mercy and tenderness of his way, Job didn't plead his innocence, and he did not argue his personal justification. But, according to his own statement, he said, "I have heard of thee by the hearing of the ear, but now mine eye seeth thee. Wherefore, I abhor myself and I repent in dust and ashes."

A plea for consideration. Look on my side. See it my way. But in every circumstance and in every case that human flesh comes in contact with the spirit of Almighty God in the person of his son, Jesus Christ, the response is the response of the publican in the temple: God be merciful to me, a sinner.

But Job also pled for deliverance. This time in Chapter 14, Verses 13 and 14. "O that thou wouldest hide me in the grave, that thou wouldest keep me secret, until thy wrath be past, that thou wouldest appoint me a set time and remember me!" A longing for an appointed occasion, a set time, a time beyond pain and suffering. The grief and the anguish would be bearable if one could know that somewhere beyond the immediate, that there would be a circumstance, that there would be a situation when sorrow and sighing would flee away. However intense the pain, however burning the throbbing ache, it could be endured if we could be assured that somewhere, some time, some place, all pain would be eradicated, and that sorrow would flee away and that the tears would be forever wiped from our cheeks.

Yes, I know the smug cynic, totally world-oriented, laughs and scoffs when we speak of heaven and blatantly accuses us of being concerned only about pie in the sky, by and by. But that argument is advanced in the absence of pain, and that argument can only be sustained in the absence of sorrow. Because every one of us, when we suffer and when we grieve, begin to long for a time and a place when the old things, the former things, will pass away, and pain and death will be remembered no more. And Job was saying, oh, if there could be something beyond the death of the grave. He raises the most zoaring consideration that I suppose had ever been formulated in man's thinking process up until that time when he raised the question, "If a man die, shall he live again?" Asking for an appointed circumstance beyond the veil of tears, but is it possible? Is it conceivable? Beyond the shadows, can there really be light? Beyond the grave, can there really be a resurrection? Beyond the darkness of death, can there really be the light of life?

And so, Job condenses it all in that plea: hide me. If you could just hide me from the violence and the pain, if you would keep me until the wrath has passed, if you would appoint me a set time.

And here it is: Oh Lord, remember me. Remember me.

As I read those words, I remember the drama of the cross. The confusion, the insensitivity to suffering, the brutal mechanism of Roman execution. The searing pain stabbed the bodies of those victims impaled upon the Roman wood. And one of those men, like Job in his hurt, as the shadows of darkness gathered around his consciousness, he looked at Jesus, who in turn was dying, and he said, "When you come into your kingdom, remember me."

Remember me.

Sometimes the Lord places us on that ash heap in order to provoke that kind of urgent plea. Remember me.

Do I speak to someone disturbed, distressed? Things don't seem to fit. Dreams are not materializing. Hopes are not being realized. Ambitions are not being fulfilled. Mystified, perplexed by the seeming senselessness and meaninglessness of the events of life. Have you turned to God, and have you cried with Job, "Remember me"? Have you? If you haven't, will you do it now at this very moment? If you're not in that anguish, if you're not in that torment, if you're not in that turmoil, rest assured, it's out there waiting. And you'll have to face it with or without the Lord.

How much more significant it can be if you could face it with him. Would you put your life in his hands? Would you be obedient to his son? Would you live for him and his glory? Would you respond to his will? Would you be faithful to his instruction, and would you be in the center of his providence? Whatever happens in the course of life, you can be if you make that decision.

SERMON: *The Confidence of Job*

Now, if you have your Bible, would you turn to the 19th Chapter of the Book of Job? I shall read Verses 23 through 27, or at least midway through 27. Job 19, Verse 23: "Oh, that my words were now written! Oh, that they were printed in a book! That they were graven with an iron pen and lead in the rock forever! For I know that my redeemer liveth, and that he shall stand at the latter day upon the earth. And though after my skin worms destroy this body, yet in my flesh shall I see God; Whom I shall see for myself, and mine eyes shall behold, and not another."

In preparation for this series of messages on the Book of Job, I resurrected a very interesting little commentary that I found two or three years ago, perhaps even longer. Despite its being located in an unlikely place, I think, perhaps, it is as appropriate a comment on much of our understanding of Job as is to be found anywhere. I speak, of course, of that deep theological, ongoing dissertation called *Peanuts*. You're familiar with *Peanuts*, and in this particular sequence of comic strip events, we find Charlie Brown in his familiar place on the pitcher's mound. Now, you remember Charlie Brown. He's the born loser, and he's talking to his catcher, Schroeder. It begins like this.

"We're getting slaughtered again, Schroeder. I don't know what to do. Why do we have to suffer like this?" And as his erstwhile catcher turns and heads back toward the plate, he throws this remark to Charlie Brown. "Man is born to trouble as the sparks fly upward." And the intrepid pitcher says, "What?"

Then here comes Linus to join the discussion. "He's quoting from the Book of Job, Charlie Brown. Seventh Verse, fifth Chapter," and he decides he'll elaborate a little bit on this. "Actually," he continues, "the problem of suffering is a very profound one." And here comes old crabby Lucy. You know, she always wants to get into the act, and she says, "If a person has bad luck, it's because he's done something wrong. That's what I always say."

By this time, Schroeder's back on the side of the mound. He says, "That's what Job's friends told him. But I doubt if—" And that's as far as he can get with his sentence when Lucy jumps right back in. "What about Job's wife? I don't think she gets enough credit." By this time, the whole ball club is assembled around the pitcher's mound. Schroeder continues, "I think a person who never suffers, never matures. Suffering is actually very important." And then Lucy, "Who wants to suffer? Don't be ridiculous."

And here's a nondescript member of the team. "But

pain is a part of life," and Linus picks it up, "A person who speaks only of the patience of Job reveals that he knows very little of the book. Now the way I see it . . ."

And poor Charlie Brown, from his lonely perch on the pitcher's mound, now looks at the reader and says, "I don't have a ball team. I have a theological seminary."

Well, it may be cruel, and it may be humorous, but that's a pretty good picture of much of the confusion and uncertainty about exactly what is being said in the Book of Job. And there are some interpreters, including some dramatic presentations[17] that miss the heart and the core of Job as completely as if they had only been reading a comic strip. Various and contradictory interpretations of Job's mysterious sufferings prevail.

The fact is Job, himself, was baffled. The torturous trail of his grief and frustration meanders through Chapters 4 through 18. And then in Chapter 19, Job makes an unexpected, zoaring leap of faith. He suddenly finds a dazzling grasp of a brilliant, eternal truth. And, therein, he seizes the key to his profound dilemma within the pit of despair. Job expresses a magnificent confidence: I know that my redeemer is alive.

He's been searching for someone to bridge the gap

---

[17] A reference to the 1958 play *J.B.* written by Archibald MacLeish.

between the unreachable God, in his lofty holiness, and Job, in his deplorable, pathetic plight. A daysman, an umpire, a mediator, an arbitrator. I know that my redeemer is alive. Now we find Job's confidence expressed in my "goel," translated my "redeemer." More appropriately, it could be translated my "kinsman redeemer" because, in some instances, this word is used to describe the nearest of kin. The term that Job employs is a word that is used elsewhere in the Old Testament with a restricted or a stylized, an almost technical type of interpretation. Because, you see, the goel or the kinsman redeemer was designated in the Mosaic law to perform some very critical vital functions in the rather primitive structure of ancient Israelite society.

For example, in the 25th Chapter of the Book of Leviticus, God's word says, "And if a sojourner or stranger wax rich by thee, and thy brother that dwelleth by him wax poor and sell himself unto the stranger or sojourner by thee, or to the stock of the stranger's family, after that he is sold he may be redeemed again; one of his brethren may redeem him."

The word used here "redeem" is the activity of a nearest of kin, conceivably the brother. And it would be this one who would take the responsibility for liberating his kinsman from a debtor's obligation. And if, because of his reverses and his financial misfortune, he has to forfeit freedom and liberty itself, it becomes the responsibility of the nearest of kin, or the goel, the kinsman redeemer, to activate processes by which this individual would be set free again.

Still in the 25th Chapter of the Book of Leviticus, the Word says, "The land shall not be sold forever." Speaking now of the inheritance in the land of Caanan, God said, "The land is mine; for ye are strangers and sojourners with me. And in all the land of your possession, you shall grant a redemption for the land. If thy brother be waxen poor, and hath sold away some of his possession, and if any of his kin come to redeem it, then shall he redeem that which his brother sold."

When the Israelites came into the land, God said, "This is really not yours. It's mine. And I give it to you as a trust, as a stewardship. And it is to be your possession to occupy. As long as the land is in existence, it is not to be sold. It is to remain in the family."

This is the background of that discussion and the dialogue between Naboth in the vineyard of Jezreel and Ahab, the King of Israel. To sell that plot of land, even to his king, would be a violation, as he understood it, of God's word. This is the reason that he balked at the proposition. But if for any reason, because of some type of reversal in family fortunes, if the land has to be put up for mortgage and it is forfeited, then it becomes the responsibility of the nearest of kin, the goel, the kinsman redeemer, to set in process the procedures that would be necessary to purchase that land back again, that it might still be possessed by a member of the family. So, it became his obligation to redeem the homestead.

In the 25th Chapter of the Book of Deuteronomy, there is a rather interesting custom that may somewhat baffle us in our Western culture, but here it is in any event. "If brethren dwell together and one of them die, and have no child, the wife of the dead shall not marry without unto a stranger. Her husband's brother shall go in unto her and take her to him to wife and perform the duty of an husband's brother unto her. And it shall be, that the firstborn which she beareth shall succeed in the name of his brother which is dead, that his name be not put out of Israel." So, the nearest of kin, the goel, the kinsman redeemer, has the responsibility, in the event of the death of a brother without seed, without a child to bear the name, it becomes his responsibility to marry the widow in order that he might bear children in his brother's name, lest that name be obliterated from the roll of the names of Israel.

Now, this again is the background of some of the meanderings, for example, in the Book of Ruth, between Ruth and Boaz, who was not the nearest of kin, and he had to secure permission from the nearest goel in order to exercise the option to be her husband. This may be something that we do not really grasp. It may somehow be to us of trivial importance. But this is a matter of great significance in the Orient. Even until today, it is a tragedy, unspeakable that the family name should not be preserved.

For example, in Japan, in circumstances such as this, we find a very interesting response. Say there are two daughters born into the family of the Itos. Just the two daughters, no sons to bear the family name. In that society, where marriages are frequently arranged and they are the result of some sort of contractual agreement, the go-between, as he is called, would then scout around and see if he could find a family that would have several boys, for example, the Takahashi family.

Let's say they have four or five sons. So, he would enter into the negotiations, and he would bring these two families together until finally an agreement would be reached that one of the young Miss Itos would marry one of those young gentlemen, a Mr. Takahashi. But when the wedding ceremony is performed, instead of Ms. Ito becoming Mrs. Takahashi, Mr. Takahashi takes her name and he becomes Mr. Ito, so that the name may be preserved in Japan.

It became the responsibility of the nearest of kin to redeem the name of his deceased brother. Then in the 35th Chapter of the Book of Numbers, we have a word concerning the judicial procedures in this rather primitive tribal society of ancient Israel. "But if he thrust him of hatred," speaking now of an assassin, "or hurl at him by laying of wait, that he die, or in enmity smite him with his hand, that he died; he that smote him shall surely be put to death, for he is a murderer. The revenger of blood shall slay the murderer, when he meeteth him."

And the expression translated the "revenger of blood" is the same word that Job uses in the 19th Chapter of his poem, the redeemer of blood, the goel of blood, the avenger of blood, as it is sometimes translated. It becomes the responsibility, then, for him to be the official executioner in order to mete out vengeance where there has been assassination or murder committed. And it became the responsibility, then, of the nearest of kin to see that righteous satisfaction is attained and achieved.

How interesting that Job would use this word, my

kinsman redeemer. My kinsman redeemer, who would somehow come to secure for me liberation and freedom from my dungeon of disease and pain and frustration. My kinsman redeemer, who would come and secure for me my homestead and my rightful heritage. My kinsman redeemer, who would come and remove the smirch and the stain from my name in light of the misunderstanding on the part of my friends. My kinsman redeemer, who would come and avenge me upon my adversary who has lied and mortally wounded me.

How appropriate that he would use that term, for it was the goel who accepted the responsibility to redeem his kinsman's lost opportunities for a successful life. Job's life was in miserable shambles. But he made this leap, in trust and commitment, "I'm persuaded that somewhere I have a living redeemer, a kinsman redeemer, who will secure for me the justification that I so desperately need."

Now, in his earlier pleas, Job has anticipated our Christ as he spoke of the mediator—someone to bridge that awesome gap between untouchable God and depraved mankind—but never has he as dramatically anticipated the coming of our Lord as here. Our redeemer, who redeems us, who grants unto us freedom. "You shall know the truth and the truth shall make you free." Said Paul, "For the law of the Spirit of life in Christ Jesus hath made me free from the law of sin." And we, who were bound to our sin and our disobedience, may anticipate a kinsman, not a stranger from some far-off land, but one who tabernacled in flesh and became as one of us to come and to liberate and to emancipate. One who would come to bring to us our heritage of an eternal city, that we might indeed approach Mount Zion, the city of the living God, the heavenly Jerusalem, an innumerable company of angels, which inheritance we have forfeited as a result of our disobedience and our rebellion against God.

A kinsman redeemer, who would come to take away the stain and the debauchery of our name of depravity, who would, according to his promise, inscribe for us a new name in that stone in heaven, who would see that our name is entered into the Lamb's book of life. One who would write upon us the name of his God and the name of the city of God, which is new Jerusalem. One who would secure for us a name in glory, one who would come to deal with our arch opponent of the ages—who has bested, who has worsted us, who has caused us to be encased in our disobedience and to be ensnared by our own unfaithfulness.

We see Jesus, who was made a little lower than the

angels for the suffering of death. We see him who became partaker of flesh and blood, that he also might taste of death and destroy him that had the power of death, that is the devil, and deliver those who, through fear of death, were all their lifetime subject to bondage.

I know that my redeemer lives. He understood that this was not some dead or some distant God, but he was alive. One who could indeed mediate between God and man, one who could see an answer, one who could respond to the heartache and the hurt. One who would be sensitive to his burdens and to his cares. Oh, Job had been searching for someone who could really understand, someone who could really care. This is the basis for it. His pathetic expression, "Oh, that thou would hide me, that thou would keep me, that thou would appoint me a set time that thou would remember me." Now I know that my kinsman redeemer is alive.

And apparently Job could understand that he also cared. That's the question that haunts us, isn't it? When God seems to tarry, when his deliverance is delayed, when his arm of strength is postponed, we begin to wonder, we are plagued with torment and doubts. Does he know? Does he see? Does it matter to him? God's people across the ages, before and since the day of Job, have had to ask that question. A songwriter once asked it like this:

(singing) *Does Jesus care when my heart is pained too deeply for mirth or song; as the burdens press, and the cares distress, and the way grows weary and long.*

You've been there, haven't you? You probably asked that same question. Does he see? Does he know? Does he care? The songwriter gave his own answer.

(singing) *Oh, yes, He cares. I know He cares. His heart is touched with my grief. When the days are weary, the long nights dreary, I know my Savior cares.*

That's what you'll be saying. He's alive and he cares. Though my skin be destroyed, and this body be lowered into the earth, yet, literally, from my flesh, I shall see God; whom I shall see for myself. Who my eyes shall behold and not another. As it is translated, "Who my eyes shall see, and not as a stranger." He'll know me when he comes to stand at the latter day upon the earth. He will take care of all of the inequities and all of the injustices. He will answer the questions that somehow baffle me in the present. Job seems to grasp the answer to the haunting question that he's formulated earlier for himself, "If a man die, shall he live again? My redeemer will stand at the last day upon the earth."

There will be a day when our next of kin, our

redeemer, our liberator will make things right. However deep and bitter the waters may be, that day will come when he'll make it right.

You remember some months ago that Fred Swank, the pastor at Sagamore Hill Baptist Church, spoke here in a series of services. I remember an experience he once shared with a group of preachers several years ago. There was a couple in his congregation who had a precious little baby girl about three or four years of age. She was smitten by a terminal disease, and that mother and father had to watch for long, excruciating weeks as that precious little body withered away. Gradually that light of their life was snuffed out, the little life gone. Brother Swank said, as they came to the graveside after a period of mourning, while the tears continued to stream down their cheeks, the mother and father came to him to say, "Pastor, we've decided not to ask 'why' until we see, face to face, the only one who can answer that question."

I know that my redeemer liveth and, at the last day, he'll stand on the earth, and he'll make things right as they ought to be.

SERMON: *The Victory of Job*

Turn with me, if you will, to the 42nd Chapter of the Book of Job, beginning in Verse one.

"Then Job answered the LORD, and said, 'I know that thou canst do everything, and that no thought can be withholden from thee. Who is he that hideth counsel without knowledge? Therefore, have I uttered that I understood not; things too wonderful for me, which I knew not. Hear, I beseech thee, and I will speak; I will demand of thee, and declare thou unto me. I have heard of thee by the hearing of the ear; but now mine eye seeth thee. Wherefore I abhor myself and repent in dust and ashes.'

"And it was so, that after the LORD had spoken these words unto Job, the LORD said to Eliphaz the Temanite, 'My wrath is kindled against thee, and against thy two friends; for ye have not spoken of me the thing that is right, as my servant Job hath. Therefore take unto you now seven bullocks and seven rams, and go to my servant Job, and offer up for yourselves a burnt offering; and my servant Job shall pray for you, for him will I accept; lest I deal with you after your folly, in that ye have not spoken of me the thing which is right, like my servant Job.' So Eliphaz the Temanite and Bildad the Shuhite and Zophar the Naamathite went, and did according as the LORD commanded them; the LORD also accepted Job.

"And the LORD turned the captivity of Job, when he prayed for his friends; also, the LORD gave Job twice as much as he had before."

Charles Crane of our church called my attention to the fact that a certain play was being presented here in the city, a drama by Archibald MacLeish entitled *J.B.* That particular play is, at least theoretically, an adaptation or a modernization of the experiences of the Biblical Job. The story, the casting, the setting are all staged in a contemporary or a modern-day circumstance. So, when he suggested that I might be interested in seeing the play, just by virtue of the fact that I have been attempting to dig around in the Book of Job these last few weeks, I very readily consented. And we went to the play, and we saw it.

I continue to amaze myself, frankly, with the magnitude of my self-control and restraint because, to be perfectly candid, I almost came unwound two or three times in the course of that play. I do not mean to be hypercritical of a playwright, but I think he made some very fundamental and some very serious mistakes in his grasp of the material that he attempted to present. In the first place, I think he missed the personality of Job altogether. The J.B., or the Job, in the play is sort of a plastic type of individual—I guess we're fairly familiar with that terminology[18]–who is really sort of a hypothetical type of a person who in effect says, "Well, the reason all of these things come my way is just because the Lord is merciful."

But it's somehow presented with tongue in cheek, as if to say, "Now the real reason that God has blessed me is because I'm such a goody-goody." And he's dressed all in white, and you somehow. . . well, Job is just not in that characterization, as I understand it.

A second mistake was the grotesque distortion of the role and the personality of both God and Satan. God somehow comes across as a very arbitrary, capricious, tyrannical boss of the universe who pops the whip and is very anxious to be sure that he exacts the full sixteen ounces in his pound of flesh and is really, somehow, the master slave driver of man and history. On the other hand, Satan comes across as, really, man's friend and bosom buddy and inveterate ally. And were it not for his work, God would just be overbearing beyond measure.

I think he also missed it concerning the nature of faith. He tries to come to grips with it. I think he chews around on the edge of it, but obviously he misses, as I

---

[18] A reference to Dallas Cowboys running back Duane Thomas's criticism of head coach Tom Landry as a "plastic man."

understood it and as it came across in that particular presentation, he missed the deep devotion of a man who was, in his heart, committed to his God, and yet even in heartache and misery, could have confidence in the integrity of his operations in his life.

But then perhaps, supremely, I think he totally failed to grasp the nature of the reality of suffering. I do not know that author. I cannot say how much heartache or how much misery or how much suffering he has been exposed to in his own personal lifetime. He may have lived with it day in and day out. If he has, somehow, I'm convinced, he has not lived with it as a Christian, because he misses the heart of the purpose of the Book of Job. And he completely fails to lay hold on the mystery of suffering in the life of the innocent and the children of God.

In fact, there were two or three times in the course of some of this that I found myself gripping the sides of the chair. It was a rather unorthodox presentation and some of the people were out in the audience for part of the time, and sometimes they were up on the stage or up in the wings there, the little balcony that was on the side of the room. And it occurred to me that I really wouldn't be so much out of keeping with the whole staging of the thing if I just stood up in the middle of it and said my piece. I think Charles

Crane could sense what I was thinking because I saw him nervously looking for the nearest exit. You know, if I were to hit my feet, he'd bolt for the door immediately and say, "I never saw him before in my life."

And then I got to thinking, well, not only would it upset the performance, but how would it read in the morning paper. You know, "Baptist Pastor Upsets Dallas Theater Center Production." But I confess that there were several times when I wanted to just leap to my feet and blurt out, "No, you've missed the whole point of it! You don't understand Job, and you surely don't understand Job's God like Job did."

This past week I had the rather unique privilege to talk to two individuals who are, at this very moment as I speak now, experiencing the deepest, traumatic, horrible experience of their lives in the deepest water through which they have ever journeyed. Right now. And in the conversations with them, the questions that bubbled to the surface as we talked were almost questions as if they were lifted up verbatim out of the Book of Job.

There are the critics who say that Job was not actually a literal, historical personage, and that all that we have in the poem of the torturous dialogue between Job and his tormenters, or comforters as the case may be, is really the projection of some later point looking back into antiquity. But it really doesn't matter, as I see it, whether Job lived in ancient times or in more recent days. Whoever penned these words had to go through what Job went through.

And the person who does not understand that here is an experience dredged up from the very bottom of the pits of despair and despondency and suffering and heartache and misery and frustration, in my judgment just hasn't been in the very deep water yet, himself. Nobody could theoretically speculate and come to grips with a heart of suffering like the words of this book except the man who had been there himself. Shorn of his health, his possessions, his children. His friends come, I think really at the beginning, with a serious intention of bringing some words of comfort and consolation to him, but I suppose his compatriots of the book are the personification of the stinging comfort that many of us can bring.

Reminds me of a friend of mine who was pastor in Mississippi while we were students at seminary. He came in one day shaking his head. He said, "Man, I just can't believe it. I just can't believe it." You know, it's sort of like this figure in the television commercial— "I can't believe I ate the whole thing."[19]

"Well, what are you talking about?" I asked. He said, "Well, we have a member of our church who's sick down in a clinic here in New Orleans. And over the weekend we decided it would be very helpful and encouraging for this person if we'd bring a group of people down from the church in Mississippi to visit." And he said, "I swear to my soul, I'm telling you the truth. We walked into that room and the last man who walked in, he stopped just inside the door, and he looked around and he said, 'You know, this is the very room my cousin died in.' And the poor patient lying over there on the bed, he said, 'Well, I didn't come down here to die.' And his comforter said, 'My cousin didn't either.'"

Boy, with friends like that, who needs any enemies? And this is apparently what happened with Job's comforters. I really think they came with a deliberate intention to bring some encouragement and some solace to his aching heart. But before they realized it, perhaps, they had been reduced to something more akin to a pack of hungry hyenas, snarling around a rotting corpse out in the wilderness as they began to pick and hack and saw and chew away on Job.

---

[19] Alka-Seltzer award-winning TV ad from 1972.

But then in 19:25 and following, that great zoaring expression of faith, "For I know that my redeemer liveth." After all of these tortured questions and all of these frustrated reflections, Job, somehow even in his misery and the squalor of his illness and his despair, is able to say, "I know that my redeemer liveth, and that he shall stand at the latter day upon the earth." I'm not able to explain it, he said, but somehow my faith assures me that even "after my skin, worms destroy this body, yet in my flesh shall I see God, whom I shall see for myself, and mine eyes shall behold and not another."

As I read Job, while the questions still elude him, at least satisfactory answers to them, somehow the scalding bitterness that tinges his words in the earlier part of the book—I find them missing after the 19th Chapter. Still perplexed, still baffled, still hurt, still unhappy, still miserable, but somehow the bitterness has been eased.

And then in the closing chapters, Chapter 38, the whirlwind, or in Texas vocabulary, a tornado, comes racing in off of the plains. And as it whirls and as it swirls out of that blinding storm, there comes a voice from God himself. And Job is confronted by the God whose integrity and whose wisdom he has come to question and concerning whose purposes he has cause, ample cause, to doubt. And in an unforgettable conversation, Job comes to see the total inadequacy, not of God's purposes, but of himself. And he comes to experience, finally, an ultimate and an unusual victory.

But I think the victory of Job is not to be found in his miraculous recovery from illness. There are those who want to measure the power of God, and there are those who want to measure the dimension of a testimony, in terms of miraculous healing or in terms of some physical demonstration of divine power to be sure he is Jehovah, the God of all flesh. As I understand it, when any medicinal procedure is applied, it is still God who ultimately heals. Whenever physical health is restored, it is a result of God's handiwork. The physicians, at best, are simply attempting to cooperate with the powers of God in operation in a man's body and in a man's personality.

But the real victory is not in his healing, not in the restoration of family, not in the confidence, regained confidence, of his friends, not in the restoration of his possessions and his wealth and his position. Oh, no. I think Job's victory is to be found at some other levels. I find his victory, first of all, in terms of his submission. In the 38th Chapter, God comes to speak out of that torrent of wind to say, "Who is this that darkeneth counsel by words without knowledge?"

He's had a lot of his wisdom and a lot of his handiwork and a lot of his design and a lot of his blueprint and a lot of his purpose and a lot of his integrity called into question by the creatures that were result of his creative genius.

"Gird up now thy loins like a man, for I will demand of thee and answer thou me. Where wast thou when I laid the foundations of the earth?"

Now, he's speaking to Job, but even as his voice thunders in their presence, it reverberates in the ears of his companions. You've had all the answers. You have all of the little patent solutions, and you are able to pass judgment upon the wisdom of what I have done. Where were you when I really needed your counsel? Where were you when I designed the blueprint of creation? "Declare, if thou hast understanding. Who hath laid the measures thereof, if thou knowest? Or who hath stretched the line upon it? Whereupon are the foundations thereof fastened? Or who laid the corner stone thereof?"

What tantalizing questions, particularly in light of the latest photographs from outer space. There is that beautiful blue orb hanging, suspended out in blackness. Who put it there and who keeps it there?

"Hast thou entered into the springs of the sea? Or hast thou walked in the search of the depth? Have the gates of death been opened unto thee? Or hast thou seen the doors of the shadow of death? Hast thou perceived the breadth of the earth? Declare if thou knowest it all. Where is the way where light dwelleth? And as for darkness, where is the place thereof?"

Well, that was a great question. When the lights turn off, where does it go? You have all the answers. You dare to question my handiwork in your life. If you've got the answers, then let's deal with some of the more complicated dilemmas of my handiwork.

"Who hath divided a watercourse for the overflowing of waters, or a way for the lightning of thunder, to cause it to rain on the earth, where no man is; on the wilderness, wherein there is no man? To satisfy the desolate and waste ground, and to cause the bud of the tender herb to spring forth? Hath the rain a father? Or who hath begotten the drops of dew?"

As these questions are flashed on the screen of his attention, Job begins to realize that, while he still has not had the answer concerning his own personal problem of suffering, if God knows the answers to questions like that, upon what basis can I dare impugn his mercy or his integrity? When I have the wisdom to grasp creation's mysteries, then, and only then, may I legitimately question his judgment.

God also brings to bear his awesome power. As Job attempts to field those questions and to respond to them, the Lord presses the issue. "Then the Lord answered Job out of the whirlwind and said, 'Gird up now thy loins like a man. I will demand of thee and declare thou to me. Wilt thou also disannul my judgment? Wilt thou condemn me, that thou mayest be righteous? Hast thou an arm like God? Or canst thou thunder with a voice like him?

"Deck thyself now with majesty and excellency, and array thyself with glory and beauty. Cast abroad the rage of thy wrath, and behold every one that is proud, and abase him. Look on every one that is proud and bring him low, and tread down the wicked in their place. Hide them in the dust together and bind their faces in secret."

When you have that kind of power, and when you are in that position of sovereignty in the affairs of history and flesh, "Then will I also confess unto thee that thine own right hand can save thee." When I have the power to rule the universe as does my God, then and then only will I be in a position to understand the verities of his conduct.

Paul was dealing with that same question when he

said, "O, the depth of the riches both of the wisdom and knowledge of God! How unsearchable are his judgments, and his ways past finding out. For who hath known the mind of the Lord, or who hath been his counsellor?"— quoting from Isaiah, then turning to Job— "Or who hath first given to him, and it shall be recompensed unto him again? For of him, and through him, and to him, are all things, to whom be the glory forever."

And so, Job simply said, "I don't have the answers, but I realize that my God has wisdom and power that baffle and simply overwhelm me. And I know he is gracious and merciful. I cannot discern the pattern of his purpose in what has taken place in my life. I cannot mark out the symmetry of his design in my calamity, but I know his will and purpose are good."

God is like an artist who has only a selected number of paints to use. The blues, the blacks, the yellows, and the reds—the reds of suffering, the reds of heartache, the reds of illness, the reds of death—and as he paints his tapestry of history, all of the colors and all of the hues must be used. Not by his choice, but by man's choice. When we selected to rebel and to disobey, we put the red paint on the palette, and he must use it because man's choice to rebel, to disobey, to be the renegade of the universe means that he must be separated from God. He must die. And in order to die, there must be suffering, sickness, and death. So, God simply takes these selected colors, the blues of his mercy, the blacks of his tenderness, the yellows of his forgiveness, and the reds—the reds. He must use all of them, but the picture he paints ultimately is a picture of love and tenderness.

And it is highlighted by the red hues in the painting.

Job came to submit to his God. I find his victory in terms of forgiveness. Not God's forgiveness, but Job's forgiveness toward his friends. Job prayed for them despite the hurting. You know, they really had lacerated his wounds. They came to bathe his sores with acid. Just listen to some of the statements of his companions. Here comes, in the 11th Chapter, for example, his friend Zophar. "Know thou, therefore," in his pontifical pronouncement, "that God exacteth of thee less than thine iniquity deserveth."

Job, he's tapping you, right? If you got what you really deserve, man you sure would suffer. Old Zophar, he's all heart.

Then here comes Eliphaz to bring some more tenderness to the scene. Said he, to his companion of the years, Job, "For thy mouth uttereth thine iniquity, and thou choosest the tongue of the crafty."

Now, isn't that amazing? None of them are able really to pinpoint with any precision exactly what they thought Job had done, and so now they're just winging it. They're just speculating. He continues, "For the congregation of hypocrites shall be desolate, and fire shall consume the tabernacles of bribery." He's accusing his intimate friend Job of some flagrant hypocrisy. Then, as if to add the supreme touch to it, he goes on to make just a sweeping blanket accusation. He, the same Eliphaz, said, "Is not thy wickedness great? And thine iniquities infinite?"

Why you're the most reprobate, nasty, dirty, old man I ever saw. I don't know exactly what you've done, but it surely must be something awful. "For thou hast taken a pledge from thy brother for nought and stripped the naked of their clothing. Thou hast not given water to the weary to drink, and thou hast withholden bread from the hungry. . . . Thou hast sent widows away empty, and the arms of the fatherless have been broken."

Boy, if you're not a scoundrel.

But praise God, after all of these bitter accusations based on nothing less than shadowy prophecy, Job is able to pray for their forgiveness. And you can't pray for the Lord to forgive somebody you haven't forgiven first. You just can't do that.

You know, this dilemma really raises two or three interesting considerations. Wouldn't it be awful to be in Job's position, really in your heart to be right, not to have compromised your integrity or your commitment, and yet to be misunderstood by all of your friends? There are those of us who find ourselves in this kind of circumstance now and again, and it's extremely bewildering and mystifying. There are times, I'm sure, when we're tempted to believe that somehow God cannot understand what it would be like to be misunderstood, even to be persecuted by friends.

That reminds me of the words in Zechariah, in his prophetic vision, when he came to say, "And one shall say unto him, 'What are these wounds in thine hands?' Then he shall answer, 'Those with which I was wounded in the house of my friends.'" Now, if you think you are hurt when your friends misunderstand you and crucify you mercilessly, why don't you talk to Jesus about it? You understand?

But even worse than that, I'm persuaded, would be to compromise your integrity and violate the friends' confidence and trust behind the facade and be thought right, but on the inside, be out of fellowship with God. That's even worse. But I believe Job was able not only to pray for them despite the hurt, I think he was able to forgive and to forget. Now that's the hard part. That's the real difficult part. Every once in a while, you might say, "Well, I can forgive him, but I sure can't forget it." You know, when I hear that phrase in an apology, I'm persuaded they haven't forgiven him.

Now, we can't just blot out memories of injustices. We cannot simply wipe our memory slate clean, to be sure, and yet the essence of forgiveness is the ability not to hold that shadow in your thinking as you approach someone. To err is human, to forgive is divine. Let's remember the Lord's Prayer. "Forgive us our trespasses as we forgive those who trespass against us."

But then very quickly, and here's the real crux of the victory as I see it. It's not just his submission, not just his capability to forgive those who had so severely abused him in his hour of greatest need. His victory is to be found in his faithfulness to his God. The Lord said, "my servant Job, him will I accept."

Obviously, Job had not abandoned his basic integrity. This, of course, goes back to that question that the arch accuser first posed in that heavenly council. When the Lord called attention to the integrity of Job, Satan answered by saying, "Doth Job fear God for nought? Take away your blessing and he will curse you to your face." The Lord permitted the first wave of calamity to overtake him. Job responded by saying, "Naked came I out of my mother's womb. Naked shall I return thither. The Lord gave, and the Lord hath taken away. Blessed be the name of the Lord." And "in all this, Job sinned not nor charged God foolishly."

Then, even as his own body raged and tormented in pain and tantalizing irritation, in all this he was obedient. "Shall we receive good at the hand of God, and shall we not receive evil? And in all this did not Job sin with his lips."

The great victory was in his demonstration to Satan, to his God, to his friends, and to the spectators of the centuries who have come to watch the suffering of Job in the coliseum of his ancient misery, to demonstrate that he was not an opportunist, that he was committed to his God, and that, however deep the waters through which he might pass, his love and his commitment would not be compromised.

I've shared this before, and I repeat it. As I lay immobilized from the waist down in the fourth floor over at Baylor Hospital, almost day and night I wrestled with a memory from while I was a student at the university. A friend of mine came to me one day and said, "You know, I've been reading in Job . . ." And then he rehearsed that heavenly council dialogue between God and Satan. Then he said, "How would you feel if, right now, you knew that Satan was appearing before the presence of God again, and the Lord was saying, 'Have you considered my servant Corky Farris? He is just and upright and he really loves me, and he's really committed to me,' and Satan were to say to him, 'He just serves you because you bless him. Take away your blessings and he'll curse you to your face.'"

I wrestled with that. Listen to me carefully. Job's victory was not in the recovery of his health and the restoration of his possessions. Job's real victory was that, even in his illness and even in his loneliness and even in his privation and even in his misery and even in his heartache, his commitment to his Lord was not for sale. And I stand here tonight to tell you I am convinced the victory, if I had any part of it, in my own personal experience is not that I am able to walk, even with the assistance of a cane. But the miracle, the wonder, the victory, so far as I am concerned, is in my effort to prove that Satan is a liar.

You see, doctors can heal, miracle drugs can restore, but I don't know any greater demonstration of God's power and adequacy than that to be found in the suffering of his children who are able to endure the deepest hurt and heartache with a pain that gives them a peace passing all understanding. Wouldn't it be strange if only Christian people were exempt from suffering and illness and death? Wouldn't that be strange?

And wouldn't Satan have a heyday to say to God that the only reason they turn to you is because you bless them at a material and a physical level? I hope God can say in my life, and I hope he can say in yours, "No, he serves me and he's faithful to me because, deep down in his heart, he really does love me, and he'll follow me the last step of the way."

Now, I want to personalize that mocking accusation of Satan. "Does Job fear God for nought?" What if it were not Job's name in that question and what if it were not the preacher's name in that question? What if it were your name? Do you serve God for nought? Do you serve God for nothing? Take away your blessing and he'll curse you to your face. Would Satan ever be right? Are you just in this for what you can get out of it? Are you in some monstrous barter game with God trading a predetermined number of hours a week at a church house in order to buy some insurance and some protection?

Surely not. Surely not.

Transitional Narrative: *"I go a fishing"*[20]

Corky loved to fish, something he tried to pass on to his sons, but it never really took for me like it did for my brother Steve. Oh, sure, I loved spending time with him, but I hated getting up before daylight to go (because apparently largemouth bass were on a schedule) and then sitting in a boat all day, sometimes in cold or rainy weather (because apparently largemouth bass are inclement weather feeders), often with little or nothing to show for our efforts at the end of the day. Even in his later years, after the plane crash that forced him to walk with a cane for the rest of his life, fishing was Corky's favorite pastime. When I think of him and his love for fishing, three particular fishing trips stand out.

The first involved a five-pound bass that I hooked, and wrestled to the boat, on a small, private lake in east Texas. I remember that day as being cold and a bit rainy, so maybe there really was something to this inclement-weather-feeding thing. I was probably ten or eleven at the time. I have a picture of me holding the fish in our backyard after we got home, with Steve staring down its gullet. This is one of my wife's favorite pictures. I think it

---

[20] "Simon Peter saith unto them, I go a fishing." John 21:3a. This story is relevant to an illustration in the sermon that follows.

allows her to see what my potential looked like even as a kid.

Or maybe not.

The second trip was also to a small, private lake in east Texas, and it involved one of the more memorable moments of my childhood, again when I was about ten or eleven. Corky had a small, flat-bottom fishing boat with an Evinrude motor that allowed us to get to all the "good spots" (because apparently largemouth bass are unable to escape boats with motors—except ours). We had found one of those "good spots," and I was about to hook the largest catch of my life.

I was sitting at the front of the boat, while Corky sat at the rear, so he could man the motor. I don't remember what he was using as a lure, but I was fishing with a purple worm (because apparently largemouth bass are color-blind), trailing it along the bottom of the lake (because apparently largemouth bass lurk there). My casting form was inelegant, at best, and on one cast (instant replay would likely have revealed it to have been accomplished sidearm), I hooked Corky in the ear.

The barb of the hook seated itself deep in the fleshy part of his earlobe, so that he was unable to extricate it. That meant a trip to the emergency room of a small hospital in a nearby town was in order because, not only was he concerned about removing the hook, but he also figured he would need a tetanus shot. Using a pair of clippers, he cut the worm in two, leaving about two or three inches dangling from his ear like a punk rocker's earring (though nobody knew what punk rock was back then), and we motored back to shore and uploaded the boat to its trailer. Then we drove to the hospital, which was surprisingly busy. There was no doctor on duty in the ER, though; just one "on call."

A nurse gave Corky the doctor's home number, and he went to a nearby phone to make the call, oblivious to the stares and giggles from others in the ER. I was not oblivious, though; I was mortified, because I was clearly the culprit in this two-man fishing team. (Obviously, only an idiot would have done that to his father.)

I listened in on Corky's side of the conversation as he explained his dilemma, and the doctor advised that he would arrive shortly. I can only infer from what was said next that the doctor had asked how he would recognize us, because Corky responded, "I'll be the only one with a purple worm in his ear."

The third trip was actually the last fishing trip I ever took with Corky. It was in late summer of 1980, shortly before I headed to Texas Tech to start law school and Steve headed to Ouachita Baptist University in Arkansas for football two-a-days. Thinking it might be a final "hurrah" for the three Farris men, Corky took us to Bell River in Louisiana, where he first fell in love with fishing in the mid-1950s while pastoring Goodwood Baptist Church in Baton Rouge. We stayed at a cabin on the river for the better part of a week and fished, arising before sun-up each day. Or at least Corky and Steve arose before sun-up; I opted to miss the early morning runs and join them when they came back for a mid-morning break.

We didn't catch much, but we had fun, though I think Steve and I had the most fun. Since Corky was a serious fisherman, we probably drove him crazy with our clowning around. We seemed to spend more time fishing for "tree bass" (getting hung up in the branches of low hanging trees along the shoreline) than actually getting our lines wet. I have a *Lord of the Flies* picture of Steve and me holding up a prize catch, a tiny fish about five or six inches long, which pretty much explains why Corky later told my sister that he would never again, on purpose, get the two of us together in the same place at the same time.

SERMON: *Whys and Wherefores of Suffering*

Tonight, at last, at long last, we will conclude our series of messages from Job, but I trust we will not tuck Job away to rest and think of his book no longer. I anticipate that, while we may not reflect on the writings of the Book of Job with great frequency, when the time comes that you need to think about it, I'm persuaded that you will need the lessons from the Book of Job as desperately and as earnestly as any lessons anywhere in God's word. Sooner or later, all of us will need to call upon them.

"But he knoweth the way that I take: when he hath tried me, I shall come forth as gold."

We have attempted to deal with the rhyme and reason for suffering and heartache in the life of the Christian. We observed that, inasmuch as disappointment and pain are unavoidable, ultimately, as a part of human experience, and that God in his mercies will let these things plague our lives, he's able to use even these bitter experiences to do a gracious work of his love. Just by way of quick review, we observed that suffering in the heart of the Christian is a way by which God shows the adequacy of his grace, in fact rather than theory. We also observed that he is able, thereby, in our lives to demonstrate the true nature and character of devotion and commitment. There is no real commitment except in the face of sacrifice.

We also notice that it is through this means that he qualifies us to minister to others. One of the most expensive parts of the Christian's education and growth process is to purchase, with his own tears, the right to minister to others in their grief and in their need. Then we also attempted to assert the fact that, in our suffering, there is always a hidden blessing and sometimes a very special blessing that can occur only in the context of our particular or individual disappointment or calamity.

I would like to go back and pick up at that juncture, and I would like to process it on to its completion. Then I would like to make just one or two observations, as limited as they are from my own experience, about how to cope with suffering when it does come.

Another reason or another purpose or another design in permitting us to experience pain and suffering is the fact that this gives an opportunity for us to have a personal and an intimate fellowship with the Lord that we might never have otherwise. Now, this is somewhat mystifying. I cannot quite explain it, but I know it to be a fact, that in our grief or in our suffering, our deep disappointment, the mists that cloud the face of our Lord somehow evaporate. And I'm persuaded that we are more conscious of his presence in times such as this than at any other moment.

In the harried press of day-to-day humdrum responsibilities and routine, we have so little time just to be with him, just to fellowship with him, just to commune with him. We're too busy. But then when we are immobile, when we're stretched out on the bed, the only way we can look is up. When the secondary matters of life are diluted by the intensity of pain, then we come to see the Lord. And somehow in that crucible, there is a sweetness of fellowship with him that we can never know at any other level of our experience.

Then I observed that he uses these events and these periods of life to grant a fresh understanding and appreciation of his Word. I do not know how you study your Bible. There are times when I study a given book. There are other periods when I may study a given subject. Now and again, in random devotional reading, I may underline some verses, but it is in the valley of travail that the Word somehow takes on a fresh and a distinctive glow, and that the verses that I underline in my moments of discouragement or in my moments of deep sadness or my periods of heartache, these verses somehow become more precious to me than they've ever been before.

In later moments of loneliness, I go back and just leaf through my Bible and—You know, I have some verses in some old Bibles that are too worn and too disintegrated in their condition for me, really, to be able to use them with a great deal of frequency. But I just somehow cannot quite bring myself to throw them away or to give them away because there are some verses, particularly in the old Bible that stays on the desk at the house, that have been marked, not with a red pencil altogether, but there are some verses that have been marked with some rather bitter tears. But those verses that bless my heart in a midnight hour mean something to me beyond measure. The Word comes alive, takes on a fresh hue and a deeper import in our sadness and in our heartache as we turn to it.

But I think Job came really to the crux of the matter when he said, "When he hath tried me, I shall come forth as gold." There is something about the discipline and the chastisement of suffering that causes us to grow and to develop and to mature that no other process I know about can quite bring to pass in our experience.

I read some time a long while ago about a man who was watching a fledgling butterfly trying to break out of its cocoon. It was struggling and it was crashing in that fragile little prison that encased it. And when he saw the extreme difficulty, he wanted to be helpful and so he very carefully and very tenderly took that cocoon and broke it apart. Ripped it asunder so that the butterfly could emerge. But only then did he realize what a tragic mistake he'd made, because the butterfly could not fly. Those very fragile little structures in the membrane-like substance of the wings were flexible and so they were not strong and rigid. Then he recognized that it was through the struggle of extricating itself from that prison that gave the little insect the strength with which to fly.

Now, there's a deep lesson about suffering in that because, as we struggle, as we agonize, as we thrash in the throes of our grief and our sorrow, if we are willing to let God develop and mature us, there will be a growth process take place in our lives. And we'll come out of it stronger than we were when we went into it. There will be a greater reservoir of determination. There will be a stronger sinew of commitment. There will be more firm muscles of commitment than we've ever had before if we will let him develop us, even through our suffering.

There's something else that the Lord does with our pain and our grief. And this, too, baffles me. Quite honestly, it eludes me. I don't understand how it could be.

I'm not quite able to grasp why, but I'm convinced that it's so. Our suffering and our travails stimulate and deepen our love for the Lord. I can't explain that. I don't understand that, but it works like that. Not in some twisted, sickly, distorted, sadistic type of way, but in a very warm and very fulfilling, in a very positive way. Somehow suffering and heartache, if we'll let it, will deepen our love for the Lord.

Have you ever been provoked and stimulated just to tell the Lord how much you love him? Have you? Have you ever just wanted to tell Jesus how much you love him? I confess that impulse is not nearly as frequent as it ought to be in my own heart. But I remember during those days of painful and excruciatingly slow convalescence, after coming out of the hospital, for quite a long period of time, I slept on a mattress that we placed on the floor. And it seemed to me that progress was so slow. Here I was the responsible breadwinner for my family, and despite the limited use of my limbs, the prospect of my being able to take care of them was pretty remote and pretty dismal. And as I would get down on that mattress and take that metal brace off my back—Oh my!

In the midnight, those were hours of an eternal discouragement. But one night, in the very pit of that experience—I don't understand this—but suddenly I felt a stirring of love deep down in the core of my heart for Jesus that I've never felt before. And even in the tears, there was a sweetness of loving him that I did not know I could ever taste or understand. It is in this kind of a crucible that we come to love Jesus with an intensity we've never known before. Strange as it may seem.

But how do we come to grips and how can we cope with the problem of our tragedies and our suffering? May I just make three or four very brief observations? I think, first of all, we need to recognize the inevitability of suffering of some kind. It's going to come sooner or later. I suppose, in the optimism of youth, we are quick to believe that tragedy may strike in other lives, but it'll never come close to us. There seems to be an eternal optimism in our attitude and in our perspective. Then when tragedy or calamity strikes, we're baffled and we're mystified, as if some strange, unique, far out, mysterious thing were taking place.

Oh, suffering will catch up with all of us. If your number hasn't come up yet, just hang on. The brass ring'll come around. After a while, tragedy will strike. Suffering, disappointment, heartache. It's inevitable. It's unavoidable. Sooner or later. It's not a question of whether, it's just a question of when. And it seems to me that we forfeit one of the real possible areas of victory if, when it does come, we are overwhelmed as if we thought we were being penalized. As if we were under the delusion that it would never take place and that somehow God has been unfair and unjust. This causes us to miss one of the vital possibilities of doing something really worthwhile with the opportunities in the events of life. We cannot decree, nor can we determine, what happens or when it comes, but we can decide how we are going to face it and how we're going to beat it. And isn't it sad that, when we have that one golden opportunity for greatness of character, we blow the whole thing by wanting to complain to God about the fact that suffering came our way.

Second thing. I think it can reinforce us against that hour to consider the transitory nature of suffering. Now, at this point, it reminds me of the story I heard. Maybe I've shared it with you, I don't know, about some people who were asking others to give their favorite scripture verse, and the old Black preacher said, "Well, my favorite verse is, 'And it came to pass.'" The other people in the group were mystified. "Why is that your favorite verse? We don't quite understand." And he said, "I'm just so glad it didn't come to stay."

I've been there. I know what he is talking about.

"And it came to pass."

We could let the drag of our disappointment pull us down, like some cursed beast of prey clutching at the jugular vein of our hope and aspiration, and we could plunge into the dusk of despair and discouragement. But remember, it's not always to be this way. I never stand at the head of a casket that I don't look at the flowers, the grief-stricken family, the evidence of death, and think to myself, "Praise God, one of these days I'll never preach another funeral sermon; it'll all be over." One of these days. One of these days. There may be grief and there may be bitter tears, but it's only temporary. One of these days, we shall be permanently and totally liberated and emancipated from the valley of shadows.

Praise God.

Sometimes I see a daddy out there playing pass football with his boys. Man, I'd love to do that. But that's all right. One of these days, on the courthouse steps of heaven, I'm going to run back and forth and pass a heavenly football with my boys. There may be a dark night, but there will be a dawn one of these days.

Something else I think can help. Let's emphasize the positive. Let's take everything we got coming. You know, some people, you ask them how they're doing today and twenty minutes later you wish you hadn't asked. I run on to people who have problems, and they tell me about all the difficulty. People who have good health, people who have two good legs, people who have a wonderful home, children, and all they can see is the problems in life. Well, there are problems in anybody's life, but let's don't let that beat us to our knees. Let's look at the things that are good, and let's concentrate on the things that we can do.

As I have already intimated, there are times when I have just a twinge of remorse about my own condition. But, you know, I try not to think about the things I can't do. Maybe I can't throw the football around, but I can fish. Some of y'all happen to know about that. I can fish just as good now as I ever could. I may not catch as many, but I can fish as good as I ever did, you know? So why should I sit around and mope and mourn over what I can't do until I don't get in the boat and go fishing? You know, some people do that.

I think we need to take all of the opportunity out of our situation and all the positive that we can get. I remember one of the doctors came into my room when I was about to begin therapy and, I don't know whether this is standard procedure or not, but that doctor came into the room, said, "Now, Mr. Farris, I do not know what the possibilities of your recovery are. But I do say this: ninety percent of it will be up to you."

I guess it sounded a little bit braggadocious, but I just went ahead and said it 'cause I really meant it. I said, "Well, I promise you one thing, I'm gonna get everything I got coming. I'm gonna fight for it."

I think we ought to take everything we got coming. Man, let's get all the goody we can. And then when we can't go a step longer, then let's not lament what we cannot do, but let's concentrate on the victories we've already achieved.

Something else I've found. Let's maintain a sense of humor. You know, we're fast becoming a neurotic society until we can no longer laugh at ourselves. Isn't that sad? Isn't that sad? We ought to be able to laugh at our weaknesses, and we ought to be able to see the humor in even our deepest of tragedies.

Following the plane crash, I lost about twenty-four pounds and when I got out, boy, I looked pretty slim compared to what I'd been. Somebody commented on it, and I said, "Yeah, I've got a special crash diet that takes weight off just like that." They thought I was being a little bit ghoulish, but man, you know, it's either laugh or cry. If that's the case, let's laugh. Let somebody else cry. Might as well go ahead and make a joke of it. Man, let's laugh. Let's have a good time. We can sit around and be sensitive about all of our problems and all of our difficulties until everybody's jumpy and uptight, and they're afraid to even use the word "cane" for fear that I'll think you're trying to spell out cripple, you know, in some kind of sign language or something like that. Man, let's just go ahead and take it and let's not be uptight and sensitive about it.

Then something else that I think helps: Let's look for the manna. You know, sometimes that hidden blessing is gonna be tucked away pretty tightly. It may not bubble to the surface at the very outset. We may have to sort of dig around, scrounge around, and look for it. I'm not talking about some blind, childish, sentimental Pollyannaism. But in every experience, if we'll look for it, there will be the special blessing of God in the manner that he provides to give us strength.

Then I think it helps to understand that whatever our limitation, we are not all alone. At a pastor's conference out in California, some four years ago now, a fella came up to me on crutches. Very difficult for him to walk. I do not know the nature of his handicap, but he had a very limited ability to talk. But as to the very point that I'm trying to illustrate, emphasizing the positive, despite his difficulty in talking, even in English, his companions indicated to me that he was one of the most eloquent preachers in Spanish in California. Now he's not Spanish; he's Anglo. And despite his limited capabilities of talking in English, he had mastered the Spanish language.

But I ran into him out away from one of the meetings on a given afternoon, and as he came up to me in his laborious fashion, he said, "You know, you're being here this week has been a real blessing to me." He said, "There are times when I become so discouraged that I'm tempted to just give up and quit. With my limitations, it's so difficult for me to try to minister and to serve in the Lord's name. But you're being here with your handicap has given me a source of encouragement."

Man, I want you to know that's the manna I'm talking about. At that particular moment, I wouldn't have traded this cane not only for two good legs, I wouldn't have traded it for two good legs and five million dollars. Man, if it could buy a little encouragement for that old boy, that's a pretty cheap price. And I said to him something I really think is so. I said, "Well, thank you, dear brother. But let me tell you what. I'm convinced that we all have our handicaps. Some of them are more obvious than others, and sometimes the handicaps you can't see are more difficult to overcome than the ones you can see. And we are all serving Jesus with our limitations." I think that's so.

But there's one other thing. Satan accused Job of serving the Lord as a cheap opportunist. By his insinuation, "Doth Job fear God for nought," he was saying he just engaged in a trade-out. He doesn't really love you and he's not truly committed to you. You take away the goodies of his life, and he'll renounce you and he'll curse you to your face.

I think the greatest challenge that any Christian will ever confront is to find the rug pulled out from under him, his world caving in on top, the bottom dropping out, and facing the challenge of proving that Satan is a liar and that we love Jesus, come hell or high water.

But this and I'm through with the Book of Job. "When he hath tried me, I shall come forth as gold." That's the way it's translated in the King James. But we might miss what I think is a real, real spiritual gem here. Real interesting. As I studied the verse, looked at the comments and the books about Job, nobody seemed to be particularly intrigued with the language. But what that verse literally says is, "He knows the way with me." And the verb "to know" here is a verb that expresses intimate, personal, spiritual knowledge. He knows personally the way with me, and I believe ultimately it is this that gives us strength.

(singing) *Jesus will walk with me down through*
the valley,
Jesus will walk with me over the plain;
When in the shadow or when in the sunshine,
If He goes with me, I shall not complain.

Jesus will walk with me in life's fair morning,
And when the shadows of evening must come;
Living or dying, He will not forsake me.
Jesus will walk with me all the way home.

Jesus will walk with me, He will talk with me;
He will walk with me;
In joy or in sorrow, today and tomorrow,
I know He will walk with me.

Dr. T. V. "Corky" Farris

Narrative: *In Memory of Dr. T.V. Farris*[21]

He walked with an unsteady gait, supported by a cane, covering up his tracks as he went. Surgical scars marked his body, mute testimony to physical suffering. His nose arced across his face, bent precariously by time and circumstance, both a badge of honor and of his own self-deprecating humor. His hair, once a shock of thick, wavy black, now combed back white from his brow and temples, adding an aura of distinction. A crooked smile graced his lips; a twinkle lit his eyes, exuding a warmth, grace, and gentleness unmatched.

He was my father. I admired him above all others. I couldn't, and still can't, speak of him without being overwhelmed with pride. He was intellect mixed with humor, seasoned by humility, tempered with sadness, surrounded by integrity, and steeped in love. I loved him with all my heart. And I miss him deeply.

I approached his casket at the funeral home with great apprehension. I think that of all the things associated with his funeral, I dreaded this the most. Maybe, in the back of my mind, I thought that if I never saw his body,

---

[21] After Corky passed away on December 14, 1993, I wrote this tribute to him, which was published in *The Messenger*, the publication of Mid-America Baptist Theological Seminary, in the spring of 1994.

then he wouldn't really be gone. But when I gazed on his body, cold and lifeless, I realized with a startling reality that I saw only a shell. The eyes were closed, their twinkle gone. The lips were solemn, their smile erased. I've heard for years that the soul and the spirit make the person and not the body, but I guess that's a lesson you have to learn for yourself. The twinkle, the smile, the warmth, the love—they came from within, not merely from flesh and bone. At the funeral home, that became real for me. Daddy wasn't in the casket; he was with the Lord. He didn't die with the body, but he lives on in the lives and memories of those whom he touched.

I'll never forget talking to the steady stream of visitors, many of whom I had never met before, as they told me of my dad. Each one had a story to tell, separate and distinct. Something funny, something poignant, something inspiring. Each story brought a smile, or a tear, or perhaps a laugh. But a common theme ran through them all—he had touched lives. He had comforted, cheered, ministered, counseled, and witnessed. He had cared, and he had loved. And everybody he touched loved him back. What a tribute! What a legacy!

What I had always known began to reinforce itself—how blessed I was to have been his son, to have received his counsel, his instruction, his discipline, and his love. How blessed to have had a little of him planted in me, hopefully to grow and to prosper.

I remembered my own stories I have to tell about him—some funny, some poignant, and some inspirational. Like the time we went fishing and I managed to hook him in the ear with a purple worm. The hook had not gone all the way through his earlobe, so we had to visit the emergency room to have it removed. He had to phone the on-call doctor at home. I'll never forget his answer when the doctor asked how he'd recognize him when he arrived. "I'll be the only one with a purple worm in his ear," he said with a chuckle.

I remember how he recounted his struggles as my mother suffered with a malignancy. He told me how his prayers underwent an evolution. They started as prayers for her healing, then changed to prayers simply that her pain be eased. Finally, he placed the entire matter in God's hands and told the Lord that whatever He did was okay by him. God gave him peace. That's why, when God took her home, he could write, "It is at this point that the message of the Gospel and the hope of eternity take on a new and sweeter meaning. To be perfectly honest, I seem to have more investment on the other side than here. Won't it be a glorious day when we can be reunited with those we love?"

I remember his determination to walk again after the plane crash in the Big Thicket in east Texas. Afterwards, the doctors told him that he'd never do it. But he did! I remember as a boy helping him with his daily exercises as he rehabilitated his body. He hurt and he perspired, but he never complained—and the braces and crutches gave way to a simple cane.

I remember weekend preaching trips with him as we drove around Texas. On Sunday, I would sit and listen to his sermons, captivated as a boy, as he shared the Gospel. I remember fishing trips and going to movies. I remember bad jokes and corny stories. I remember his pet expressions, like, "That's where the water hits the wheel" or "Now, the beauty of this is . . ." or the inevitable nearing the end of a sermon: "Now this and I'm through."

In his last years, I could see his body, wracked with pain from the crash, wearing down, his step growing more unsteady. He seemed tired, but he still kept on the go. There was much left that he wanted to do. I welcomed his every visit to our home, where he talked about his unfinished work. I can still see him sitting on the end of our couch, going on and on about his computers, his writings, his plans, and his goals. So much of that went right past me. Susan and I used to laugh at how he always put on his glasses to eat. That *eatin'* was serious *bidness*.

Every time he came to visit, and I helped unload his car, I was reminded of others who visited our home when I was a boy. Daddy never wanted the visitor to carry his own luggage. He always voiced his concern by saying, "Here, let Mike get that." He was always free with my labor. I never really minded, though. I would have moved mountains, stone by stone, for him.

I remember how proud he was of us when we were in school. He'd come to football games or school productions, just beaming with a father's pride. Waving his cane in the air was his way of showing support. It always embarrassed us, and we'd laugh about it afterward. I'd give anything to see that cane waved just one more time or to have him sit in my home and go on and on, again, about his computers.

My memories of him are dear. I remember much laughter, a few tears, and a lot of love. I remember gentleness, kindness, and caring. I also remember a touch of discipline every now and then, but that's not bad. It helped make me what I am today.

When I come to the end of my road, I can only hope that people will remember me as one who cared, one who loved, and one who touched lives. That's how they remember Daddy. That's why I can join with the psalmist in saying, "Precious in the sight of the LORD is the death of his saints." I can almost hear as God greeted him in Heaven on December 14, 1993: "Well done, thou good and faithful servant."

APPENDIX

Photographs and Documents

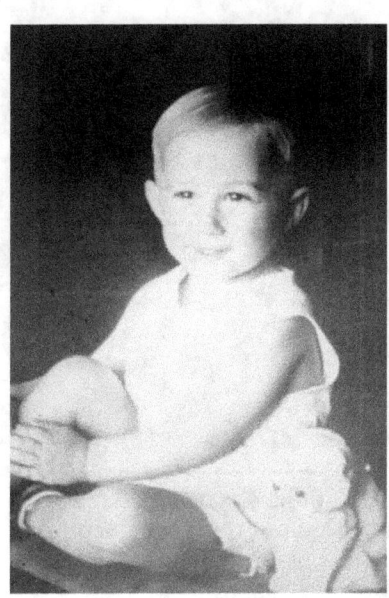

Theron Vernelle Farris was born in Fort Worth, Texas, on July 4, 1927

He detested his name. Fortunately, at an early age, someone gave him a nickname "Corky"– though no one is sure who, when, or why– which he went by for the rest of his life.

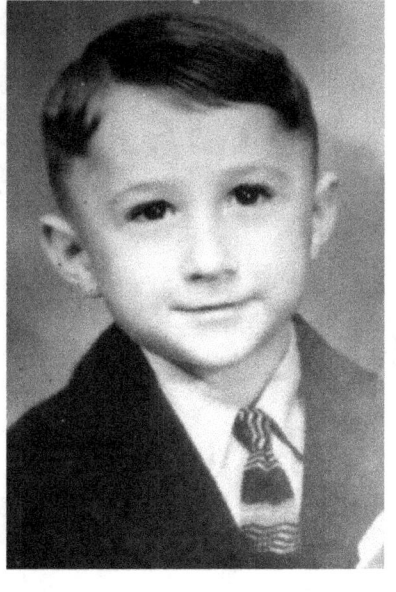

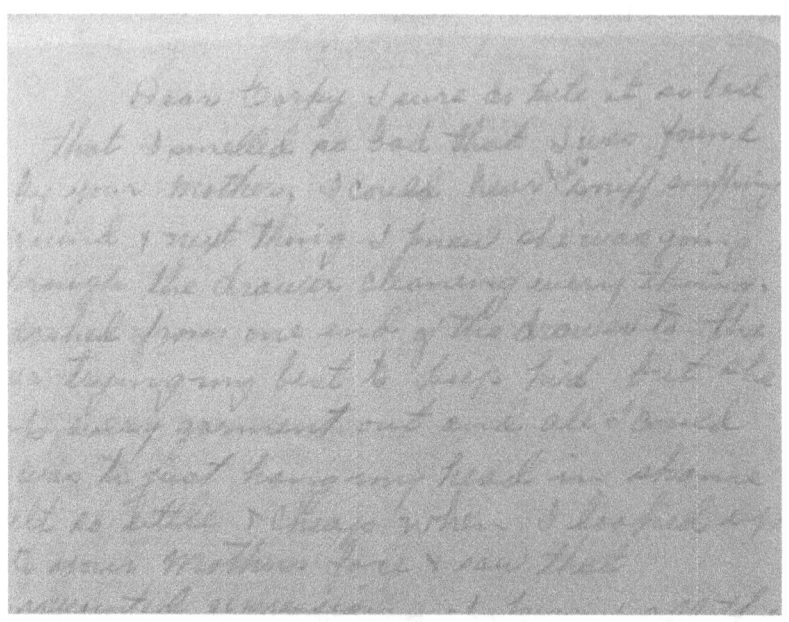

By his own admission, Corky adopted some bad habits early. One of those was smoking a pipe -- which his mother found hidden in a drawer. She took it and replaced it with a letter, ostensibly written by the pipe, chastising him.

He played football at Fort Worth's Polytechnic "Poly" High School, earning honorable mention all-district honors.

During a time of teenage rebellion against God, Corky (front left) began singing in a men's quartet at Polytechnic Baptist Church in Fort Worth under the direction of Dallas Alford (center).

While singing in the quartet, he met and fell in love with Juanita Peacock (far left).

Corky joined the Army at the end of World War II and served in Japan as part of the post-war occupation by the US military.

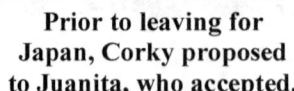

Prior to leaving for Japan, Corky proposed to Juanita, who accepted.

They were married on June 27, 1947.

While a student at Baylor University, Corky participated in several mission trips to Japan. In this photo, he is front row, center, of a group of Texas college students on one of those trips.

While a student at New Orleans Baptist Theological Seminary, daughter Darlyne was born, and two years later, son Mike.

In 1958, the Farris family prepared to travel to Japan where Corky and Juanita would serve as missionaries.

The family traveled aboard the *SS President Wilson* to their new place of service in Tokyo.

(Left) Steve was born in Kyoto, Japan, in 1960, bringing the family to five. (Right) Corky initially preached with an interpreter, but after completing language school in Tokyo, he was able to preach in Japanese.

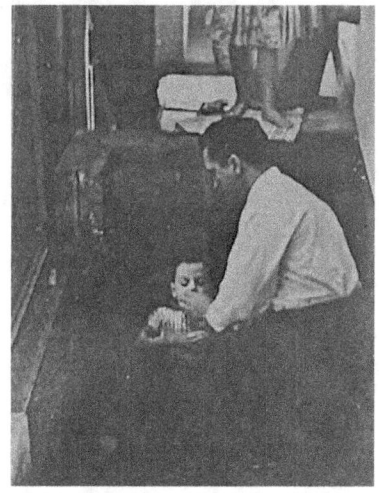

In addition to preaching, Corky baptized new believers (left), including son Mike (right).

Corky, Juanita, and family spent five years in Japan before Corky accepted a position as an associate in the Evangelism Division of the Baptist General Convention of Texas.

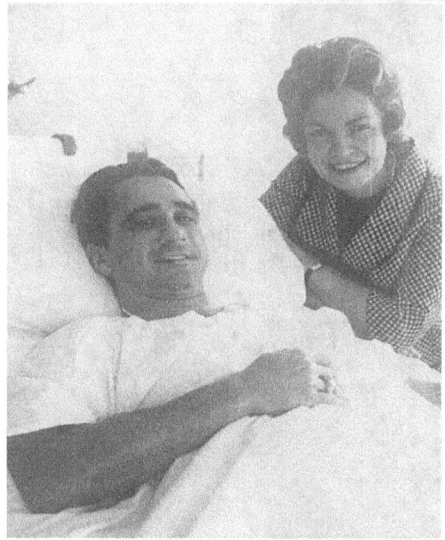

On January 12, 1965, Corky and pilot Len Rogers were in a plane crash in the Big Thicket region of southeast Texas. The pilot was killed while Corky survived but broke his back and was paralyzed from the waist down. Forty hours passed before he was found by rescuers.

(top) Groundbreaking for Forest Meadow Baptist Church in the Lake Highlands area of Dallas in the mid-1970's. (bottom) Preaching at Forest Meadow Baptist Church.

Corky didn't just preach about joy as a
fruit of the spirit, he lived it.

Corky enjoyed teaching at Mid-America Baptist Theological Seminary (MABTS), where he spent the last seventeen years of his life as Chairman of the Old Testament and Hebrew Department.

Book signing at MABTS for his book
Mighty to Save: A Study in Old Testament Soteriology.

Corky always thought
it was significant that,
in John 21:3, Simon
Peter didn't say,
"I go a golfing."
Instead, he said,
"I go a fishing."
So did Corky.

Sons Steve and Mike pose beside Corky's portrait in the library at MABTS.

FARRIS: WHAT'S IN A NAME - 424

Corky and Mike at Mike's wedding in 1983.